BECOMING A TRIAL LAWYER

Becoming a Trial Lawyer

Steven P. Grossman

Michele Gilman

Fredric I. Lederer

Carolina Academic Press

Durham, North Carolina

ISBN: 978-1-59460-187-3
LCCN: 2007940221

Several of the chapters in this book are adapted from *Trying the Case*, written by Steven P. Grossman and published by MICPEL. MICPEL has the copyright to that material and the aforementioned chapters are being published with their consent.

Carolina Academic Press
700 Kent Street
Durham, North Carolina 27701
Telephone (919) 489-7486
Fax (919) 493-5668
www.cap-press.com

Printed in the United States of America

CONTENTS

ACKNOWLEDGMENTS

For their help and assistance with this project, Professor Grossman would like to thank Norman Cooper, Forensic Engineer, Michael Dorfman, Esq., Dr. Kenneth Fine, Fire Captain Christopher Gauss, Eileen Grossman, Robert Michael, Esq., Professor Arnold Rochvarg, Andrew Slutkin, Esq., Marcus Shar, Esq., Professor Stephen Shapiro, Professor Adam Todd, and Barbara Jones.

Professor Gilman would like to acknowledge the assistance of Professors Jane Murphy, Robert Rubinson, Leigh Goodmark, Wendy Seiden, Dan Hatcher, Yoanna Moisides, and Helen Harnett; students Monty Smith, David Burkhouse, and Stephen Mutschall; Laura Garcia; Dr. Karen LaFace; Julia Gilman; Stephanie Travis; and the many clinical students in the Civil Advocacy Clinic from 1998–2007.

INTRODUCTION

This book is the product of our desire to share what we have learned about the art of being a trial lawyer from our combined 60 years of experience trying cases, and teaching lawyers and law students to do so. It is written primarily for law students, designed to acquaint them with the basic knowledge, skills and techniques they will need to start on the road to becoming effective trial lawyers.

Trying a case is an incredibly exciting and terrifying experience, especially for new lawyers. While thorough preparation is crucial to performing effectively in court, the trial is a dynamic process that often requires even the most comprehensively prepared attorneys to adapt on the spot to the shifting sands in the courtroom. This book teaches fundamental trial advocacy skills, and it helps students both prepare systematically for what they can expect to face and to handle those sands in the courtroom as they shift.

In addition, we recognize that not all trials involve juries and unlimited time and resources, as many trial advocacy books assume. Trials are not cookie cutter, and neither is this book. We discuss the wide variety of forums in which lawyers try cases, ranging from jury trials to bench trials to administrative hearings. We discuss how to sharpen and shape your advocacy for these different settings. Further, we discuss creative strategies for trying a case with limited financial resources. The chapter on litigating poverty cases will be helpful to students in law clinics, attorneys in legal services and public defender practices, and pro bono attorneys who serve our profession and society by representing low-income clients for free. We also recognize cutting edge issues in the art of litigating. Thus, we have an entire chapter devoted to using courtroom technology to enhance your case. Courtrooms are changing, as are jury expectations and attorney capabilities. You need to understand the state-of-the-art developments in trying cases.

Our belief is that while not every trial lawyer can develop into a true artist, most can learn to become very effective in court and every attorney can at least become a competent litigator. Maximizing one's knowledge and skill as a trial lawyer is obviously important to attorneys who appear regularly in court. Less obvious is the benefit to attorneys whose practice does not regularly involve court work. For these attorneys, possessing some knowledge of the ways of the trial lawyer will increase their confidence that they can perform ably in court should the need arise. With such confidence, the attorney may be less likely to feel the need to refer out a relatively simple case merely because it could possibly lead to a trial. Additionally, alleviating the fear some lawyers have of trying a case will reduce the psychological pressure that may cause reluctant trial lawyers to accept an unfavorable settlement.

Our experience trying cases and teaching others to do so has convinced us that the only way to become an effective trial lawyer is to actually try cases or to work on trial skills in a simulation format. Books such as this one provide necessary information and open the mind to acquiring the techniques that the lawyer needs to become a skilled advocate. As with other skills, however, those techniques can only be developed fully through practice and performance. A concert pianist needs to understand music but will become a virtuoso only through hitting those keys over and over. The same need to get one's hands dirty is true for auto mechanics, brain surgeons and golfers hoping to become experts at their craft. Accordingly, this book has an accompanying set of case files that will allow you to practice the skills and strategies discussed in this book. The case files allow you to practice all core trial advocacy skills. You will make opening and closing statements, examine fact and expert witnesses, practice impeachment techniques, and handle a wide variety of real and demonstrative exhibits. You will develop these skills through repeated practice in an assortment of cases. The case files include criminal and civil cases, as well as jury and bench trials.

Two of the case files are designed specifically to provide realistic simulations of typical poverty law cases. We hope the child custody and landlord/tenant cases will assist clinical students and attorneys in legal services offices in training for the realities of representing low-income clients in court. These two files are also appropriate for standard trial advocacy classes, because they cover the essential skills discussed in this book while exposing lawyers to new practice areas.

Allow us to offer two qualifiers before you begin reading the substance of the book. First, while the book necessarily discusses evidentiary rules and principles and offers examples of how to deal with certain specific evidentiary issues (evidence is after all the essential tool of our trade), this is not an evidence book. Second, all litigators know that the effective use of the rules of discovery and pre-trial practice in general can play a significant role in the outcome of a lawsuit. This book's focus on courtroom skills is not an implicit rejection of that notion but reflects the need to concentrate on one set of skills in order to improve them in a meaningful way. Therefore, the chapters of the book for the most part are devoted to the various facets of a trial.

It is our hope that this book will not only begin the process of helping you develop the skills of a trial lawyer but will also make trials seem less terrifying and even enjoyable for would-be litigators. Good luck!

Steven P. Grossman
Michele Gilman
Fred Lederer
July, 2007

Becoming a Trial Lawyer

CHAPTER 1

OPENING STATEMENTS

The trial has begun, and you are about to speak to the jury for the first time. Given the concept of primacy, it is unlikely the jury will ever again be as intently focused upon your words as they are at this moment. The presentation at this stage of a dynamic, goal-oriented opening statement can be a significant contributor to the successful outcome of the case. The attorney who fails to accomplish the important purposes of the opening statement, however, has experienced a golden opportunity forever lost.

I. Purposes

The particular nature of the issues and the identity of the parties in any case will affect the goals that the attorney needs to achieve in his or her opening statement. There are, however, certain purposes, common to every opening statement, that attorneys should consider as they prepare to address the jury for the first time.

A. Putting the Case Together

The traditional purpose of the opening statement and the one most frequently mentioned is to provide the attorney a means of laying out for the fact finder what he or she needs to prove and the form which that proof will take. To accomplish this, prosecutors and plaintiffs' attorneys identify for the jury the elements that comprise the relevant crime or cause of action and explain how each witness and piece of evidence will help them satisfy their burden of proving those elements. This approach to opening statements is sometimes called the "road map method". In fact, attorneys who bear the burden of proof sometimes tell juries, " Think of my opening statement as a road map through which I will show you where I am going and how I am getting there."

Another analogy commonly employed for opening statements designed to put the case together for the jury, especially where some of the evidence is opaque or circumstantial, is the jigsaw puzzle. "This case is like a jigsaw puzzle consisting of many individual pieces. When we have finished presenting the evidence, you will see how each piece fits together to complete the puzzle and to prove the case." Defense attorneys in both civil and criminal cases also use these analogies and advise the jury to be on the lookout for roads that don't go through or key pieces of the puzzle that are missing.

B. Establishing the Theme

While the goal of putting the case together for the jury is an appropriate purpose for the opening statement, substantially more should be accomplished before the attorney has concluded his or her opening remarks. The most fundamental purpose of the opening statement is to begin the process of establishing and selling your THEME to the jury. The theme of a case is the central reason why the case should be decided your way. It provides the fact finder with an overall way of looking at the case that frames the issues in their most favorable light. Perhaps the best way to decide upon the theme of a case is to imagine completing the sentence, "this case is about...," in terms that strategically define and characterize what the attorney regards as the principle issue of the trial.

By way of example, imagine an accident case in which the defendant is alleged to have sped through a traffic light as it was turning red. The plaintiff was crossing the street drinking a beer and allegedly more worried about talking with his friends than looking for cars before crossing. The plaintiff disputes the claim that he paid no attention to oncoming cars, and the defendant disputes that she ran a red light. While the plaintiff will spend time at trial showing he looked before crossing, his theme should be that the case is about a serious injury caused by a driver in too much of a hurry to stop for a red light. In his opening statement, plaintiff's counsel should begin the process of establishing that theme and of persuading the fact finder that this is the principle issue in the case. The defendant, on the other hand, should focus the attention of the fact finder on someone too preoccupied with partying in public to exercise reasonable caution before crossing the street. This is her theme. The successful litigant is often the party that gets the jury to adopt its theme concerning what the case is primarily about.

The trial of Terry Nichols for his role in the bombing of the federal building in Oklahoma City offers another example of the importance of developing a trial theme. Nichols' attorneys wanted to turn the case into a verdict on the credibility of conspirator turned government witness, Michael Fortier. They hoped to portray Nichols as a decent family man in contrast to the "drug-using proven liar" who was his chief accuser. This strategy could only work, however, if the jury accepted the defense theme that the prosecution's case came down to whether one believes Fortier. In its opening, the prosecution spoke of the mountain of physical and circumstantial evidence that demonstrated the substantial accuracy of Fortier's testimony and the connection of Nichols to Timothy McVeigh and the bombing. One point of argument that could ultimately emerge from this approach is that of coincidence. That is, " given the confluence of events and incriminating evidence, what an amazing series of never-in-a-lifetime coincidences had to occur for anyone but Terry Nichols to have been the man who helped Timothy McVeigh build the bomb that destroyed so many lives." In order for the jury to be substantially influenced by such an argument, they had to first accept that the case was about much more than just Michael Fortier's personal credibility. It was, instead, about a mountain of incriminating evidence that, taken together, allows for no reasonable explanation other than Nichols' involvement. This battle of competing themes began as it should have with the opening statements.

An attorney should never take a case to trial without having a theme. There may be trials when the lawyer calls no witnesses or even conducts no cross-examinations and is still successful. Without having a central reason why the jury should find in his favor or an overall approach to the case that will lead them in the right direction, however, the trial lawyer is doomed to fail. It often takes the entire trial for the attorney to develop fully the trial theme and persuade the jury of its centrality to their verdict, but it is well worth the effort (as will be discussed later in the chapter on "Closing Argument"). With the opening statement, the attorney takes the first important step in that direction.

C. Striking the Right Emotional Chord

Anyone who has ever tried a case to a jury will agree that the jurors decide upon their verdict with their hearts as well as their heads. Attorneys should never forget that both individual jurors and the collective institution called the jury are human beings. As such they are possessed of emotions such as sympathy or contempt, and they are full of likes and dislikes, biases and predispositions. Notwithstanding instructions from the court that sympathy and other human emotions are to play no role in the jury's deliberations, human beings are often unable to separate entirely their thoughts from their emotions. The successful trial lawyer accepts this reality and uses it to his or her advantage.

The opening statement is your initial opportunity to bring the jury into your case emotionally as well as intellectually. In developing your theme, you began to get the jury to accept what you regard as the key issues in the case and to characterize them most favorably. Now you want the jury to see the people and issues involved in the case in a manner that will strike the right emotional chords. You want them to *feel* as well as think about the people and issues involved in your case. It is more difficult for the jurors to return an unfavorable verdict against someone for whom they feel affection, sympathy or better still, empathy.

1. Plaintiffs and Crime Victims

While some cases present obviously sympathetic parties and issues, others require that the attorney work harder to evoke the sympathetic elements of his or her case. One way to accomplish this is to give the jury a feeling of the impact that the incident had on the parties. The plaintiff whose life has been changed fundamentally from the injuries he suffered in the construction accident should find the jury, at least initially, predisposed to wanting to help him. The prosecutor in a rape trial should have no difficulty getting across how profoundly the victim was affected by her attacker. It is easier for a jury to return a favorable verdict when it is impressed with the depth of the suffering that the plaintiff or crime victim has suffered. The attorney should ensure that his or her opening statement makes clear to the jury the impact of the incident on his or her client.

There are times when evidentiary requirements limit the ability of the attorney to discuss impact with the jury. For example, in a bifurcated personal injury case in which damages will be considered only after liability is proven, the plaintiff is severely limited in divulging the impact of the incident during opening statement. In a burglary case where the issues are the defendant's illegal entry into the victim's home to commit a crime therein, the prosecutor may be restricted in how much can be discussed about the victim's loss of a feeling of personal safety. Nonetheless, a little creativity on the part of the attorneys in these cases can leave the jurors with the clear impression of the loss that was incurred.

Other cases may involve plaintiffs or crime victims who have not been so obviously impacted by the events leading to the trial. While getting the jury involved emotionally in these situations may require more effort on the part of the attorney, the results are well worth it. The plaintiff in a breach of contract case is suing for money damages accrued as the result of the defendant's failure to deliver the items agreed to. In the opening statement, the plaintiff's attorney should speak with the jury about not just the money lost but also the loss of ability to conduct business in a predictable manner and the danger all businesses face if they cannot rely upon contracts being enforced. While this hardly has the emotional force of a victim who has lost his leg in an auto accident, it creates a feeling about the case that should resonate with at least some members of the jury.

2. Defendants in Criminal Cases

Defendants in most civil and criminal cases are unlikely to be regarded as sympathetically by the jury (at least at the outset of the trial) as are their opponents. Still it is often crucial to bring the jury into the defense case by painting the defendant as sympathetically as possible. This involves first deciding what is the best emotional response, consistent with the facts and issues in the case, that the jury can have to the defendant. In Terry Nichols' case, the defense labored mightily to have the jury feel for the family man charged with this crime. While it is impossible to match the feeling the jury will have for those innocent people who were brutally murdered in the bombing, painting Nichols as a good family man allows several different appeals to the jury's emotions. It allows the defense to address the unlikelihood that Nichols would risk being separated from the family he so loves were he apprehended for the bombing. It invites the jury to ask the core question of whether a man who cared so deeply about his family could so cruelly destroy the lives of other families. Perhaps most importantly in Nichols' case, some members of the jury might be less likely to convict a good family man, even if guilty, of the most serious charges alleged and opt instead to convict him of a lesser offense.

Some defendants in criminal cases have little in their personal backgrounds that will cause the jury to view them sympathetically. Even in these cases, the attorney must get the jury to feel a certain way about the case. No jury wants to convict the wrong person. If the defense is misidentification, the attorney should go beyond the facts and use the opening statement to have the jury feel the depth of the wrong that would ensue were they to convict someone without being certain of their decision. Effectively explaining to the jury the significance of the requirement that the prosecution prove the defendant's guilt beyond a reasonable doubt and connecting that requirement to the evil of convicting the wrong person can get the jury to feel as well as understand the importance of the burden of proof. While most criminal defense attorneys allude at some point in their opening statements to the presumption of innocence and the high burden of proof required of the prosecution, their presentation often comes off as a dry, formulaic description of the law. Instead, attorneys should make the jury feel the crucial importance of these protections and their applicability to the defendant and the issues in the instant case.

3. Defendants in Civil Cases

Defendants in civil cases may be able to elicit certain emotional responses from the jury that are normally unattainable for those charged with crimes, especially serious ones. The driver whose car has severely injured the plaintiff may be able to use empathy to aid in his or her defense. "Any one of us could have been driving down the street as John Smith was, on January 6, when a pedestrian came out of nowhere and caused an accident". Additionally, the defense attorney should endeavor to make his client likeable by eliciting the positive aspects of the driver's background and the helpful actions he took after the accident. Even seemingly minor actions such as trying to help the victim after the accident or cooperating fully with the police during the investigation can cause the jury to feel more favorable about the defendant.

Among those attorneys facing the greatest challenge in making their clients sympathetic are those who represent corporate or institutional clients. It is one thing for the court to instruct the jury that it must treat such a party in the same manner that it treats other parties, and quite another for jurors to actually give the same benefit of the doubt to a big company that it does to a sympathetic human party. Despite this reality, or perhaps because of it, some of the best attorneys at getting jurors to feel positive about their clients come from the ranks of those who customarily represent corporate or institutional parties.

When their named client is an insurance company, these attorneys often use their opening statement to educate the jury about how insurance companies work. Jurors are told how fraudulent claims are not only wrong but can result in increased premiums for all who are insured. Some attorneys attempt to put a human face on their corporate and institutional clients by choosing an appealing personal representative of the company to sit by their side and referring to that person instead of the company as often as feasible. Others make particularly good use of the issues in the case to get the jury to sympathize with their client. For example, the defense attorney may attempt to have the jury grasp fully how false claims of harassment made by employees can ruin a company's hard-earned reputation and strike at its ability to do business.

Whatever method they use, attorneys should say something in their opening statement about their client or the issues in the trial that will incline the jury to *feel* some emotional connection to their case. They should, however, guard against overplaying their hand by appealing too obviously or repeatedly to the sympathy of the jury.

D. Expose a Weakness in Your Case

For some of the same reasons that attorneys during their direct examinations anticipate a line of questioning likely to occur on cross-examination (see discussion of anticipating cross-examination in chapter on Direct Examination), they should consider exposing a weakness in their case during opening statement. When there is something detrimental to the case that the attorney knows the other side will exploit, he or she should consider the benefits of raising the topic during opening statement. Doing so will allow the attorney to say during summation that his or her client never sought to conceal the issue, as well as allowing the issue to be presented in its least damaging light. Additionally, if discussed first by the attorney who is harmed by the issue, it drains some of the emotional impact of the issue when presented by the opposing attorney.

Defined broadly, a weakness is any aspect of the case that can make it more difficult to prevail. It may be something in the background of a key witness that detracts from his credibility, some aspect of the case that will be proven only circumstantially or a problem that runs through the overall presentation of the case. It may relate to a particular witness or piece of evidence, or the lack of a witness or piece of evidence. Imagine a situation where an essential witness for the plaintiff or prosecutor has in his background a 5 year old conviction for forgery. When that witness takes the stand, the opposing attorney can impeach him through use of the conviction under FRE 609. The defense attorney, wishing to damage the witness before he ever testifies by pre-conditioning the jury to his criminal background, can be expected to discuss the conviction in her opening statement. In such a situation, the plaintiff's attorney or prosecutor may be well served to address the subject himself as follows:

> During the course of this trial you will be hearing from Lloyd Gooner. Mr. Gooner will tell you that he saw exactly what happened on the night of March 3 and how the defendant seriously injured Mary Smith. Now, we want to you to know that at one difficult time in his life, Mr. Gooner did something which he has regretted ever since. That act led him to plead guilty to the crime of forgery. You will hear from Mr. Gooner how he turned around his life and has gotten in no trouble since that day. As you consider Mr. Gooner's testimony, lis-

ten particularly carefully to the supporting testimony of Jane Jones and Officer Miller, who will corroborate each of the critical aspects of Mr. Gooner's description of what happened.

In exposing the weakness in his case, the attorney above achieved the following benefits: he made clear that there will be no attempt to conceal the witness's background, he discussed the conviction in as favorable a manner as possible, he pointed out how, notwithstanding the witness's background, his important testimony is strongly supported by other witnesses and he minimized the impact on the jury when the issue is raised by the defense.

Defense attorneys, as discussed above, know they must often confront the sympathy that the jury is bound to have for the victim of a violent crime or a severely injured plaintiff. In certain cases, this can be the chief obstacle that the defense has to overcome in order to prevail. It is often helpful for the defense attorney to raise the issue directly during opening statement:

It is certainly understandable that you would sympathize with the plaintiff because of the injury he has suffered. As the judge will tell you, however, sympathy cannot be allowed to play a role in your verdict. Our jury system depends upon your being able to consider the facts in this case objectively and to apply the law dispassionately to those facts. We are confident that you will abide by your oath and do just that.

When the plaintiff's attorney has been especially blatant in appealing to the jury's sympathy, the defense attorney may wish to supplement the above by contrasting the defense's case with that of the plaintiff. This can be accomplished simply by noting, " Unlike the plaintiff, our case will rely upon the evidence you will hear from the witnesses, not appeals to your sympathy".

Another example of being able to expose and deal with a weakness in opening statement involves a prosecutor in the familiar position of having only one eyewitness to the crime:

The State wants you to know at the outset of this case that there is only one eyewitness to this brutal crime, Mary Smith. The law requires no more to convict the defendant. When you finish hearing Ms. Smith's account of what happened, I'm sure you will agree that it is the quality and not the quantity of the testimony that matters.

Note that in each of the above examples, the attorneys exposing the weakness in their case did not dwell upon it. They made mention of it, diminished its importance and moved on.

E. Specific Purposes for Specific Cases

The purposes of the opening statement discussed above apply generally to all cases. Certain cases involve issues that require the attorney to consider additional purposes for the opening statement. As each case is different, it is impossible to enumerate all of the specific purposes to which opening statements in particular cases can be put. By way of illustration, I offer two such purposes for consideration in specific cases.

When much of his or her case depends on complex testimony, the attorney may wish to use the opening statement to explain those aspects that will be particularly difficult for lay jurors to understand. Such an explanation can be especially helpful when the witness is not particularly articulate or seems unable to testify without constantly lapsing into jargon. Beginning the explanation of how damages should be assessed or giving the jury some understanding of what is contained in the detailed business records that will be introduced can facilitate the jury's comprehension of this testimony when it is offered.

In some cases, evidence may be introduced or witnesses called whose connection to the issues in the case may not be immediately apparent to the jury. Using the opening statement to put such testimony into context may be important in these cases. While the jury does not need to be told why the accident victim will be testifying or how the testimony of the eyewitness to the crime fits into the presentation of the case, the role of other witnesses or evidentiary items is not so apparent. Although the attorney can explain the relevance of testimony during closing argument, if the jurors did not understand the purpose of the testimony when it was presented, they are less likely to have assimilated the testimony and will probably have largely forgotten it before closing argument. During the opening statement the attorney can explain why the meteorologist's testimony about the lack of rainfall on May 2 is important or how the absence of a certain entry in the medical record is germane to the issue of negligence. When this testimony is presented at trial, the jurors will immediately see why it is relevant and will remember the testimony more fully, and the attorney's comment upon it during closing argument will register with maximum effect.

One caveat is in order about the purposes to be achieved through opening statements. The attorney should bear in mind that the more that is included in the opening, the less emphasis the listener is likely to place on each point. Therefore, in choosing what purposes he or she wishes to accomplish in the opening, the attorney needs to prioritize among the possible options.

II. Organization and Content

The content of the opening statement and the manner in which it is organized contribute significantly to the ability of the attorney to accomplish the purposes discussed above. While no one organizational scheme fits the goals of every opening statement, attorneys planning their openings should consider the following organizational elements:

A. Capture the Interest of the Jury at the Outset

> Ladies and Gentlemen of the jury, my name is Henry Lott and I represent the plaintiff in this case. Over there sits Ann Lee, she represents the defendant. Judge Hoff sits up there on the bench, and this is the court stenographer who will record everything that we say. The case will proceed this way. First, I will present my case, and then Ms. Lee will present the case for the defense. The judge will charge you on the law and then we have an opportunity to sum up to you.
>
> This is my opening statement in which I will show you what has to be proven and how I will prove it. Remember, neither my opening nor Ms. Lee's is evidence. You should base your verdict on the evidence presented to you. Pay careful attention to all of the testimony from the witness stand as well as those items that are placed into evidence. Keep an open mind throughout the presentation of evidence and through the summations and the judge's instruction on the law.

How often have you heard an attorney begin his or her opening statement with the type of largely purposeless recitation of introductory matters or trial procedure as that illustrated above? Such a beginning is more than just a waste of time, it is an important moment squandered. The instant that you rise to address the jury for the first time is likely to be a moment when the jurors are focusing most intently on what you are about to say. Use that moment to accomplish something that you hope will be meaningful to the outcome of the case.

There is no moment too early to capture the interest of the jury in your client and his or her case. While juries usually pay maximum attention to attorneys as they begin their opening statement, the attention span of the average juror is not long. If they lose interest at the beginning of the opening statement, the attorney is unlikely to ever again gain the full attention of the jurors.

The attorney who captures the interest of the jury at the outset of the opening statement not only brings the jury into his or her case but, additionally, increases the likelihood that jurors will stay focused throughout the remainder of the opening. Furthermore, the jury is anxious to hear what the case is about and who the parties are. Jurors become impatient when attorneys talk for a period of time without ever satisfying their curiosity. Accordingly, after some brief introductory remarks, the attorney should launch rather quickly into the themes of the case, who the parties are and how they have been affected by events. Consider the following approaches for beginning the opening statement once the attorney has made brief introductory remarks:

Scenario 1:

On May 6, at 4:00 p.m., Ellen Rose was walking home from work on her way to pick up her children as she did every day. Then she encountered the defendant. He was leaving the bar where he had spent the afternoon drinking beer. As Ms. Rose crossed Elm Street, the defendant's car came barreling around the corner from Ash Road and smashed into Ellen Rose. This knocked Ms. Rose 20 feet down the road, caused her skull to crack open and ultimately killed her. As a result of the defendant's negligent driving, Ellen Rose won't be picking up her children anymore.

Scenario 2:

Right now, and at the end of this case, you will feel terrible about what happened to Ellen Rose. John Fallo is a decent and good man who has felt terrible about what happened to Ellen Rose from the day of the accident. This case and your job as jurors, however, is not about how terrible you feel but instead about what caused this accident. When you have heard all of the evidence, you will understand how it was largely the actions of Ellen Rose that caused this accident.

Scenario 3:

This case is about a doctor who did everything she could have and should have to help her patient. Dr. Leslie Frommer treated her patient by conforming to the accepted medical approach for dealing with the plaintiff's symptoms. Because the plaintiff is unhappy that his condition has not materially improved, he is suing Dr. Frommer. Your role in this case is to carefully examine the evidence and determine not whether the plaintiff is satisfied with his condition but whether he meets his burden of proving that Dr. Frommer committed serious errors that resulted in the plaintiff's current condition.

Scenario 4:

As the prosecutor has said, rape is indeed a serious crime. Joan Gault was raped and is the victim of this terrible crime. I tell you this right at the outset of my opening statement because Leo Falk wants you to know that there is no dispute about what happened to Ms. Gault or its seriousness. What this case is about is whether an innocent man will have to pay the price for this crime. Your role as jurors is to hold the prosecution to meeting its heavy burden of proving to you beyond a reasonable doubt that Leo Falk committed this crime. As the evidence unfolds you will see and hear many things that will cause you to doubt—doubt the accuracy of the victim's identification, doubt the reliability of the police investigation and doubt why Mr. Falk was even charged with this crime.

The above scenarios were each designed to accomplish important purposes of the opening statement right at the outset and to maintain the jury's interest in the attorney's case. Scenario 1 introduces the jury to the plaintiff's version of the accident and the case theme that emanates from it. Additionally, it begins the task of getting the jury to understand fully the impact of the accident on the victim and her family. In Scenario 2 the defendant counters the plaintiff's appeal to the jurors' emotions in two ways. First, the issue of sympathy is placed directly before the jurors and then they are reminded of their responsibility to disregard that sympathy. Second, the jury is introduced to the defendant as a decent man who, like the jurors, feels terrible about the accident.

Scenario 3 begins the characterizations of the parties that will continue throughout the trial of the defendant as a capable physician who did everything she should have for her patient and the plaintiff, a person suing because of dissatisfaction with results, not negligent treatment. Scenario 4 begins by acknowledging that the victim was raped. This is done in order to get that issue off the table or at least reduce its importance. Then it focuses the jury's attention on the concept of reasonable doubt and connects events in the case to such doubts.

B. Tell the Jury the Story of the Case

Now that you have captured the interest of the jury, keep them interested by telling them the story of your case. As discussed more fully in the chapter on Direct Examination, jurors are accustomed to hearing stories and assimilate more of what is told to them if related in the form of a story. Every case has its story. Although some cases require more creativity on the part of the attorney to tell the story in a compelling manner, it is not difficult to conjure up the story of the crime victim or one who suffered a disabling personal injury. It is equally important, however, for the attorney to communicate to the jury the story of the client when that story might not be so apparent. For example, take the story of the AC Bolt Co., which is suing for breach of contract:

> Members of the jury, I want you to get to know the AC Bolt Co., so you can understand the degree of the loss it suffered when the defendant failed to honor its commitment to deliver the metal necessary to make bolts. AC is really Alan Anderson and Charles Clark, who founded and run the company, and the 15 men and women whom they employ.
> Seven years ago, Alan and Charles were working at a large metal supply company when they realized there was a shortage of places where automobile manufacturers could purchase the particular kind of bolts they need to build automatic transmissions. They pooled their resources, borrowed money from the bank and started their own business, AC Bolt Co. Over the next seven years, the company grew substantially, because the automobile manufacturers came to know they could rely upon AC to provide the specialized bolts they need WHEN they need them. Because of this reputation for reliability, AC recently landed its biggest account yet, with Ford Motor Co.
> In order to make the bolts that Ford needed, AC had to increase substantially the amount of steel it purchases. In response to AC'S solicitation of offers, the defendant metal supply company agreed to provide the necessary steel by February 1 of this year. You will hear testimony regarding how Mr. Anderson emphasized to the general manager of the metal company how crucial it was that the steel be delivered on time and how that requirement was put into the contract. Well, February came and went, and so did March, and still the defendant did not supply the steel that was agreed upon. Mr. Anderson called the metal company on many occasions and was repeatedly told it was on its way. You know, the check is in the mail. Finally, Ford

Motor Co. had to cancel its agreement with AC and purchase its bolts elsewhere. AC lost hundreds of thousands of dollars because they could not fulfill their deal with Ford, but Alan Anderson and Charles Clark lost much more than that. In a business which is based on your ability to deliver the product when it is needed, Alan and Charles lost their reputation for reliability. This is why these two men and their company come before you seeking to recover the money lost as a result of the defendant's failure to honor its commitment and hoping to recover that which they value most, their reputation.

Through this portion of the opening statement, the jury gets to hear the story of the company plaintiff. Although one company suing another for damages incurred due to breach of contract is hardly going to bring the jurors to tears, telling the jury the story of the plaintiff accomplishes several benefits. It keeps the interest of the jury in the opening statement and the plaintiff's case. It explains the events leading to the lawsuit in a manner by which the jurors are used to acquiring oral information, through the telling of a story. Therefore, they are likely to assimilate this information more fully and to remember it as the trial proceeds. Additionally, through the story the company is humanized and its loss made more meaningful to the jury.

C. Identify and Characterize the People Involved in the Case

During most trials, the jury hears the names of numerous people involved in the case. Some of these people will appear as witnesses at the trial, others the jury will get to only know by reference. If a person's role in the events leading to the trial is significant, that person should be introduced to the jury during the opening statement regardless of whether that person is scheduled to testify. In this way, the attorney can describe for the jury the relevance of that person to the issues in the case. Then, when the jurors hear the person referred to during the trial, they will know who the person is and his or her connection in the case.

In addition to explaining the person's involvement in the case, mentioning that individual during the opening allows the attorney to characterize the person in the light that he or she desires the jury to view that person. The criminal defense attorney who knows that much of the government's case depends on the testimony of the former co-conspirator should lose no time in characterizing this witness as a criminal who is willing to falsely accuse the defendant in order to escape a long prison term. It is crucial to the defendant's case that the jury come to regard the co-conspirator as a criminal and a liar. Painting this picture as early and often as possible will prepare the jury in advance to listen with a great deal of skepticism to this witness's testimony.

The manner in which favorable witnesses are regarded by the jury will also be impacted by the characterization of those witnesses offered during opening statement. Describing the 12 year old witness during the opening statement as a bright, relatively mature and aware young person will condition the jury to better acceptance of the child's testimony. Referring to positive traits of the eyewitness to the accident, such as his objectivity (because he knew neither party to the accident) and his ability to observe, will bestow upon him a degree of credibility even before he testifies to what he saw.

D. Describe the Applicable Law

In some form, the jury will be instructed by the court to arrive at its verdict by applying principles of law to the facts of the case. While the primary responsibility for describing the applicable law to the jury rests with the court, the attorney should help the jury understand how the law relates to the particular issues in the case. This is true with respect to specific legal principles that arise out of the case and to more general principles applicable to all such cases.

All crimes and civil causes of action contain elements that must be proven factually. Both the attorney who has to prove the elements and the one trying to show that one or more of the elements is lacking should explain to the jury how the testimony adduced at trial will impact upon this legal requirement. The plaintiff in a defamation suit will want to explain to the jury what evidence will be offered to show 1) the defendant actually made the defamatory statement; 2) it was false; 3) the statement was published to others; and 4) that the plaintiff suffered economic and other damages as a result of the harm to his reputation. The defendant may have no defense to the first three elements, but intends to put on evidence of the already tarnished reputation of the plaintiff. In her opening statement, counsel for the defendant should explain to the jury how the law requires the plaintiff to prove that he has suffered damage as a result of the defamatory statement. Here, because the reputation of the plaintiff was already substantially sullied well before the defendant's statement, no further damage under the law resulted from the statement.

In defending an automobile case in a contributory negligence state, the attorney whose client claims the plaintiff crossed the street from between cars should explain how such conduct constitutes contributory negligence, and that under the laws of this state, the plaintiff cannot recover when he is even somewhat at fault for the accident. The criminal defense attorney should not refer to the prosecution's burden of proving the case beyond a reasonable doubt in the abstract, but should point out factual aspects of the case that will create such doubt.

A word of warning is appropriate at this point. It is within the prerogative of the court to describe and explain the applicable law to the jury. With varying degrees, however, judges allow attorneys to touch upon the law when addressing the jury. No clear line of demarcation exists to determine how far the attorney may go in explaining the law to the jury. Given this uncertainty, the attorney should not delve too far or in too much detail into the law. Additionally, the attorney may help to avoid a successful objection by quickly relating whatever legal principle he or she is discussing to some fact or piece of evidence that will emerge during the trial.

E. Emphasize the Theme of the Case

It will be recalled that the fundamental purpose of the opening statement is to establish the theme of the case. The attorney is likely to have introduced his or her theme when capturing the interest of the jury or telling the story of the case. Despite having done so already, it is important for the attorney to come back to the case theme somewhere near the conclusion of the opening statement.

Among the most valuable strategic tools available to the trial lawyer is EMPHASIS. What aspects of the case to emphasize and how to do so are decisions that relate to virtually every function that the attorney performs during trial. The attorney should choose most carefully the matters to be emphasized. By definition, only a limited number of things can be emphasized. The more items the attorney attempts to emphasize, the less emphasis the jury will place on any one of those items. Additionally, if repetition is the means of emphasizing a particular matter, the attorney should be aware that juries are not very receptive to listening to him or her discuss the same matter again. Therefore, when discussing a matter for a second time during opening statement, the attorney may wish to raise the issue in different words or a different context. Most importantly, the attorney should repeat only those items that are of profound importance. Such an item is the case theme.

Returning to the Terry Nichols case, his attorneys might have concluded their opening by alluding again to their dominant theme:

Therefore, when all of the evidence is in, you will see that the government's case really boils down to the word of Michael Fortier, a proven criminal and liar. We will ask you not to ruin the life of a good man and his family on the word of a person such as this who is out to save his own hide.

F. End on an Appropriate Note

Just as the jurors pay particular attention to the attorney at the outset of the opening statement, so they will focus intently on the attorney's final remarks. Therefore, the attorney should end on a high note.

To ensure that the jury is focused on the final remarks in the opening statement, the attorney must make certain that the jury knows that the concluding words are indeed the concluding words. Accordingly, the final comment in the opening statement should never leave the jury hanging or anticipating that further statements are forthcoming.

Some attorneys believe that the only proper conclusion to the opening statement is a request for a favorable verdict. The following two conclusions exemplify this approach: "I am confident when you have heard all of the evidence you will return the only proper verdict … for John Jones and against Beth Smith." "At the conclusion of this case I will stand before you again and request that you do right by May Lee and do justice for the people of this State by finding the defendant guilty of all the charges he faces."

While requesting a particular verdict is an appropriate way of concluding an opening statement, it is not the only way. Leaving the jury with the theme of your case ringing in their ears is another manner of finishing strong and letting the jury know these are your final remarks. "As the evidence unfolds, listen with particular attention to all of the testimony showing the careless manner in which the plaintiff crossed the street at the time of the accident. After the judge instructs you as to the meaning of contributory negligence, you will have little difficulty deciding what the correct and proper verdict in this case should be. Thank you."

III. Style and Delivery

Saying the right thing is only the first aspect of giving an effective opening statement. The manner in which you address the jury plays a significant role in determining the effectiveness of the opening. Because the stylistic elements that make an attorney persuasive in addressing the jury are common to both opening statements and closing arguments, they will be discussed only once, in the chapter on Closing Arguments.

IV. Don't ...

The focus of the discussion so far has been upon those things that the attorney should do to make the opening statement successful. The attorney should also be aware of those things that detract from the effectiveness of the opening.

A. Take Too Long

The attention span of a jury is notoriously short. Knowing that you have a number of things to accomplish in the opening, make sure you do so while the jury is still paying attention. The longer you drone on, the more jurors will turn you off. Accordingly, say what you must as efficiently and briefly as possible.

Some cases, because they involve many witnesses or complex material, will necessitate a longer opening statement to achieve their purposes. More explanation of the testimony may be required during the opening statements in such cases. It is especially important in these opening statements to keep in mind that you must maintain the interest of the jury. In longer openings, it is particularly helpful to use stylistic techniques such as pace, voice modulation and movement (see section on Style and Delivery in chapter on Closing Arguments), in addition to the methods for maintaining juror interest discussed above.

B. Go into Too Much Detail

A successful opening statement creates the desired *impression* in the mind of the jury about the case and the people involved. Specific details regarding the evidence that will be adduced at trial should be included in the opening statement only to the extent they help create the correct impression or directly achieve one of the purposes of the opening.

There are several reasons for not delving too deeply into or recounting too specifically the details of the testimony the jury will be hearing. First, as the trial progresses, the jury is unlikely to remember any but the most essential details that were provided during the opening statement. Jurors might recall the prosecutor's remark during opening statement that the victim saw "Slick" tattooed on the arm of her attacker, but are unlikely to remember that she also described him as 5' 10"–6' 1", 165–180 lbs., wearing a blue sweatshirt and black hat. Therefore, the prosecutor generally should avoid going into all of the details of the description during the opening statement. If the prosecutor's goal in detailing the description given by the victim is not for the jury to absorb the description's specifics but is, instead, to create the impression that the victim got a good look at her assailant, then providing this information in the opening statement may be effective.

Each clause of the contract and all of the terms embodied therein may be germane to the breach of contract case, but this is not the type of information jurors are apt to remember. Accordingly, discussing the contract in such detail during the opening statement is not only likely to be a waste of time, but also may exhaust the jury's limited attention span and make it difficult to accomplish the goals of your opening statement. It is preferable for the plaintiff's attorney during opening statement to provide a sense of what is contained in the contract and how the defendant failed to honor his commitments.

Describing the witness's testimony in too much detail may create inconsistencies that can be exploited by opposing counsel. The witness may have said during the preparatory session that the defendant's car was about 25 feet from the crosswalk and moving 35 m.p.h. at the moment of impact, and the attorney is considering incorporating these details into his opening. While looking at a map during direct or cross-examination, however, it is not uncommon for the witness to give somewhat different numbers for what is, after all, only an estimate. Why open the door for a closing argument from opposing counsel such as:

> You recall plaintiff's key eyewitness testifying that my client's car was going between 25 and 35 mph and that impact occurred about 30 feet from the crosswalk. That is not what Mr. Smith told you during his opening statement about the speed of the car or the location of the accident. Is Mr. Smith incorrect or is his key eyewitness? In either event, it should lead you to have real doubts about the plaintiff's version of the accident.

One final reason to avoid describing the witness's testimony in too much detail relates to the purpose of direct examination. The primary purpose of direct examination is to impart information to the jury in a manner that will make the information credible and memorable. Where the testimony is dramatic, the attorney should be especially concerned that the drama and the emotion of the witness (the person who experienced the event) be transmitted fully to the jury. If the attorney covers all of the material the witness will later testify to, the testimony will be robbed of some of its impact on the jurors who have heard it already.

C. Lapse into Argument

Laypersons often think of opening statements and closing arguments as chronological bookends of the trial, the former telling the jury what *will* happen, the latter reminding them what *did* happen during the trial. In fact, the purposes of the opening statement and closing argument differ from one another, and the difference between the "statement" attorneys make at opening and the "argument" they deliver during closing is a distinction that attorneys need to understand. The opening statement is designed to clue the fact finder into the evidence the attorney will produce and how, once adduced, that evidence warrants a certain legal conclusion. Closing argument, although often labeled inaccurately as "summation," allows the attorney to do substantially more than merely sum up the evidence that has been elicited. During closing argument, attorneys can characterize the evidence, interpret the meaning of specific responses, and assess the credibility of witnesses—in short, argue the case.

Anyone who understands the variety of purposes that can and should be achieved through the opening statement, as discussed above, should realize that in practice, the distinctions between opening and closing can become somewhat blurred. In discussing the theme of the case, it is not difficult to see how the attorney may characterize the evidence somewhat or say something suggesting that a witness for the other side is not worthy of belief. While such remarks are more appropriate during closing argument, opposing counsel is unlikely to object and most judges will not sustain an objection during opening statement where the attorney has made only occasional and brief comments that might constitute argument. Problems do arise, however, with attorneys who use a good deal of their opening to "argue" their case. The solution, then, is to make sure you do not unduly lapse into argument during your opening statement. Such lapses are likely to cause your opening statement to be interrupted by objections and to become disjointed in the event that the objections are sustained.

D. Institutionalize Your Client

From the discussion concerning striking the right emotional chord and capturing the interest of the jury, it should be apparent that the attorney must *humanize* his or her client during opening statement. To this end, the attorney should avoid institutionalizing the client. Repeated references to one's client as "the plaintiff," "the accused" or "the driver" make it easier for the jury to see the client as a legal entity instead of as a human being who will be severely affected by an unfavorable verdict. It is easier for the jury to return a verdict detrimental to a legal entity than one which will harm a real person.

E. Promise More Than You Deliver

The rules of evidence tell us that every witness who takes the stand puts his or her credibility at issue. What the rules don't tell us is that the credibility of the attorney is also quite relevant to the outcome of the case. Juries view attorneys as the personification of their cases and assess the credibility of the attorneys, as well as the testimony, throughout the trial. During closing argument, when the attorney looks into the eyes of the jurors and attempts to sell the case for the final time, the attorney will face an unreceptive audience if he has lost credibility.

One of the first ways the attorney loses credibility with the jury is by promising too much during opening statement. Attorneys are normally keyed up for their opening statement and probably believe firmly in their case after working on it for weeks. Additionally, attorneys are trained to describe the testimony in as favorable a light as possible. The combined effect of these factors can lead attorneys to overstate what the evidence will show. Aside from raising substantive questions about the reliability of the testimony in the minds of the jury, such overstatement can result in the jury losing faith in everything else the attorney says.

Be careful not to forecast that "all of the evidence will show ..." unless it will—or that "none of the plaintiff's witnesses are worthy of belief" if some of them are. Don't promise that the witness will positively identify the defendant if the witness has previously been only tentative in her identification. If the witness told you he thought the car was traveling at 30 to 40 m.p.h., don't tell the jury the car was driving at least 40 m.p.h. All of the above will cost the attorney valuable credibility points with the jury.

V. Should You ... ?

A. Discuss the Other Side's Case

Whether you should discuss the other side's case and how much you should discuss it depends to some extent on whom you represent. Prosecutors, of course, are barred from suggesting, or even inferring, that the defendant will put on a case. Therefore, although the prosecutor has been served with notice that an alibi witness will testify for the defense, he or she cannot comment upon such testimony during opening statement. Neither criminal defendants nor parties to civil cases are prohibited from doing so and, accordingly, must consider the strategic benefits of discussing the opponent's case in the opening statement.

Defense attorneys have an opportunity to respond somewhat to what the prosecutor or plaintiff's attorney has said in his or her opening statement. If the opposing attorney has laid out a convincing theme and effectively portrayed the people and issues in the case, there is a danger that if the defense attorney does not at least raise some questions about the other side's case, the jury will be predisposed to regard the testimony favorably for the plaintiff or prosecutor. If a certain view of the case is allowed to go unchallenged until later in the trial, there is a danger that the jury will arrive at a premature conclusion about the case (despite being instructed by the court to keep an open mind until all of the evidence is in).

When the prosecutor has painted a compelling picture of a victim who confidently identified the photograph of the defendant as his assailant, the defense attorney may wish to prevent this image of a reliable identification sinking in with the jury. Therefore, during her own opening statement, the defense attorney may wish to inform the jury that the initial description of the assailant given by the victim was very vague and did not become more specific until the photograph of the defendant was presented to him in a highly suggestive manner. The defense attorney in the automobile accident case will want the jury to know that the eyewitness described by plaintiff's counsel as offering positive proof that the defendant ran the red light happens to be a close friend of the plaintiff.

The plaintiff's attorney cannot respond to defense counsel's opening statement, but because of the liberal rules of discovery should anticipate the thrust of the defense case. Therefore, it may be helpful for the plaintiff's attorney to include in his opening statement the following:

> I expect the defense in this case will put on witnesses who will testify
> they were with the defendant prior to the accident, and they never

saw him drink any alcoholic beverage. As you listen to this testimony, see if any of these witnesses were with the defendant during the hour before the accident, the crucial time period in this case.

B. Object during Your Opponent's Opening Statement

Most attorneys prefer not to object while their opponent is addressing the jury. A combination of reasons accounts for this reluctance. To some extent, it is a vestige of days past, when trial lawyers were perceived as exhibiting a greater degree of courtesy toward each other. Objecting during opening statement was just not the thing to do. Judges often viewed these objections as unwarranted interruptions, rarely sustained objections during opening and closing statements, and sometimes admonished the objecting attorney in the presence of the jury. Additionally, attorneys realized that objections from them during their opponent's remarks would likely result in the opponent responding in kind.

These same concerns continue to exist today and continue to minimize the frequency of such objections. The widely held view is that "my opponent gets his chance to present his case to the jury, and I have mine." Therefore, occasional lapses into argument during opening statement, overstating what the evidence will show and references to matters of questionable relevance often do not bring objections. Although there are some attorneys who object to "break the flow" of their opponent's remarks, such objections are of questionable propriety and often are counterproductive with the jury as well as the judge.

Having noted the above reasons not to object, however, there are times when attorneys must do so to protect their clients when opposing counsel is addressing the jury. Comments referring to evidence that will not be produced at trial, those that can be seen as violative of court orders not to discuss certain matters (or not to discuss them in certain ways), serious misstatements of the law or any remarks that improperly prejudice one's client should bring an objection.

As with other decisions trial lawyers have to make, no clear line of demarcation exists to signal the lawyer when to object during opposing counsel's opening statement. Perhaps the key criteria in deciding whether to object during opening statement is whether the improper remark of opposing counsel is sufficiently important to cause real damage. The objecting attorney should be confident the objection will be sustained to avoid providing opposing counsel with the opportunity to repeat the harmful remarks—this time with the court's explicit approval. Such a result only emphasizes the matter for the jury.

CHAPTER 2

WITNESS PREPARATION

I. Why Prepare Your Witness

Attorneys expect to have some damage done to their case when their witnesses are being cross-examined. Far harder to bear is having your case harmed during the direct examination of a friendly witness. Such a situation is, for the attorney, that most painful of experiences: the self-inflicted wound. Too often that wound is caused by the failure of the direct examiner to adequately prepare the witness prior to his or her taking the stand.

Testifying at a trial is an extremely traumatic event for most non-professional witnesses. Imagine having observed a crime or serious auto accident 9 months ago and being called as a witness to testify about the event. Having to remember precise details about the event and testifying under oath to such recollections are upsetting enough. Combine that with having to tell the story to a group of 12 strangers, knowing your every word is being taken down in an official transcript and exposing yourself to hostile cross-examination, and you'll understand why witnesses are tense about testifying. This tension is only heightened if the witness is a party who has a strong interest in the outcome of the case and, thus, in the effectiveness of his or her own testimony. Since it is the attorney who puts the witness through this traumatic experience, the attorney should do whatever possible to ease the process for the witness. This should be done not only because we owe it to the witnesses we are about to call to reduce their level of apprehension, but also because the most effective witnesses are usually the best prepared witnesses.

II. Preparing the Witness Regarding the Substance of the Testimony

Witnesses should be prepared with respect to both the substance of their testimony and the method in which they should communicate with the jury. As to substance, I am not speaking of what is sometimes referred to as "coaching the witness." I am assuming that the witness has already related her story to the attorney and the two are now meeting for a final preparatory session prior to trial. Thus, the attorney has heard from the witness in her own words the substance of her testimony. The preparation session is about how that information can be presented most coherently and persuasively to the jury.

A. Have the Witness Review Her Previous Statements

Witnesses sometimes forget details or remember things somewhat differently over time. It is therefore helpful to begin the preparation session by showing the witness her most recent accounting of events (perhaps the transcript of a deposition or preliminary hearing) and inquiring of the witness whether she still remembers the incident the same way. You want to learn of any change in recollection during the preparation session rather than when the witness is on the stand. During preparation you can ascertain whether the witness's memory has actually changed or, instead, whether she is merely phrasing something differently or relating more or less of the story than she did previously. If there is a substantive change, you can discuss with the witness whether she will account for the change in direct examination or be prepared to explain it away on either cross or redirect examination.

B. Ask the Witness the Same Questions You Will Ask at Trial

In proceeding through the details of the witness's testimony, it is best to ask the witness, during the preparation session, the exact questions you will be asking her on the stand. While the meaning of your questions may be abundantly clear to you, it may not be so clear to the witness. Additionally, the witness may not understand the scope of your question. "What happened after that?" might lead to, "I saw a strange man enter the store. Then I bought a loaf of bread, a quart of milk and some napkins. I waited for the bus at the corner on Main and Oak for 20 minutes, then took it home. At home I fed my cat and turned on the television." You could interrupt the witness after she tells of seeing the man enter (the testimony you were seeking), but this may disconcert the witness or seem impolite to the jury. At times, the witness who misunderstands the scope of the question might volunteer information that is more directly harmful to your case than in the previous example. If you ask the same questions during preparation that you intend to ask at trial, you can learn the extent of the witness's answer and explain to her the limits of your question and the extent of the response you seek.

Another advantage of asking trial questions during the preparation session is that it gives the attorney the opportunity to see if problems exist with respect to how the questions are framed. This permits the attorney to rethink precisely how the question should be phrased in order to obtain the desired response from the witness. Such a process may be particularly important with an expert witness, who is reluctant to draw certain conclusions, but entirely comfortable providing the necessary information if the question is worded differently.

Witnesses may use inappropriate, imprecise or even misleading wording in response to certain questions. "How long were you stopped at the traffic signal before you felt the impact from behind" might lead to, "Oh, just a few minutes." It is extremely likely that the witness did not think through the precise meaning of those words before she uttered them. In your office you can calmly inquire as to approximately how many seconds she is referring, or ask her to recreate the approximate time span as you time her. When you inform her that the time she estimated was about 30 seconds and she confirms the accuracy of that estimate, you have diffused a problem that otherwise could have arisen for the first time on direct examination and resulted in confusion, or worse.

C. Tell the Witness the Points of Emphasis

After taking the witness through the questions you will be asking and dealing with potential problems, it can be helpful to let the witness know what parts of her testimony are particularly important and require emphasis. Regardless of how well the witness is prepared, due to the stress that accompanies giving testimony, it is still possible the witness will forget certain aspects of her testimony. By discussing with her points of emphasis, the attorney markedly reduces the likelihood that key pieces of information will be omitted during direct examination.

D. Ask the Witness If She Has Questions for You

Before you conclude your final preparation session with the witness, ask her if she has any questions for you. It is sometimes surprising what the witness may not realize about a trial or the process of giving testimony. One attorney remembered to ask this of his witness as she was walking out the door of his office on the way to the courtroom. The witness responded by inquiring whether she had to swear under oath to tell the truth or whether that just happened on television. When informed that such an oath was in fact administered, the witness indicated she did not believe she could take such an oath. Upon further inquiry, the attorney learned that the witness thought that as she was less than 100% certain about specific aspects of her testimony, she could not testify "truthfully" to the events in question. The attorney explained to the satisfaction of the witness that she could express her lack of certainty during the direct examination, and that her testimony would be entirely truthful. Had the attorney not asked the witness if she had any questions, the witness might have initially refused to take the oath in front of the jury.

III. Preparing the Witness Regarding the Manner in Which She Testifies

No matter how well prepared a witness is regarding the substance of her testimony, her effectiveness as a witness can be significantly enhanced or diminished due to the manner in which she provides that testimony. The goal here is not to turn your witness into Robert DeNiro or Meryl Streep but to remove the barriers that interfere with the witness's ability to communicate most effectively with the jury. You may have observed some physical or verbal habits of the witness during your preparation sessions that detract from her ability to provide her testimony as clearly and persuasively as possible. Some witnesses speak too softly, others too quickly, still others tend to go on too long. The attorney should make the witness aware of any barrier to effective communication and speak with her about overcoming the problem. I noticed that during a preparation session my witness tended to look down into her lap when responding to my questions. I spoke with her about this and explained that while I knew she was telling the truth, it was of vital importance that the jury believe her. Unfortunately, some jurors may be less likely to believe someone who refuses to look them in the eye. Therefore, it was important that, at least when delivering the crucial aspects of her testimony, she try to look at the jurors. I told her that if she forgot, I would remind her by prefacing my question with, "would you please explain to the jury ..."

A. Identify Problems

There are an infinite number of behaviors a witness can exhibit that may interfere with the effective presentation of her testimony. Asking the precise questions during preparation that you will ask on direct will aid you in identifying these behaviors and working on them. A note of caution is appropriate here. *Do not dwell on the problem to such an extent that you heighten the anxiety level of the witness.* You do not want the witness concentrating so hard on not playing with his tie that he forgets part of his testimony. Additionally, avoid trying to turn the witness into someone he is not. Jurors may not pick up every factual nuance presented, but they are usually adept at spotting a phony when they see one. Therefore, do not try to polish the witness to the extent that he is unrecognizable.

B. Familiarize the Witness with What She Will Encounter

If the witness is relatively unsophisticated about trials and courtroom decorum in general, you may want to talk to her about matters such as appropriate attire and proper conduct. Be careful what you say, however. A judge tells the true story of a rural couple who were about to walk into a courtroom for the first time. Their attorney told them to wear their best clothes to the trial. On the first day of the trial the man walked into the courtroom wearing a tuxedo, the woman wearing her wedding dress.

The more relaxed your witness is when taking the stand, the more effective he is likely to be. Familiarizing the witness with what he is about to encounter can markedly reduce his anxiety level. Explain to the witness the courtroom procedure—e.g., objections, breaks, etc. Identify where the parties to the trial will be located. Indicate the proper response to certain events that will occur in the courtroom, i.e., "Don't answer when the judge says, 'sustained.'" Some attorneys take their witnesses to the courtroom where they will testify and show them the witness chair, the jury box, the judge's bench, counsel tables and the location of other relevant items. If your witness will be illustrating his testimony through the use of demonstrative evidence, such as a diagram, it is particularly useful to show the witness where the diagram will be placed and the sight line to the jury box.

The witness who understands basic courtroom procedure is less likely to commit certain preventable errors. Tell the witness, for example, to stop his answer immediately when you object, and say nothing unless the judge overrules your objection. To the attorney this may be self evident, but many nonprofessional witnesses are unaware of this. Explain to the witness the importance of answering your question and not going beyond it in his response. Party witnesses or those with a strong interest in the outcome of the case may think they are aiding the cause by volunteering additional "helpful" information. In fact, they may be damaging your case, risking a mistrial or at least losing credibility in the eyes of the jury by seeming to be too much the advocate.

IV. Preparing the Witness for Cross-Examination

Although you have thoroughly prepared your witness for both the substance of her direct examination and the manner in which she will testify, your preparation of the witness is far from over. Your witness, in all likelihood, will face some form of hostile cross-examination. If she is not prepared for what she will encounter on cross-examination, your case can be significantly damaged. Some years ago, I was prosecuting a routine armed robbery case. The likelihood of a conviction was weakened by the shaky identification of the defendant given by the victim, the only eyewitness to the crime. Fortunately, the defense bailed us out. The defendant took the witness stand to offer an alibi in his defense. I was prepared to conduct a standard cross-examination of the defendant, using a prior burglary conviction to impeach his credibility. To my great and welcome surprise, when asked by me about the conviction, the defendant paused and then denied he was ever convicted of a crime. This enabled me to explore with the defendant in some detail his recollection of having entered a home at night only 2 years earlier and stealing several items while the homeowner and her family slept in adjoining rooms. The defendant's denials turned into grudging admissions, all of which made him appear to be quite the liar. My summation to the jury focused more on why the defendant would take the stand and lie rather than on the tentative identification offered by the victim. I learned later from the defense attorney's partner that the defendant was never told he would be asked about his prior conviction, certainly among the most obvious questions prosecutors are likely to ask.

Had he been adequately prepared, the defendant would have known the importance of readily acknowledging his conviction and in fact probably should have been asked about it on direct examination. Instead, unprepared for the question and being something less than a rocket scientist, the defendant thought he could avoid looking bad by denying his involvement in previous criminal activity.[1] I am relatively certain that the conviction in my robbery case was largely attributable to the fact that the attorney failed miserably to prepare his client for cross-examination.

A. Preparing the Witness for the Substance of the Cross-Examination

As with preparation for direct examination, you need to speak with your witness about the substance of the questions you anticipate he will be answering on cross-examination, as well as his method of answering hostile questions. Experienced attorneys prepare their witnesses for cross-examination in different ways. Some discuss generally the areas they believe will be probed on cross-examination and ask the witness for explanations of weaknesses or inconsistencies. Others conduct their own mock cross-examination of the witness (or have a colleague do so) to see how he will respond to questions framed in a leading and adverse manner. There are advantages to seeing how the witness responds to adverse questioning, but be aware that if the actual cross-examiner's method is substantially different than the mock cross, the witness may be somewhat confused on the witness stand.

Whatever method you choose, it is vital that the witness be made to understand how badly his credibility will be damaged if he attempts to fudge in his acknowledgment of certain demonstrable facts. Additionally it is important for the witness to begin thinking about explanations for any weaknesses that exist in his testimony. Assume, for example, that the pedestrian victim of an automobile accident is asked by the police immediately after the accident what color the traffic light was for the defendant driver. The police report indicates her re-

---

1. When discussing prior convictions with your client or witness in preparation for testifying, explain that serving time in jail is not required to constitute a "conviction," and that it is not necessary to explain the circumstances of the crime in response to the question unless there are tactical reasons to do so.

sponse was, "I'm not sure." At her deposition six months later, when asked the same question, the victim responds, "I am pretty sure it was red." The victim in your preparation session tells you her memory now is consistent with her statement during the deposition, and you intend to elicit that testimony from her at trial. The attorney needs to ask the witness during her preparation whether she said to the police officer what appears in his report, and, if so, why. Once the attorney learns from the witness that she was shaken by the accident, concerned about herself and her car when the officer questioned her, the attorney can discuss with the witness how best to deal with this discrepancy. Perhaps the attorney will anticipate the cross-examination and bring the issue up on direct, or perhaps the strategy will be to see how it develops on cross-examination, with the witness to offer her explanation on redirect (see chapter on Direct Examination). In any event, the witness will not be surprised and confused when she gets the question, nor will she engage in the type of denial or obfuscation that can ruin her entire credibility with the jury.

Unlike direct examination, it is difficult to prepare your witness for all of the questions or even all of the areas that may be included in the cross-examination. In preparing the witness for cross, the attorney should review thoroughly everything the witness has said on the matter at hand as well as any information that goes to the credibility of the witness. It may be helpful to have other lawyers peruse the material as well to suggest possible directions in which the cross-examination may go.

B. Preparing the Witness Regarding the Manner of Responding to Adverse Questions

The dynamic that exists between your witness and the attorney cross-examining her can affect dramatically the degree to which the jury accepts her testimony. Therefore, it is incumbent upon you in preparing the witness to speak with her about the appropriate manner in which to respond to adverse questions. Again, having gotten to know your witness should provide you with some sense of the witness's attitude toward unfriendly questions. Some witnesses exhibit overt hostility toward the cross-examiner, some attempt to show they are more clever than the questioner, while others can be curt or dismissive. In preparing your witness, you should explain the need for him to maintain his composure, answer the question he is asked and not try to win the case by out-debating the cross-examiner. While juries expect attorneys to challenge opposing witnesses to some degree, they react best to witnesses who appear to be delivering their testimony as straight as possible. Of course, if the cross-examiner challenges the witness too aggressively, the attorney is likely to lose points with the jury, and a stronger reaction from the witness may be more acceptable.

In preparing his or her witness, the attorney should realize that witnesses are often reluctant to say things on the stand they think will sound bad to the jury. For example, many witnesses are hesitant to acknowledge they do not know or are unsure of something. This hesitation can lead the witness to guess or exaggerate a part of his answer. Either can make excellent fodder for cross-examination, often through the use of a prior statement in which the witness indicated no specific knowledge of the subject matter he now claims to know with precision. Therefore, part of every preparation should be informing the witness that there is nothing wrong with not knowing the answer to every question or answering, "I am not sure" to others. Another example of this reluctance to sound bad is the witness's denial that he has discussed his testimony with the direct examiner before being called to the stand. The witness should be told of this possible question and advised to answer it truthfully. If need be, you can inquire on redirect examination regarding how the witness was instructed to answer this and all questions truthfully.

C. Special Consideration When Preparing Your Client

If the witness is your client, it is particularly important that his manner of answering questions reinforces his credibility. Additionally, with a party witness in a civil case, the attorney must remember the impact of the adverse party rule in considering when to prepare the client for his testimony. As the rule allows the opponents to call your client during their case, you should have your client prepared at the outset of the trial. If your client is not called until later in the trial, you can always review his testimony with him shortly before he testifies.

V. Preparation for Redirect Examination

Finally, the attorney should prepare with his or her witness for the possibility of redirect examination. Let your witness know that if the cross-examiner did not afford her the opportunity to explain her actions or statements, you will provide that opportunity on redirect examination. The decision regarding whether and how to conduct a redirect examination is discussed below, but, regardless of what is decided, it can relieve some of the witness's anxiety if she knows there will be an opportunity to explain away some damaging information that may be elicited on cross-examination.

CHAPTER 3

Direct Examination

Trials are usually won by the attorney who is able to present his or her direct case most effectively. In order to present an effective direct examination, it is essential that that attorney understand the primary purpose of direct. The best means of explaining the primary purpose of direct examination is to contrast it with the sharply different purpose of cross-examination.

The primary purpose of direct examination is to have the witness communicate *information* clearly and persuasively to the fact finder. On cross-examination, as the information coming from an adverse witness will seldom be helpful to the cross-examiner, he or she should seek to limit any information flow from the witness to the jury. This is best accomplished by framing questions designed to elicit only *responses* from the witness. This difference between information and responses can best be understood by reference to B.F. Skinner's experiments in operant conditioning.

You may recall that Skinner, working with chickens, received the pecking response he sought through the application and withdrawal of the correct stimulus (in his case, food). Skinner elicited responses, not information, from the chickens. The adept cross-examiner, using the correct stimulus (in his or her case, the leading question), limits the information flow by eliciting only responses from the witness (see chapter on Cross-Examination). As the purpose of the direct examiner is to have the witness inform the jury about a subject matter, the attorney planning the direct should think about how speakers best communicate, and listeners best absorb, information.

An effective communication of information between the witness and the jury is one that is both clear and persuasive. The attorney must keep these dual goals in mind and prepare the direct examination using techniques designed to ensure that the jury will understand the witness fully and be persuaded by her testimony.

I. Making the Testimony Clear

If jurors cannot understand what the witness is saying or have difficulty following the flow of her testimony as it is being elicited, it is likely that they will not assimilate important aspects of the testimony. What jurors do not assimilate they will not be able to recall and, therefore, are unlikely to reconstruct during their deliberations. The first job for the direct examiner, then, is to help the jury assimilate the information provided by the witness. This can best be accomplished by attending to the organization of the examination and by using a style of questioning that facilitates the clear flow of information from the witness to the jury.

A. Organization

It is difficult for a listener to follow any story in which the facts are jumbled. In eliciting testimony from their witnesses, attorneys must keep the facts straight by proceeding in a sequence that is easy for the listener to follow. There are essentially two means for sequencing the facts of the testimony in a manner that is easy to follow: by chronology and by topic. When the direct examination is organized so that the facts are elicited in the same sequence in which they occurred, the chronological method, jurors can stay with the witness as she relates the story. If the witness goes back and forth in time in no discernable pattern, it is easy for the jury to become confused and, thereafter, lose focus on the remainder of that witness's testimony. The second method of sequencing the facts is to cover with the witness all matters that relate to a specific topic before moving on to the next topic. While this is likely to take the testimony out of chronological order, if done well, it can serve to emphasize key aspects of testimony without making the story difficult to follow.

To see both methods of sequencing in operation, imagine a simple breach of contract case. Using the chronological method, the plaintiff would testify to coming to the attorney's office on January 29, where he signed a document with the defendant. The plaintiff would then testify to each clause of the document: that in consideration for full payment, the defendant agreed to build the plaintiff a 1) three story; 2) brick house; 3) to be completed by November 7. Next, the plaintiff would relate how he went to the job site on November 9 and saw a two story straw house that had not yet been completed. Using the topic method, the plaintiff would testify to only the first clause of the contract before telling how he visited the site and observed that the house was not three stories. He would then testify to each clause separately and show how, as to each, his observations on November 9 revealed that the terms were not honored by the defendant. Using this method, the witness stays on the topic of the particular contract term and how it was breached before moving on to another term.

A criminal case according to the chronological method might proceed as follows:

> Q: *Officer, what did you do when you arrived on the scene?*
> A: I arrested the defendant, recovered a gun from him and took him down to the station.
> Q: *What did you do next?*
> A: I gave the defendant his Miranda rights, then took my nightstick, struck the defendant several times about the stomach and obtained a voluntary confession from him.
> Q: *What action did you take next regarding this case?*
> A: I tested the gun the next day and found it to be operable.

Using the topic method, the officer's testimony, in part, would go this way:

> A: I arrested the defendant and recovered a gun from him.
> Q: *What did you do with the gun after you recovered it?*
> A: I tested it the next day and found it to be operable.
> Q: *Now, returning to the day of the crime, what did you do after you arrested the defendant?*
> A: I beat a voluntary statement out of him.

While going out of chronological order, the story is still easy to follow because it proceeds in a clearly discernable pattern. In addition, the attorney's use of transitional phrases such as "returning to the day of the crime" or "now I would like to turn your attention to" better enables the jury to stay with the witness as he proceeds through the testimony.

B. Conversational Manner

The manner in which the attorney questions the witness can contribute to the effective flow of information between the witness and the jury. We know that people assimilate more of a story if the information comes to them in a manner to which they are accustomed. When people acquire information through oral communication, they do so generally from listening to a conversation, not from observing a formal question and answer session. To the extent possible, then, attorneys should create the impression that they are having a conversation with the witness in the presence of the jury. Obviously the rules of the courtroom limit the attorney to use of a question and answer format, but there are things that can be done within that format to create the feel of a conversation.

"At the time of the alleged incident, describe your location in relation to the subject vehicle?" In all human endeavors outside a courtroom, the questioner might ask, "Where were you, where was the car?" During a trial, however, something from within drives us to attempt to "sound like a lawyer." The result of this tendency is that we forego the use of one-syllable words when four-syllable words can be found, take an understandable sequence of events and turn it into confusion, and change an interesting, at times exciting, incident into a clinical recitation of the "occurrence." The first thing to remember, therefore, about maintaining a conversational style with the witness is to use the language of normal conversation as often as possible. Both the witness and the jury will have an easier time staying with the testimony, and you will help to achieve that feeling of a conversation that maximizes the likelihood that the jury will assimilate the testimony.

Trial lawyers, apprehensive about omitting a question or wording something improperly, often look down at their pads while questioning witnesses. We seldom have conversations, however, while looking down or reading from notes. It is important to look at the witness when questioning her just as you would in conversation. Some lawyers, conscious of not wanting to read their questions, look down instead when the witness is responding. This can be even worse because, in addition to detracting from the conversational setting, such behavior may convey to the jury an unintended and undesirable message. When jurors observe you looking down as the witness is responding to your question (and make no mistake about the fact that at least some in the jury will notice this), they may sense either that you do not care about the response or that you already know precisely what answer the witness will give. If the former, jurors are unlikely to care about the response if they see that you do not. If the latter, jurors may begin to regard the testimony as canned or scripted, an image that obviously does not contribute to the credibility of your witness. In addition, you may be the only person in the courtroom that the already nervous witness knows, and she may be looking to you for some type of non-verbal support as she answers questions. The top of your head is unlikely to provide that support.

I am not suggesting you try to remember everything you wish to ask the witness. Few of us have photographic memories. It is wise to have a pad to which you can refer at counsel table in order to avoid omitting an important area of questioning. I suggest glancing at the pad after your witness has concluded an answer and before you begin your next question. The brief moment of silence in the courtroom is not problematic if it does not repeatedly interrupt the flow of the examination, and it will not detract from your conversation with the witness. While some attorneys write down the precise questions they intend to ask, I prefer putting down on the pad those areas I plan to cover with the witness and some key words which will highlight specific questions in each area. I write down verbatim only those questions that should be asked exactly, such as those that lay the foundation for the introduction of an exhibit into evidence or that enable an expert witness to render an opinion. Writing down all of the questions verbatim works well for some attorneys, but others find that it causes them to lose eye contact with the witness and makes the presentation seem too canned. Try both approaches to the use of notes and see which works best for you. Whatever method you choose, maintain eye contact with your witness when either of you is speaking.

II. Making the Testimony Persuasive

"I established everything I needed to," "I got it all on the record," "at least the jury heard it," are examples of comments uttered by attorneys relieved that their direct examination is over. So concerned is the attorney with "getting it all out" that he or she has forgotten that an important purpose of the trial is to persuade the jury. Often filled with images from books, movies and television, many new trial lawyers imagine themselves winning cases with devastating cross-examinations. Most experienced attorneys, however, are convinced that the majority of cases are won on direct examination. It is important, therefore, that the witnesses you call do an effective job of selling your case to the jury. Attorneys are, of course, limited somewhat by the character and abilities of their witnesses. Within those limitations, however, there remains much that can be accomplished by the attorney to make the case on direct more persuasive to the jury.

Some attorneys find it difficult to come up with a well-crafted series of questions through which the witness can effectively tell her story. Most of us naturally think in terms of direct statements rather than evocative questions when we consider communicating information. Therefore, prior to crafting questions for the witness's direct examination, it can be helpful for the attorney to think in terms of the *statements* she intends to make about the witness and his testimony during closing argument. If you wish to argue that the witness had a good view of the accident, for example, you know you need to elicit information from her that allows you to make that comment. Thus, you might frame questions inquiring about the location of the witness, her line of sight, her distance from the accident and what first drew her attention to the scene. Thinking through the statements you wish to make about the witness and her testimony often facilitates the task of devising the right questions.

A. Organization

The overall organization of the direct examination can contribute to a more persuasive presentation by the witness.

1. Accredit the Witness

People are more likely to be persuaded about something if the source of the information is someone they know, like and trust. Direct examiners should make a concerted effort to get the jury to view their witnesses positively before eliciting the important details of the their testimony. Often called "accrediting the witness," bringing out positive personal and professional information about the witness at the outset of his testimony has an additional benefit as well. Remember what a traumatic experience it can be for a witness to answer difficult questions under oath. Answering easier questions about his background and interests at the beginning of his testimony will put the witness at ease with the pressures of testifying and will enable him to develop a facility for answering the tougher questions that will follow.

The technique of accrediting a witness, while not difficult, can take different directions depending on who your witness is. A child who witnesses an auto accident will be accredited differently than a co-conspirator testifying for the prosecution with a grant of immunity. An orthopedic surgeon, testifying as an expert (see chapter on Expert Witnesses for discussion of their accreditation), is not accredited with the same questions asked of the mother of the criminal defendant offering an alibi for the defense. However, the purpose of the accreditation process is largely the same: to do whatever possible to make the jury receptive to the witness and his testimony before eliciting the key aspects of that testimony.

To achieve this purpose, start by giving the jury an opportunity to get to know the witness. They will be more apt to like someone they know and more likely to believe someone they like. Background questions about the witness, his family, his occupation and, to the extent the judge will allow, his interests can familiarize the jury with the witness. Next, think about specific traits of the witness that might make his testimony more persuasive, and design questions that will reveal those traits. For example, your eyewitness to the auto accident who will testify in support of your client's claim that the traffic light was red is particularly worthy of belief due to her neutrality. That is a specific trait of the witness that you intend to comment upon during summation. To inform the jury of that trait, you may want to ask the witness if prior to the accident she knew any of the parties to this action and whether she has any financial interest in the outcome of the litigation. The witness's negative response to both of these questions helps to establish the witness's credibility based on her neutrality. Another example of accrediting the witness with respect to a specific trait is having the witness testify about the detailed nature of the tasks she performs as part of her job in order to show the jury she is a careful person.

B. Set the Scene

Once you have accredited the witness, you want to set the scene for the jury. The purpose of these questions is threefold: 1) to give the jury the context in which to understand the testimony that is about to follow; 2) to cover certain details with the witness so that you will not feel the need to interrupt her recitation of the key aspects of her testimony in order to explain or clarify some detail; and 3) to build the story up to its climax. To achieve these goals, the eyewitness to the auto accident could be questioned as follows:

> Q: *Where were you at 3:00 p.m. on Dec. 6, 1996?*
> A: I was in my car waiting for the light to turn at the corner of First and Main.
> Q: *What were the weather conditions at the time?*
> A: It was clear and dry.
> Q: *Were you alone in the car?*
> A: No, my husband was with me.
> Q: *Where in the car were you seated?*
> A: My husband was driving, and I was in the passenger seat.
> Q: *Did something unusual happen at that time?*
> A: Yes, I saw a terrible accident.
> Q: *How far away were you from where the accident happened?*
> A: No more than a few feet.

Q: What was your view of the accident itself?

A: I had a clear view out the passenger's window with nothing in the way of what I saw.

This series of narrow (but not improperly leading) questions is designed to show the jury the view that the witness had of the accident scene, to reduce the likelihood that the witness will interrupt her narration of the accident that is about to follow, and to lead up to the witness's story of the accident so that the jury will rivet its attention on the witness as she relates the crucial aspects of her testimony.

C. Let the Witness Tell the Crux of the Story without Interruption

The witness is accredited. The scene is set. It is now time for the witness to give the crucial part of her testimony. An example of how *not* to adduce the critical portion of the witness's testimony comes from a rape trial I observed. The prosecutor questioned the victim as follows:

Q: Now, tell the jury what happened as you walked through the park that night?

A: All of a sudden from out of nowhere …

Q: What do you mean, from out of nowhere?

A: I mean I didn't see where he came from.

Q: Okay, go on.

A: Anyway this man came at me and …

Q: I'm sorry to interrupt you, but could you describe this man?

A: All I remember is that he was tall, blonde and had a mustache.

Q: Could you estimate his weight?

A: Not really.

Q: Okay, continue.

A: He jumped at me, pointed a knife and said …

Q: Before you tell us what he said, please describe the knife.

A: It was black and sharp.

Q: Which hand was it in?

A: You mean the knife?

Q: Yes.

A: I think it was in the right.

Q: What happened then?

A: Where was I?

Q: *He was about to say something to you.*

A: Right. He said if I opened my mouth he'd cut me and then he pulled at my blouse.

Q: *With which hand did he grab your blouse?*

This prosecutor forgot that the role of the attorney on direct is to facilitate the information flow from the WITNESS to the jury. You do this best by opening the door and getting out of the way. Questions such as "What happened" and "What happened next" may not get you into the Litigator's Hall of Fame, but they will allow your witness to tell the story in her own words and most likely capture the drama of the moment as well. The attorney should avoid interrupting the witness's recitation of this crucial part of her testimony unless such an interruption is absolutely necessary (i.e., if the recitation is difficult for the listener to understand or the witness is going on far too long).

Matters that the witness omits from her recitation should be elicited with follow-up questions rather than interruptions that break the flow of the story and cause it to lose much of its impact. Done this way, the jury will be paying maximum attention to the witness during the crux of her testimony, and her story will have a powerful and lasting effect upon them. While most of the questions asked by the prosecutor above were designed to elicit important facts, he should have waited to ask them until the victim told the story of the rape in her own words and without interruption.

Once the witness has given the key part of her testimony in response to an open ended question, the attorney should ask narrower questions intended to elicit any details that were omitted by the witness. Other important twin purposes of these follow-up questions are to emphasize certain strong points within the testimony and to deal with weaknesses that exist in the witness's account of the story or in her credibility.

D. Emphasize the Strong Points in the Testimony

Attorneys often conduct their direct examination in too linear a pattern. Each point is covered in roughly the same period of time and with the same degree of focus. That is not, however, how juries evaluate the evidence. Certain points carry greater weight than others and play more of a role in the jury's ultimate decision. The direct examiner should guide the jurors to the appropriate points of emphasis by focusing their attention on the strengths of the witness's testimony. The attorney can emphasize a certain point by: 1) having the witness discuss the matter again in response to a different question; 2) prefacing subsequent questions with the testimony to be emphasized; or 3) through the use of a demonstration or demonstrative exhibit. Imagine the attorney who wishes to emphasize the testimony just given by an eyewitness that after the defendant's car hit the pedestrian, the latter went up in the air and landed on the hood of the car. Using each of the above techniques, respectively, the questioning might proceed as follows:

Method 1:

Q: *How high did the body go into the air after the crash?*
A: About four or five feet.
Q: *Where was the body when it reached its highest point?*
A: Right in front of the driver's windshield
Q: *How long before the body came down?*
A: Probably a few seconds
Q: *How could you tell it came down?*
A: I saw it land on the hood and I heard another loud thud.

Method 2:

Q: *After you saw the body fly into the air, what did you do?*
A: I yelled to my wife.
Q: *When the body landed on the hood, what did you do?*
A: I ran over to see if I could help.

Method 3:

Q: *I show you what has been introduced into evidence as Plaintiff's Exhibit Three. Do you recognize it?*
A: It looks like a photo of the car that hit the pedestrian.
Q: *Does it fairly and accurately depict the way the defendant's car looked at the time of the accident?*
A: Yes
Q: *Please take this marker and place a number 1 where the body was at its highest point.*
A: It was here (marking on the photo).
Q: *Let the record reflect that the witness drew a number 1 directly in front of the driver side windshield.*

The attorney would then replicate the questioning with respect to where the body landed and ask the judge to publish the photograph to the jury. The actual procedure for using demonstrative evidence will be discussed in the chapter on Exhibits. For now, it is enough to see how physical or demonstrative evidence, and the other techniques illustrated above, can be used to emphasize certain points and make the testimony more meaningful for the jury.

E. Deal with the Weaknesses in the Testimony

As with the strengths of the witness's testimony, the attorney must be prepared to deal with any weaknesses that emerge. Anything that detracts from the likelihood that the jury will accept the witness's testimony can be characterized as a weakness. A weakness may derive from something within the witness's fact recitation, or it may result from factors that bear on the credibility of the witness. The central issue the attorney has to resolve with respect to any weakness is whether to bring out the point on direct or, instead, to wait to rehabilitate the witness on redirect examination if the witness has not satisfactorily responded to the issue on cross-examination.

Eliciting a weakness on direct, often referred to as anticipating cross-examination, has several benefits. First, when the proponent of the witness brings out the negative fact, it takes some of the sting out of the cross-examination. Having heard it already, the jury is likely to be less affected when the cross-examiner has the witness respond to the issue a second time. Additionally, anticipating cross-examination affords the witness the opportunity to explain or limit the weakness somewhat and thereby mitigate its damage. Finally, during opening statement and closing argument, the attorney can point out that there was no attempt on the part of the witness to conceal the negative fact, as she brought it out herself. Take the following example:

Q: *Mr. Jones, have you ever been convicted of a crime?*
A: I was convicted of robbery nine years ago.
Q: *What actions did you take after that conviction?*
A: I got treatment for the drug problem that caused my criminal behavior and then got a job, which I still hold today.
Q: *Have you been involved in any criminal activity since you got off drugs?*
A: None whatsoever.

Even the simple effort taken by the direct examiner above has reduced the negative impact on the jury that will result from learning of the witness's felony conviction on cross-examination. It permitted the witness to minimize the substance of the weakness in response to supportive questions and allowed for comment in opening and closing to the effect that the witness wished to provide this information himself so as not to conceal anything from the jury.

The attorney considering anticipating cross-examination needs to be aware of certain issues pertaining to that decision. Obviously, if you believe your opponent may be unaware of a weakness in your witness's testimony or is unable to elicit the information on cross-examination (perhaps because such a question may "open the door" to areas that will hurt your opponent), you should avoid covering the weakness on direct. If you do cover the weakness, do not do it in a way that will emphasize its importance in the eyes of the jury. Such emphasis can result from dwelling on the weakness too long or choosing to elicit it at a crucial time, such as in your last series of questions. Most experienced trial lawyers try to bury the weakness somewhere in the middle of their examination.

F. The Use of Displays, Demonstrations and Experiments

The defendant is charged with assaulting John Smith primarily because he wanted to bully the victim into doing something against Smith's will. Smith will testify that the defendant is a "very large man", but when the prosecutor gets the defendant to stand up in front of the jury, the menacing nature of the defendant will resonate much more profoundly. While the plaintiff may testify to how the injury he sustained as a result of the defendant's negligence has made it difficult for him to walk, allowing the jury to see the plaintiff limping will bring home the point far more directly. Can anyone forget the impact on the jury in the O.J. Simpson murder case when the gloves used by the prosecution to link Simpson to the murders appeared to be too tight for him when he was asked to try them on before the jury? If the gloves don't fit, you must acquit became the mantra of Simpson's attorney, Johnnie Cochran, as Simpson was acquitted of the murders. In a products liability suit, an experiment that shows just how little time it takes for a supposedly flame-retardant fabric in children's pajamas to catch fire will dramatically illustrate the danger to a child wearing those pajamas.

Displays, demonstrations and experiments, such as those alluded to above, can be a potent tool in the hands of the trial lawyer. First, however, she must know how to get them before the jury. Each method can raise evidentiary challenges that need to be considered.

Generally speaking, displays of real evidence are likely to be permitted by the trial judge. Plaintiff's counsel can ask his client to show the scars and burn marks that resulted from the injuries he suffered due to the defendant's careless driving. The prosecution can show the jury the switchblade knife that was used by the defendant when he stabbed the victim. The attorney representing the auto manufacturer can display for the jury the shredded tire she claims was the cause of the fatal accident. There are some displays however which may violate FRE 403 and its exclusion of evidence whose probative value is substantially outweighed by its prejudicial impact. Thus it is highly unlikely than any judge will allow the leg severed during the construction accident to be shown to the jury.

Demonstrations raise similar issues but additional ones as well. When a witness is asked to demonstrate her injury for the jury, there is a real danger that the witness will either consciously or subconsciously embellish the extent of the injury during the demonstration. Day in the life videos, which purport to show how an injury has affected the ability of a litigant to conduct her normal everyday life, are particularly susceptible to this danger. Such behavior could lead to an objection from the opposing party or to very damaging cross-examination casting doubt not only on the extent of the injury to the party, but to her credibility as well. The message then to the attorney using a demonstration is to avoid having it come off as if the party is exaggerating or playing for the jury's sympathy. Remember too that trial judges traditionally are afforded considerable discretion in deciding which demonstrations are permissible.

Judges tend to be even more wary of experiments conducted in their courtrooms. The purpose of conducting an experiment in the courtroom is to show that the result of the experiment is the same or similar to the result that occurred during the incident itself. The plaintiff's attorney wants to show that the pajama fabric caught fire 3 seconds after being exposed to a certain heat source. To do so, she has an expert witness use the same or similar heat source to set fire to an identical pair of pajamas. Note that such an experiment can be done before trial and testified to by the expert, but performing it in the courtroom, if permitted, would have substantially more impact. When the jury sees the pajamas catch fire in 3 seconds, the point regarding the danger to a child of the supposedly flame-retardant fabric is demonstrated dramatically and unforgettably.

To be permitted to conduct an experiment, its proponent must show that the conditions surrounding the courtroom experiment are the same or substantially the same as those existing at the time of the incident that generated the lawsuit. If the opponent of the experiment can show any material change in conditions between the two times, then the result of the courtroom experiment will be irrelevant or misleading, and the court is unlikely to permit it. In the above case for example, if the defense attorney is able to show that the conditions in the courtroom that led to the fabric quickly catching fire do not mirror the conditions that existed at the time that the pajamas at issue burned, the plaintiff will not be allowed to conduct the experiment.

In addition to considering the evidentiary issues generated from the use of displays, demonstrations and experiments, attorneys considering their use need also to think about how to get the most out of them. Most important in this regard is insuring that the jury can see exactly what the witness is doing. This evidence is not oral as with most of the testimony that takes place during a trial, but visual. If the jury cannot see it, the display, demonstration or experiment loses much of its value. Attorneys should therefore look carefully throughout the courtroom and determine where the witness should testify from that affords the jury the best line of sight. This is not always from the witness stand. Once such a place is determined, the attorney should check with the judge to make sure that having the witness testify from that location is permissible. You don't want to find out during the middle of the witness's demonstration that the court won't permit it from the place you thought best.

It is most helpful to the jury to know the relevance of the item displayed, or the purpose of the demonstration or experiment performed before it takes place. Such advanced knowledge will aid the jurors in assimilating what they have just seen and is likely to increase its impact upon them. The purpose of some displays demonstrations and experiments is obvious. Others are not so obvious, and so greater attention must be paid to educating the jury in advance about them. This can be done during opening statement as well as during the testimony of the relevant witnesses.

Done right and done well, displays, demonstrations and experiments can go a long way towards insuring that important trial points are brought home to the jury in ways they will not forget.

III. Style

Along with the organization and content of the testimony, the attorney's style contributes significantly to the overall effectiveness of the witness's presentation. The means through which the attorney relates to the witness and the personal mannerisms the attorney displays can add to, or detract from, the clarity and persuasiveness of the testimony.

A. Attorney's Relationship with the Witness

The first person to whom the jury sees the witness relate is you. Long before they begin to assess the content of the witness's testimony, they observe how you treat the witness. Therefore, the jurors' first impression of the witness often mirrors what they perceive to be your view of her. Accordingly, treat the witness in a manner consistent with the way in which you want the jury to regard the witness. Your expert should be treated with the utmost respect, the child witness with care, and the injured witness with concern. You manifest this relationship with your witness by the way you address her, your tone, your body language and the form of your questions.

For illustration, consider the following: When addressing your expert or professional witness, use titles to convey your respect. Addressing "Doctor Smith," "Officer Miller," and "Inspector Lane" create the appropriate first impressions for the jury. Assume a gentle tone with a child witness, a formal tone as a prosecutor questioning a co-conspirator giving evidence for the State. Be aware that although you may like to stand with your arms folded, such body language can convey a negative impression with respect to how you are responding to the witness's answers. While the use of leading questions may aid certain witnesses in getting through their testimony, it may also leave the jury with the impression that the witness lacks knowledge or recall of the facts. There are many other verbal and non-verbal cues we give off which communicate to the jury our relationship with the witness. The attorney should be aware of these cues and refrain from exhibiting those that convey a negative impression.

B. Personal Mannerisms That Distract the Jury

Attempting to listen carefully to all that goes on during a trial can be an onerous task for a juror. It is hardly surprising, therefore, that the attention of a juror can wander at times during the trial. Your style of questioning and personal mannerisms can either contribute to, or detract from, the degree of attention the jury is paying to your witness.

In stressful situations, it is common for people to exhibit nervous habits. Since few professional situations are more stressful than jury trials, it is understandable that attorneys display a wide variety of mannerisms that distract the attention of the jury. Perhaps the most common stems from an often sub-conscious fear of even a momentary silence during questioning. To fill this void, we say "okay" or "uh" or use the word "and" as a bridge between questions. Constantly hearing this becomes distracting for the listener, and some jurors looking for a break from the tedium of following the testimony choose instead to count the "okays." When the attorney fails to say "okay" after one response, the jury may wonder if the attorney was not happy with that answer.

When nervous, some attorneys play with the change in their pocket, others wave their pen around or tap it annoyingly on the table. Some speak quickly when the adrenaline starts pumping while others manifest nerves by speaking with a flat affect. I have seen attorneys during their examination constantly wiping imaginary hair from their foreheads, opening and closing the same button repeatedly, and fixing their ties every 30 seconds. When told about their distracting mannerisms, many reply that they were not aware of what they were doing. Unfortunately, the jurors usually are. The first step on the road to rehabilitation, therefore, is to have someone observe your examination technique and let you know whether you exhibit some mannerism that may distract the jury's attention from the testimony of your witness.

Habits are not easy to break, but developing an awareness of what we do enables us to think about ways of modifying our behavior.

Regardless of how clear or persuasive your presentation of the direct examination is, it will have little effect if members of the jury are unable to hear parts of your questions or the witness's answers. To avoid this, assume that at least one juror is somewhat hard of hearing, so that you are always conscious of ensuring that both your voice and that of the witness is clearly audible. If your witness has a tendency to drop his voice (and reminding him to speak up has not helped), you may want to position yourself at the far end of the jury box during your direct examination. In addition to the likelihood that he will speak louder in responding to you from a greater distance, the witness will more often address his statements in the direction of the jury. Auditory problems occur frequently when attorneys and witnesses are working with exhibits. Some attorneys feel safer if they stand close to the witness as he is illustrating his testimony with a diagram or reviewing a document on the witness stand. To avoid shouting at each other at close range, the voices of both parties are likely to get softer, causing the jury to miss some of the presentation. After handing the witness the document or showing him the diagram, the attorney is well advised to step back and resume a normal questioning position. Finally, if questioning from counsel table, do not let your hands get in front of your mouth. Some jurors pick up words they are unable to hear clearly by watching your lips.

C. Pace and Position

Two other stylistic concerns that arise frequently are pace and position. The pace of your questioning should be slow enough so that the jury can understand and absorb your dialogue with the witness yet quick enough to maintain the jury's interest. I am often asked whether the attorney should stand or sit during his or her examination. The answer to this question is more complex than it would appear. First, find out whether the jurisdiction you are in or the judge you are before requires attorneys to stand or sit while questioning witnesses. While most courts give the attorney the option, some do not, and you do not want to be admonished about your choice. Assuming you have the option, you may want to begin by thinking in general of the contrasting roles of the attorney in direct and cross-examination.

While the effective cross-examiner essentially provides the information to the jury himself or herself, with the witness acting as a mere deflector of the information (see chapter on Cross-Examination), the direct examiner should be merely a facilitator of the flow of information between witness and jury. With this in mind, many attorneys prefer to sit during direct to make it easier for the witness to be the focus of the jury's attention and to stand on cross when the attorney is the star. Other matters, however, should be factored into the decision of whether to sit or stand. Is the configuration of the courtroom such that it is particularly conducive to one position over the other? Are there communication concerns, such as the audibility issue discussed above, that favor one position? Finally, do you feel more comfortable sitting or standing? The way in which you intend to arrange and use your notes and your ability to relax better in one position than the other are among the matters that may affect your level of comfort.

As with many issues involving something as individual as your style of communication, there is no one right answer for everyone in every situation to the question of whether to sit or stand during questioning. Be aware, however, that when addressing the court, it is often deemed to be a sign of disrespect if the attorney remains seated. While you may not need to pop out of your chair each time you say, "Objection," you need to be on your feet for any other colloquy with the court.

IV. Redirect Examination

If your witness has been adequately prepared (see chapter on Witness Preparation), you have discussed with her the weaknesses of her testimony that are likely to be probed on cross-examination. Some of these weaknesses may have been dealt with through anticipating the cross-examination during direct, while others were handled satisfactorily by the witness during the cross. Despite the thoroughness of your witness preparation, the cross-examiner may have raised other issues or the witness may not have handled a question as well as possible, thus raising doubts about some aspect of her testimony. If such a situation developed during cross-examination, the attorney should consider the benefits of doing a redirect examination.

The purpose of conducting a redirect is to rehabilitate the witness, not to rehash what was already covered adequately during direct. If no real damage was done to your witness during cross-examination, there is usually no need to do a redirect. Furthermore, if you believe your witness is unlikely to have or unable to articulate a satisfactory explanation for an answer given during cross, you may not wish to risk causing greater damage by exploring the issue again during redirect examination.

If your witness has been damaged during cross and you are confident she can be somewhat rehabilitated through supportive questioning, conducting a redirect can be helpful. The focus of the redirect is often on the reason *why* the witness said or did something. Assume that the witness testified on direct examination that the traffic light was green when the defendant driver went through it. On cross-examination, he was impeached by the plaintiff's attorney with a statement he made to a police officer immediately after the accident to the effect that he was not sure of the color of the traffic light at the time in question. The defense attorney may wish to proceed as follows on redirect:

Q: *The plaintiff's attorney asked you about a statement you made to the officer immediately after the accident. Do you remember making that statement?*
A: Only vaguely.
Q: *Why is that?*
A: I was real shaken up having just seen a serious auto accident from close up. That has never happened to me before.
Q: *What led you to say that you did not know the color of the traffic light?*
A: When the officer spoke to me, it was immediately after the accident and as I said, I was still quite upset about what I had seen. I

felt lucky that I wasn't involved and at the same time was concerned about the people in the accident. It was a pretty awful moment. I was not really thinking about the color of the light. When
I got home my wife asked me what happened and in thinking
about the accident somewhat more clearly, I realized that I had
seen that the light was green.

The focus of this redirect was to allow the witness to explain away a weakness in his testimony and hopefully mitigate its damage before the jury. The
attorney should have been aware from reading the police report that the plaintiff would elicit the inconsistent statement. During preparation, the witness
would have been asked why he told this to the police and then informed that
he would have a chance to inform the jury of his explanation on redirect.

CHAPTER 4

CROSS-EXAMINATION

A witness for the other side, who swore to tell the truth and appeared to do exactly that, has just told the jury a compelling story that offers significant support to your opponent's case. Given the opportunity to question the witness, you now face what attorneys regard as the most difficult task confronting the trial lawyer, doing an effective cross-examination. As with direct examination, before an attorney can perform effectively on cross-examination, he or she must understand its purpose and know how to prepare for the difficult encounter that lies ahead.

Regardless of what we see on television or read in novels about trials, witnesses are seldom devastated on cross-examination. The images of witnesses being trapped into admitting the "truth" or having their testimony broken down by the Perry Mason-like skill of the clever cross-examiner should be confined to the fiction from which they emerged. When planning a cross-examination, attorneys should begin by setting realistic goals for what they hope to accomplish. Raising meaningful questions about adverse testimony or devising ways to limit its scope or impact upon the jury are reasonable expectations the attorney might envision for his or her cross-examination. To see a witness "destroyed," read John Grisham.

I. Preparation

A. Preparing for the Witness's Testimony

In preparing for cross-examination, the attorney should make good use of the rules of discovery and whatever other investigative resources are at her disposal to obtain everything the witness has written or said about the subject matter of the testimony. Additionally, as every person who takes the witness stand puts his or her credibility at issue, the attorney should endeavor to learn as much as possible about the witness, even beyond the subject matter of the testimony. As the attorney reads this material, she should remember that every word spoken by or said about the witness may serve to limit the witness's response to a question or be used to impeach the witness during cross-examination. Accordingly, the attorney should read this material carefully, making note of where she can locate each piece of information that may be germane to an area of inquiry on cross-examination. Then, during the cross-examination, the attorney will have these references in the written material ready at her disposal, so as not to break the flow of the examination by frequently taking extended time periods to locate them. The rhythm of the cross-examination is an important factor in its effectiveness. During the time it takes to scour a 50-page deposition, the jury's attention level will wane and the sharpness of the point being made through use of the prior statement will be diminished.

B. Preparing for Objections

In preparing for cross-examination, the attorney should do his or her best to anticipate what will be covered on direct. Not only will this help to shape the cross-examination, but it will allow the attorney to be better prepared to make necessary objections in a timely and effective manner. Even experienced litigators often have trouble knowing when to object, and articulating their objections persuasively if asked by the court to do so. In part, this is due to the rapid pace of the question and answer format for witness examinations. Imagine the attorney listening carefully to the substance of the direct, thinking about her own cross-examination to come and simultaneously attempting to decide whether a particular question is objectionable and why. "That out-of-court statement may be hearsay. It seems to be offered for the truth of the matter asserted, but does it go to the declarant's state of mind or is it pathologically germane?" "He is not offering the original of the letter into evidence but only a memorandum purporting to embody its contents. That could violate the Best Evidence Rule. Under the Rules, I remember there are exceptions. If I can just look them up...." Unfortunately, in the time it takes to think through whether the question is objectionable and weigh the benefits of objecting, the other attorney has long since completed that question and the judge is likely to view any objection as untimely.

Some experienced attorneys report that they can sense instantly when a question is objectionable and think through their arguments as they rise to object. For everyone else, however, anticipating what questions the direct examiner is likely to ask and what exhibits he may use affords the opportunity to prepare for when to object and what to argue should the need arise. Obviously, no attorney can envision every question that the direct examiner will ask or the precise form those questions will take, but the cross-examiner should have a fairly good idea of the key aspects of the direct and what evidence she wishes to have kept from the jury. Now when your opponent offers into evidence a document that he claims falls within the business record exception to the hearsay rule, you can argue that entries within the record were not made contemporaneously as required by the exception, and that the record contains hearsay within hearsay.

II. Organization

Unlike direct examination, cross-examination does not lend itself to any obvious organizational patterns. The cross-examiner, unlike the direct examiner, is not attempting to have the witness relate information to the fact finder by telling a story. Proceeding chronologically through the testimony or covering all questions related to one event or aspect of the witness's testimony, therefore, is not necessary on cross-examination, and may not be the most effective means to limit the damage done by the witness during her direct testimony.

A. Break the Testimony into Component Parts

In planning how to organize your cross, it is helpful to keep in mind the daunting task that lies ahead. The typical witness, having taken the oath to tell the truth, has probably just done that to the best of her ability. The jury is likely to view the witness as a decent person, worthy of belief, who has just related an event or conversation with which she is obviously familiar. How do you limit the damage to your case that this witness has done? Your first effort should be directed toward making your job less daunting. This can be accomplished organizationally by coming up with a sensible manner of breaking the witness's testimony into component parts and focusing on any weaknesses with respect to each part. It is significantly easier to plan an attack on a certain piece of a witness's testimony than to try to think in a gestalt-like way of going after the whole.

Each cross-examination will require a different set of component parts, but the effort expended to find the most helpful ones should enable the attorney systematically to consider each area of questioning, determine whether any particular area is likely to be fruitful, prioritize each area so as to decide where emphasis should be placed and help develop overall themes for the examination.

1. Example of Creating Component Parts for Cross Examination of Eyewitness

Envision a situation where the prosecutor has just examined Dr. Jan Smith, an eyewitness to a bank robbery who has implicated the defendant in the crime. An apparently honest, thoughtful, careful and caring physician has testified under oath that she is certain that your client was the culprit. How do you go about structuring a cross-examination of so effective a witness? First, realize that the cross-examination of the eyewitness is among the most frequent you will encounter in both civil and criminal cases. Studies show that the testimony of the eyewitness is likely to have a profound impact upon the jury unless that testimony can be challenged in some way. Your first job is to find an effective way to separate the testimony into component parts.

One way of segmenting eyewitness testimony is to apply what we have learned about the process of perception from psychologists. Most people believe that observing an event with our eyes is similar to the operation of a camera. That is, seeing and assimilating the event is similar to taking the picture, and telling about the event we saw is the equivalent of developing the film and revealing the photograph. Perceptual psychologists tell us that far from being camera-like, witnessing an event and testifying about what was observed involves several separate processes, any one of which could contain flaws that lead to inaccuracy. In order to challenge eyewitness testimony effectively, the cross-examiner may need to educate the jury, through his or her questions, to overcome popular misconceptions about eyewitness testimony.

One way to so educate the jury is to organize the cross-examination of an eyewitness by using as component parts the various mental processes involved in perception. Psychologists tell us that perception encompasses three separate phases: data acquisition, impression, and memory. The accurate acquisition of data depends upon the physical conditions that surround the act of observing an event. Data that makes little impression on us when we receive it is less likely to be recalled accurately. Even data acquired accurately that formed an impression when acquired can be forgotten over time. The cross-examiner can devise questions that probe each of these phases of eyewitness testimony in order to detect the presence of flaws that could lead to inaccuracy.

Applying the above component parts to our cross-examination of Dr. Smith, the eyewitness to the robbery, would lead to consideration of the following types of questions. Regarding the acquisition of the data, we might inquire about the lighting conditions, the witness's distance from the man she claims to be the robber, impediments to her view of that individual and any events in her own life, such as lack of sleep, that might have affected her ability to acquire the data accurately. If we know that the doctor saw the perpetrator in broad daylight, from a distance of 5 feet, entirely unimpeded and after 8 hours of sleep, we may wish to turn our attention to impression.

If the witness saw the man she believes to be the robber only *enter* the bank, questions may be designed to elicit that the man was dressed similarly to others on the street that day, the vague and incomplete description of the man she provided to the police, that he was carrying no weapon, had no particular distinguishing marks and that the doctor had no idea what was about to happen when she saw the man. The point of these questions is to be able to argue to the jury that the witness is unlikely to remember a man who made little impression on her at the time she saw him, and that her generic description of the suspect demonstrates this. We see many people do exactly what the witness saw the man she believed to be the robber do, yet take little notice of them and would be hard-pressed to positively identify such individuals at a later date. Should, however, the doctor say that she observed the man come bolting out of the bank with a shotgun in one hand and a money bag with a big dollar sign in the other hand, perhaps we'd best refrain from questions related to impression and look to the witness's memory of the event.

A number of things can affect and alter our memory of events. Discussions we have with acquaintances or other witnesses, seeing accounts of the event in the media, a variety of suggestive behaviors on the part of the police related to identification procedures, other events going on in our lives, or merely the passage of time can all result in flawed memory.

Inconsistencies in previous accounts of the event given by the witness can serve to illustrate these memory flaws. Questions designed to probe these memory-related topics might reveal that although Dr. Smith may have gotten a good look at the man she claims to be the robber, she may have forgotten or remembered incorrectly important features of her identification.[2]

---

2. In a civil case, you can learn about facts surrounding an identification by deposing the witness. In a criminal case, you should attempt to conduct a thorough interview of the witness pretrial, if possible obtain a signed or recorded statement. Don't risk cementing the credibility of the witness by eliciting facts that only enhance the witness's ability to perceive.

2. Example of Creating Component Parts for Cross Examination of Witness Connected to the Opponent

While the testimony of the identification eyewitness above may be best divided and organized for cross-examination purposes by using the component parts of the process of perception, other witnesses testifying to what they claim to have seen require different treatment. At a personal injury trial, the defense has called an investigator that it hired to follow the plaintiff to see if her activities were consistent with the severity of the injury she claims to have suffered. On direct examination, the investigator testified he observed the plaintiff picking up her young child, taking several practice swings with a golf club and carrying shopping bags into her house. In support of this testimony, the defense introduced into evidence a photograph of the plaintiff holding her child. The purpose of this witness's testimony is to show that the plaintiff is vastly overstating the extent of the injury to her shoulder that she suffered when hit by defendant's car. Since there is no dispute that the investigator has correctly identified the plaintiff in each of these observations, the cross-examiner should create different component parts than those used in the robbery case above. Ascertaining the best way to divide and organize the cross-examination requires thinking about the different ways in which you can raise questions regarding the claims of the investigator.

Begin your planning by considering who the witness is and whether any bias he might have could lead to exaggeration or coloring of his testimony. Where, for example, the witness has a relationship with your opponent, hostility toward your client, or has been hired by your opponent, the possibility exists for cross-examination designed to expose this bias. Through your questions, you want to show the jury the reasons why the witness may be viewing events with a slant most favorable to your opponent. Additionally, there may be aspects of the witness's character, background or the nature of what he did in this case that allow you to discredit him as a witness. Consider the following questioning:

> Q: *You were hired by the defendant in this case to keep tabs on Ms. Tyler?*
> A: I was.
> Q: *To do this you were paid $400 a day by the defense?*
> A: That is the standard rate.
> Q: *And you are here today testifying for the folks who paid you?*
> A: I'm telling what I saw.
> Q: *One way in which you get new business is to get favorable references from previous clients. Is that correct?*

A: I suppose so.

Q: *I imagine you would like a favorable reference from the defendant in this case on a job well done?*

A: Sure.

Q: *You are aware that the defendant would benefit from your claiming that Ms. Tyler could use her shoulder to help her perform difficult physical tasks?*

A: I guess so.

Q: *Is it true that you followed Ms. Tyler to work, sat secretly outside of her office, followed her home, observed her through the windows of her home and then followed her car when she drove her children to child care?*

A: I had every right to observe her at those times.

Q: *And for following Ms. Tyler, spying on her, consulting on several occasions with the defense and testifying for them today, they paid you a total of $3,200?*

A: I was compensated for the time I spent on this matter in the amount you stated.

Note that the above questioner never directly confronted the witness with the accusation that he colored his testimony to assist his client. Such direct accusations are counterproductive, leading invariably to a strong denial and often to bickering with the witness that produces sympathy for him from the jurors. You will be better served by returning to the issue of bias point during your summation when you are providing the jury with reasons for discounting the investigator's testimony. Remember, in the real world you will not "break down" the witness with these or other questions. Your goal is to cause the jury to question the testimony, in this case due to the bias of the witness.

A second means of challenging the thrust of an adverse witness's testimony is to accept *arguendo* the factual accuracy of parts of the testimony, but reveal to the jury there are different conclusions that can be drawn. From the testimony of the investigator, the defense is attempting to convince the jury that the witness could not have been feeling great pain in her shoulder as she was able to perform the acts described. While conceding that the plaintiff did have shopping bags in her hands and did pick up her child, you can, through your cross-examination, raise questions about whether this should lead to a conclusion that the plaintiff's shoulder was fit. Your questions regarding the shopping bags could ascertain that from his vantage point the investigator could not discern what was in the bags and, (assuming your client has so informed you) therefore, was unaware that the bags each contained one lightweight blouse that Ms. Tyler was about to return. As to lifting her child, did the investigator see the child fall, hurt his knee and hear him cry uncontrollably immediately before Ms. Tyler lifted him? Was he aware that Ms. Tyler suffered great pain from doing so and thereafter iced down her shoulder and had to take strong medicine to alleviate the pain? You may choose to elicit this testimony directly from the plaintiff during your rebuttal case, but it is helpful to raise questions about the damaging implications of the investigator's testimony before they sink in too deeply with the jury.

The third avenue for raising doubts about the witness's testimony is to challenge the accuracy of certain aspects of his story. This can be accomplished either by showing that the witness can be honestly mistaken (as with the eyewitness to the bank robbery discussed above) or by suggesting through your questions that the witness may have deliberately exaggerated or colored his version of events (see discussion below regarding how to treat the witness). Assume that your client has vigorously denied ever having taken a practice swing with a golf club since the time of the accident. The approach here is to challenge the accuracy of the testimony. Where the witness has made no prior inconsistent statements about seeing the swings, this can be a difficult task. You may wish to raise questions about the witness's opportunity to observe the swing, possibly asking about how long the supposed swing took, under what conditions he observed it and suggest that what the investigator thought was a swing could have been something entirely different. Most professional witnesses, however, are likely to be adept at fielding such questions concerning what they did. The better path with such witnesses often is to ask them about what they did not do that could have affirmed their testimony. The examination of the investigator could proceed as follows:

> Q: *You testified that you have been an investigator for 10 years and conducted hundreds of surveillances during that time?*
> A: That is correct.
> Q: *You have also testified in court on numerous occasions about your investigations.*
> A: Yes.
> Q: *Surely, you have used a camcorder to record your observations on some of your investigations?*
> A: I did not think that was appropriate or needed here.
> Q: *I gather you didn't, but my question is whether you have used such equipment previously.*

A: Sure.

Q: *In fact, isn't it true that you have presented to juries in other cases in which you testified video footage of what you observed?*

A: Yes.

Q: *Apparently, you did think it was appropriate to use a still camera in this case. Is that correct?*

A: Yes.

Q: *In fact, you brought into court today a photograph you took of Ms. Tyler holding her child.*

A: I did.

Q: *You took that photo because you believed that event was significant regarding the issues in this case.*

A: In part.

Q: *And based on your vast experience as an investigator and a witness, you thought the photo was important to confirm your testimony.*

A: I thought it would be helpful for the jury.

Q: *Do you have any photographs that you can show this jury to confirm your claim that Ms. Tyler took several practice golf swings?*

A: No.

Before questioning the witness about what he did not do, it is helpful first to make clear to the jury both that he *could* have and that he *should* have taken the action you are asking about. One way of doing this is to elicit that he has done so on previous occasions in similar situations. Additionally, you want to get the witness to acknowledge the benefit that could have been achieved had he done what you suggest. Where, as here, the witness has actually taken the suggested course of action with respect to another aspect of his testimony (the photograph of the plaintiff holding her child), his failure to do so on this occasion casts even stronger doubt on his claimed observation or at least suggests that he did not regard the event as particularly significant.

The final manner of challenging the damaging inferences that your opponent wants the jury to draw from his witness is to elicit from the witness those matters he observed that affirmatively support your position. From discovery materials (later to be supplemented by what you hear from the witness during direct examination), you may learn of things that the witness can testify about that are favorable to your theory of the case. You want to ensure that you are not in such an adverse frame of mind regarding the witness that you ignore those aspects of his testimony that help your case and that he is likely to acknowledge. Once again be aware of what the witness said and what he did not say.

Q: From your report, I see you watched Ms. Tyler and her husband shop for food?

A: That is correct.

Q: You watched as Mr. Tyler carried each bag to the car?

A: I did.

Q: In fact, isn't it true that Mr. Tyler had to make several trips back and forth to the car with shopping bags because Ms. Tyler was unable to help?

A: I don't know if she was able to help, but he did carry all of the packages.

Q: You conducted surveillance on Ms. Tyler for about a week. Is that correct?

A: Yes.

Q: You testified that during that time you watched her for several hours each day?

A: Yes.

Q: In all that time you saw Ms. Tyler pick up her child one time?

A: I didn't see her every moment.

Q: You did see her with her child on many occasions, however, and saw her pick him up only the one time you testified about. Is that correct?

A: I saw her lift him one time.

Q: I note from your report that you refer to her lifting packages only on the one occasion you testified about?

A: That is correct.

Q: In fact, during that entire week, you never saw Ms. Tyler lift anything else that you thought was significantly heavy enough to include in your report?

A: Not that I recall.

Q: And you know now those bags contained only lightweight blouses?

A: That's what she says.

Planning the cross-examination of different witnesses will yield different component parts in which to divide their testimony. In the above example, the component parts were: 1) the witness as a person; 2) accepting *arguendo* the accuracy of parts of the witness's testimony but offering different conclusions that could be drawn from the testimony; 3) challenging the accuracy of other aspects of the testimony as being either mistaken or biased; and 4) eliciting from the witness those observations that are favorable to your theory. To identify the best component parts for any cross-examination, closely analyze the witness and the testimony he is likely to give. After you analyze the testimony and learn all you can from independent sources, write down the points you want to make during summation that raise questions about both the witness's factual allegations and the conclusions your opponent draws from those allegations. At this stage, you are in a position to organize an examination that will develop each point fully before moving on to the next. Furthermore, you can determine which areas of inquiry are likely to be the most fruitful and decide how to best emphasize those areas for the fact finder. Then you can begin to think of how to frame your questions to accomplish these goals.

III. Framing the Question and Limiting the Response

As with direct examination, writing down the exact questions to be asked will work well for some attorneys but not for others. It is particularly important for attorneys to maintain their flexibility during cross-examination. Regardless how thoroughly the cross-examiner has prepared for the examination, it is not unusual for the witness to say something during direct or cross that requires a change in the way a question should be asked. A witness may have exhibited a degree of uncertainty concerning a fact at issue for the first time during trial or, conversely, become more precise in his recollection of an event than he had been previously. In the first instance, a question or series of questions designed to show that the witness could not be certain of the fact would likely need to be changed in substance and tone from what was originally envisioned by the cross-examiner. In the second case, the cross-examiner may wish to expand the questioning beyond what was prepared to demonstrate that, given his prior statement, the witness is unlikely to be as accurate as he is precise. In both situations, the cross-examiner should be flexible enough to account for modifications in the manner in which the witness handled an area of questioning. If you benefit from writing down your questions verbatim and can adjust as the situation warrants during trial, do so. Even if you do not write them down verbatim, considerable thought still needs to be given to how you will frame each of your questions.

A. Elicit Responses Only

To achieve the goals of cross-examination, it is important to remember that, in contrast to direct examiners, cross-examiners seek to elicit only responses from the witness, not information or explanations. Recall from the discussion in the chapter on Direct Examination the limited nature of the response sought by the cross-examiner, and how the desired response is analogous to that which B.F.Skinner elicited from his chickens. Skinner was not interested in explanations or interpretations of the behavior of his chickens, but primarily in eliciting the responses he desired from the stimulus applied. In the same way, cross-examiners use leading questions to get the desired responses from adverse witnesses.

Ideally, from eliciting these responses, the cross-examiner puts the witness in the position of either having to acknowledge a certain point or, in failing to do so, the witness's losing credibility with the fact finder. Assume, for example, that the cross-examiner wishes to demonstrate that it was unlikely for the eyewitness to the auto accident to know the color of the traffic light immediately prior to impact. A successful examination might proceed as follows:

> Q: *Immediately before the accident, you were approximately 200 feet from the traffic light?*
> A: Approximately.
> Q: *Isn't it true that you were talking to your wife at that same time?*
> A: Yes.
> Q: *You were facing her while speaking to her?*
> A: Sure.
> Q: *Is it correct that your wife was sitting directly to your left?*
> A: Yes.
> Q: *And the traffic light was directly to your right as you have indicated previously on the diagram marked as plaintiff's Exhibit #6?*
> A: I guess so.

Should the attorney now choose to ask whether the witness actually saw the color of the light immediately before the accident, the witness must bend, at least somewhat, to the cross-examiner's point or, in maintaining his position, lose credibility with the jury. The cross-examiner arrived at this desirable position through the use of questions that in essence provided the important information to the jury. The witness was a mere reflector of the information that came from the questions on its way to the jury.

1. Use Leading Questions

Witnesses are much more likely to answer with limited responses if the questions put to them are leading in nature. Leading questions, generally prohibited on direct examination, are permitted and should be the norm during cross-examination. Such questions presume the answer, so that instead of asking when someone arrived at the store, the leading question would be, "is it true that you arrived there at 6:00 p.m.?" Assume we are attempting to raise questions about that portion of the robbery victim's direct testimony in which she offered a positive identification of the gun she claims the robber was wielding during the crime. Using leading questions, the cross-examination might proceed as follows:

> Q: *It was late at night when you were robbed, Ms. Watt?*
> A: Yes.
> Q: *And your testimony was that it happened on a dark street with no light directly overhead?*
> A: Yes, but I could still see.
> Q: *Isn't it true that your description of the gun was that it "looked dark"?*
> A: Yes.
> Q: *But you could not determine whether it was black, brown or even dark gray?*
> A: Not for sure.
> Q: *You saw no distinguishing marks on the gun, did you?*
> A: No.
> Q: *Have you ever had a gun pointed at you before?*
> A: No.
> Q: *So I'm sure you were quite shaken by what happened here?*
> A: Of course I was.
> Q: *You testified on direct that this all happened fairly quickly. Is that right?*
> A: Yes.
> Q: *And in the brief period of time you had to look at the robber, you said you were looking mostly at the bandanna he wore across his face. Isn't that true?*
> A: I guess so.
> Q: *You have almost no familiarity with guns, do you?*
> A: No. I hated them even before this happened.
> Q: *So you really cannot distinguish between a .38 caliber semi-automatic and a .44 caliber revolver, can you?*
> A: I don't think so.

> Q: *When you identified the gun in the police station, the police showed you only one gun. Is that correct?*
> A: Yes.
> Q: *So they never showed you a number of guns and asked if you could select the one used in the robbery. Did they?*
> A: No.

At this point, should the above attorney wish to ask the ultimate question (the wisdom of actually doing so will be discussed later in this chapter) regarding whether the witness is certain that the gun produced in court was the one used by the robber, she would either have to acknowledge some degree of uncertainty or, by sticking to her guns (sorry), lose credibility with the jury. This cross-examination did not "destroy" the witness, but it raised questions about an important aspect of her testimony and reduced the impact of the witness's positive identification of the gun. Note that this was accomplished in large part because the information provided to the jury really came from the attorney, with the witness merely acknowledging the information through her responses to leading questions.

2. Avoid Explanations by the Witness

When a person gives an answer that makes little sense or is inconsistent with what he has said previously, the inclination of any intelligent, curious listener is to ask for an explanation of the answer. "How could you say such a thing?" or "Why do you now say 'maybe' when you said 'yes' two weeks ago?" are logical follow-up questions to ask in such situations. Similarly, when a witness describes an action he took that is incongruous with a position he is asserting, the tendency of the questioner is to ask the witness to justify his position in light of his action. Recalling that the cross-examiner seeks only Skinner-like responses from the witness and not information or explanations, however, the natural inclination to ask "why" type questions must be resisted. Rarely will the explanation from an adverse witness be helpful, and the cross-examiner is apt to spend 10 minutes getting back to where he was with the witness before he asked "why." Furthermore, that 10 minutes is likely to take the cross-examiner off track, cause the attorney to bicker with the witness (creating an unfavorable impression with the jury) and result in diminishing the impact of the point that was made before the "why." Acquiring the discipline to resist asking the witness for a reasonable explanation for his response or actions, the logical next question, is one thing that makes cross-examination so difficult.

Legal lore is filled with anecdotes—some real, some apocryphal—of lawyers who "asked one question too many." Analysis of those stories reveals that the actual problem of the cross-examiner was not the number of questions asked but that they invariably invited the witness to explain, justify or interpret his actions or responses. Perhaps the most often repeated of such examinations involves the attorney defending his client against an assault and battery charge based on biting off the ear of the victim. The witness is a man who testified on direct examination to seeing the horrific incident as it unfolded. After asking a series of effective leading questions that showed the jury that the witness did not actually see the bite, the cross-examiner decides to hammer the point home. "If you did not see the bite, HOW can you say my client bit the victim's ear off?," he asks. "I saw him spit it out," comes the immediate reply. The correct message of such an anecdote is that if you ask the adverse witness to explain or justify his response, he will do so, usually to your detriment.

> Q: *Ms. Benn, is it true that immediately after the collision you left the scene?*
> A: Yes, it is.
> Q: *So you were unable to see the condition of the plaintiff right after the accident.*
> A: I guess that is true.

At this point the attorney is well advised to stop, having made her point. Instead she continues as follows:

> Q: *So you thought it was more important to reach your destination than to see if you could help after a serious accident?*
> A: No, I thought it was important to get to a phone and call the police rather than add to the mass of people crowding around the victim. I came right back and saw how badly hurt the plaintiff was, if that is what you wanted to know.

This examination serves to illustrate several points regarding asking the witness to explain her actions. First, once the point is made, it is generally best to proceed to another area of questioning. Once the answer you seek is elicited, avoid asking the witness to explain or characterize her actions. While the witness can be rehabilitated somewhat on redirect examination when your opponent asks her to explain why she left the scene, the point you made has had an opportunity to sink in with the fact finder and will not be completely undone. Furthermore, your success at having damaged the witness without lying or bickering with her can affect positively the manner in which the remainder of your examination proceeds.

Instead of seeking the witness's own characterization of her actions and then disputing it with her, wait until your summation and offer unopposed the interpretation that you feel is warranted. "Members of the jury, you recall Ms. Benn telling you she left the scene immediately after the accident, before seeing what happened to the plaintiff. Regardless of whether you believe her actions in leaving the area were warranted, I suggest her testimony on the plaintiff's condition is far less meaningful than that of the two witnesses we provided you who stayed and saw the plaintiff emerge from his car."

Another lesson to be learned from the above illustration is that a question that asks the witness to explain, sometimes referred to as the "why" question, can take several forms. In addition to obvious prefatory words in the question that call for an explanation, such as "why," "how come," or "how can you say," sometimes what sounds like a leading question is really an invitation for the witness to explain or characterize. The damaging question above, beginning with the words "so you thought," appears at first to be a leading question that calls for a yes or no answer. Whether the answer to that question technically should be limited to a yes or no answer hardly matters, as judges invariably will allow the witness to respond in full to such an argumentative question. The longer the cross-examiner pursues the area of questioning once the key point has been made, the more likely it is that the witness will be given an opportunity to explain her actions. For those who like to analogize cross-examination to competitive contests, think of yourself as the fencer who makes his or her point and then withdraws, rather than the boxer trying to bludgeon his opponent into submission.

B. Limiting the Response

Regardless of how well crafted a leading question on cross-examination may be, witnesses sometimes go beyond the limited response called for in the question. When this happens repeatedly, the cross-examiner may have a difficult decision to make about how best to confine the witness's answer to the question posed. While the attorney can request the judge to instruct the witness to limit his answers, the potential drawbacks to such an approach should first be considered. If the judge believes the witness cannot fairly answer the question without being permitted to provide a fuller explanation of his response or the judge is predisposed against becoming involved unduly in the examination, she may deny your request. In such a case, the attorney risks appearing to the jury as one who is attempting improperly to keep information from the jury and has lost control of the witness.

Consider, instead, self-help. Although attorneys should generally refrain from interrupting the witness, where the witness continually exceeds the scope of the question, the cross-examiner may want to politely interrupt at appropriate points and ask the next question. If the witness is continually and deliberately engaging in such conduct, the judge may be inclined to view with disfavor appeals by opposing counsel to prevent the cross-examiner's termination of the witness's response. Better still is increasing the likelihood of getting the desired response by asking the question again. Especially in situations where the witness is being evasive, re-asking a question in as focused and leading a manner as possible can put pressure on the witness to answer the question and serve to alert the jury to the fact that the witness is being evasive. Consider the following:

Q: When you spoke with Officer Johnson immediately after the accident, what color did you tell him the light was as you passed through the intersection?

A: Things happened very quickly and, as I said, that pedestrian came out of nowhere. I was nervous and upset when I spoke to the officer. In fact, I'm not even sure I saw the color clearly at that time.

Q: Let us try again. Isn't it true that immediately after the accident you told Officer Johnson you had gone through a yellow light?

At this stage, the witness, knowing what she told the officer and knowing you can prove what she said, is far more likely to answer the question posed. If she again avoids the question, it should be clear to the jury that she has done so purposefully. Furthermore, when her earlier statement is presented before the jury, its significance will be enhanced by the witness's earlier failure to acknowledge it. If you are particularly fortunate, your opponent will object to the question as having already been asked. This allows you the opportunity to point out that while the question was asked, it was never answered, and is therefore unobjectionable.

IV. Treating the Witness Appropriately

Similar to direct examination, the attitude you exhibit toward a witness on cross-examination can have a significant impact on how the jurors regard the witness and how they regard you. Lawyers who behave improperly with an adverse witness risk damaging their own credibility and antagonizing the jury. The results of such a jury reaction can affect how the jurors assess the attorney's final argument and the case as a whole. It is, therefore, important to develop a strategy for how the witness should be treated and to act at trial in accordance with that strategy.

A. Decide What Category the Witness Fits In

When planning a cross-examination, most attorneys envision the responses they believe should be forthcoming from the witness to each of their questions. At trial, however, the adverse witness often resists giving the responses that the examiner thinks the questions deserve. In the hurly-burly of the trial atmosphere, it is easy for the lawyer to get upset or frustrated when this occurs. Depending on their individual personalities, cross-examiners react in different ways to uncooperative witnesses. Some become aggressive, others sarcastic and still others downright rude. Except where the witness is deliberately and obviously being evasive or misleading, the jurors tend to identify with the witness (far more than they identify with the lawyer) and to be highly critical of lawyers whom they perceive are acting with disrespect toward the witness.

To minimize the chance of such a dynamic developing during the cross-examination, it is wise for the lawyer to think in advance about the appropriate demeanor to display with each witness. Witnesses to be cross-examined will usually fall into one of three categories, and determining the category appropriate for each witness will help you decide the proper attitude to exhibit with that witness.

The first type of witness is one you are trying to show is deliberately exaggerating or even lying. The second and far more common type of witness is one who is honestly mistaken. While people can make honest mistakes for all kinds of reasons, only those with a strong motive to lie or shown to be pathological liars will be viewed by the jury as having lied under oath. The third type of witness is one offering testimony that is largely undisputed or harmless. The treatment accorded these witnesses by the cross-examiner should be consistent with the category into which each falls.

The witness who the cross-examiner is presenting to the jury as honestly mistaken needs to be treated differently than one who is deliberately concealing, avoiding or exaggerating the truth. While the cross-examiner should always avoid being perceived as unfair, nasty or obnoxious, the latter type witness can be confronted more directly and pointedly than the honestly mistaken witness. The greatest danger that attorneys face regarding their attitude toward adverse witnesses is that they will be seen as treating the honestly mistaken witness harshly or unfairly. As the attorney becomes more dissatisfied with the witness's responses, the danger that the attorney's frustration will show increases. This is when it is crucial for the cross-examiner to remember that the witness is being presented to the jury only as one who has made an honest mistake. The attorney should make the points that need to be made without bickering with such a witness or behaving unpleasantly toward him.

Most trial lawyers have seen cross-examiners damage their case by treating witnesses in a manner that is viewed as unduly hostile by the jury. I have watched a plaintiff's lawyer in an auto accident case become overly aggressive with an eyewitness who had no relationship to any of the involved parties and was obviously telling what he saw to the best of his ability. The lawyer had some good impeachment material at his disposal to show that the witness's recollection of the accident was faulty. Instead, he—at first implicitly (through tone and body language) and later more overtly—tried to show that the witness, with no motive to do so, had purposefully changed his story. The jury was clearly not pleased with his treatment of the witness. Worse still was the criminal defense lawyer who became so frustrated that the rape victim was not acknowledging the possible flaws in her identification of the defendant that he became sarcastic and then nasty with the victim. The anger on the faces of the jurors was apparent as this woman, an undisputed victim of a horrible attack, was mistreated by the cross-examiner. In each of these cases, effective cross-examination points were not only lost but turned into negatives because the lawyer forgot that he was trying to show only that the witness had made an understandable, but still important, mistake.

The final type of witness is the neutral witness with whose testimony you have no quarrel and who, in fact, may offer some information helpful to your case. An example of this third type of witness can be a police officer in an auto accident who responded to the scene and made certain observations. The plaintiff may call such a witness to testify to the physical surroundings of the accident scene and the damage that he observed. The defense may have no dispute with this testimony and wish to cross-examine this non-adverse witness only to elicit favorable information about the defendant, such as his sobriety and cooperation. The cross-examiner may wish to show the jury through his or her attitude and demeanor that this witness is either unimportant or, alternatively, supportive of the cross-examiner's case.

V. Prior Inconsistent Statements

The witness you are about to cross-examine testified on direct about an important fact in a manner that is inconsistent with what the witness had said or written previously. This presents you with the opportunity of impeaching the witness with his own words. You can barely constrain yourself during the remainder of the direct examination, as you are chomping at the bit to get at the witness to expose his contradiction. When the witness is turned over to you, you leap out of your seat and ask, "How could you possibly say this now when you said that then?"

The witness will then gladly offer to you the infinite number of reasons why there might be small differences in the way he described events previously and how he testified about them during direct. Quite often, both the point you were attempting to make about the inconsistency and the impact you hoped it would have on the jury are diminished, if not lost. What you need is a systematic method for establishing the inconsistency and making clear its significance without allowing the witness to explain it away.

A. Decide upon the Specific Purpose for Showing the Inconsistency

Before developing a systematic approach for impeachment through prior inconsistent statement, you must first decide what message you wish to communicate about the witness through use of the prior statement. At times the witness may have misspoken about a fact that is really not in dispute but that you need corrected in order to continue with your line of questioning. In correcting such an error, your goal is really not impeaching the witness so much as getting him back on track. The method you use to correct his mistake, therefore, will be different and more abbreviated than the method you would use to perform a standard impeachment. One means of correcting witness error quickly is to provide the witness orally with the correct information through your next question. "You meant October 2 rather than October 3, didn't you?" is an example of this technique. If such an approach is unsuccessful, you may wish to show the witness his previous statement and ask whether this refreshes his recollection of the subject. While technically a witness cannot be given a document to refresh his recollection unless he has first indicated some lack of memory about the subject, few judges or opposing attorneys will interfere with this efficient manner of eliciting what you clearly have the right to elicit. Should a judge sustain your opponent's objection to such a procedure, you can use the standard method of impeachment described below but in a more abbreviated form. Remember, your point here is not to communicate anything negative about the witness due to his mistake nor to highlight the error for the jury (dwelling on an understandable and largely insignificant error can make you seem to be one who, out of desperation, is grasping at straws) but only to correct the error quickly so as to proceed onto the rest of your questions.

Where the witness's discrepancy involves an issue in dispute, especially one that may be important in determining the outcome of the case, a more pointed and systematic means of impeachment should be utilized. The primary purpose of any such impeachment is to make clear that indeed a difference exists between what the witness has said previously and what he maintains now. There are several possible conclusions the cross-examiner may wish the fact finder to draw from this discrepancy once it has been established. The most common conclusion desired by cross-examiners is that what the witness said on the earlier occasion is more likely to be correct than what he is saying now. In order to develop an effective line of questioning aimed at having the fact finder arrive at this conclusion, it is helpful to understand first what could have led to the change in the witness's story.

Over time, witnesses tend to feel an affiliation with the cause of the party on whose behalf they are testifying and often wish to see that party prevail in the litigation. While this is obvious with respect to the party himself, witnesses who have a prior relationship with the party, and paid professional witnesses, this bonding between witness and party (or lawyer) or antipathy between the witness and the adverse lawyer occurs frequently with seemingly unbiased witnesses as well. This feeling can lead any witness, at least subconsciously, to shade the testimony as favorably as possible for the side calling him or her to the stand.

Another factor that could cause changes in the witness's recollection of an event over time is evidenced in studies performed by experimental psychologists. These studies reveal the discomfort experienced by people feeling any degree of uncertainty or ambiguity over their recollection of an important event. To overcome this discomfort, it is not uncommon for the mind to remember an event with more precision or certainty (although not more accuracy) as time goes on and to fill in any gaps that might exist in the person's recollection of events. This may explain why a witness who said at a deposition that "the light could have been red" testifies during direct examination, "I'll never forget that the light was red." It could, in part, account for the crime victim,who told the police that she was robbed by a dark haired man of average height, between 150 and 180 lbs., later testifying at trial (after having seen the defendant on numerous occasions) that her assailant was between 5' 7" and 5' 9", weighed between 160 and 175 lbs. and had long black hair and sideburns.

For the above reasons and others, the earlier statement, writing or testimony of the adverse witness is usually more favorable to the cross-examiner than what the witness has said at trial. Therefore, in such a situation, you will want to do everything possible to convince the jury that the first statement is closer to the truth than what the witness claims now.

B. Build up the Witness's Earlier Statement before Eliciting the Inconsistency

As you plan your impeachment, it is helpful to regard the witness's earlier statement and her testimony at trial as two distinct pieces of evidence. It follows that your first effort should be directed toward accrediting the earlier statement and the conditions under which it was produced. An important benefit achieved by building up the earlier statement of the witness at the beginning of your impeachment is that it makes it more difficult later for the witness to avoid the impact of the inconsistency by diminishing the importance of the earlier statement. Consider the two lines of questioning below, each designed to build up pre-trial witness statements.

> *Q: Ms. Hyde, do you recall coming to my office a few months after the accident?*
>
> A: I do.
>
> *Q: You were accompanied by the attorney for the plaintiff?*
>
> A: I was.
>
> *Q: It was explained to you that you were at a deposition during which the plaintiff's counsel and I were going to ask you some questions about the accident. Is that correct?*
>
> A: Yes.
>
> *Q: Before you began answering questions, were you administered an oath during which you swore to tell the truth?*
>
> A: I was.
>
> *Q: And of course you told the truth about what you saw?*
>
> A: Of course I did.

Q: *You realized then how important it was to tell what you saw as accurately as possible?*
A: I guess so.

Q: *After you testified at the deposition, do you recall being given an opportunity to read what you said and to make any changes you felt were needed?*
A: Yes.

Q: *I show you what has been marked Defendant's exhibit #6 for identification, the transcript of your deposition. Is that your signature on the last page?*
A: It is.

Q: *Right above your signature it reads, "I have read the foregoing and it is correct to the best of my knowledge." Is that what it says?*
A: That is what it says.

Q: *The testimony you gave at that deposition was only 4 months after the accident whereas the testimony you gave yesterday is more than 3 years after the accident. Is that correct?*
A: I believe so.

The second examination is designed to build up the arrest report of a police officer before asking him about a discrepancy between the report and his testimony on direct examination.

Q: *Officer is it true that you prepared an arrest report in this case?*
A: It is.

Q: *You know the importance of an arrest report, don't you?*
A: Yes.

Q: *You are aware that it goes to the prosecutor first and then can be used during trial?*
A: I am.

Q: *In fact, given the vast experience you have testified about on direct, surely you know when you prepare such reports that a jury might ultimately see them. Isn't that correct?*
A: That is possible.

Q: *When you were in the police academy, they taught you the correct way of preparing arrest reports?*
A: Among other things.

Q: *During your ten years as a policeman, is it safe to say that you have prepared hundreds of such reports?*
A: I haven't counted, but I have written many arrest reports.

Q: *Knowing their importance, I'm sure you try to prepare them as accurately as possible. Is that correct?*

A: Sure.

Q: *Is it true that when the report is finished, you sign at the bottom attesting to its accuracy to the best of your knowledge?*

A: Yes.

Q: *And, naturally, you don't sign the report without first reading it over carefully?*

A: I read it before signing it.

Q: *I show you what has been marked Defendant's exhibit #3 for identification. Is this the arrest report you prepared in this case?*

A: It is.

Q: *Is that your signature on the bottom attesting to its accuracy?*

A: That is my signature.

Note that the questions in each of these examples are non-adverse in nature, unlikely to result in bickering with the witness, yet are almost certain to elicit the desired response. The questions magnify the importance of the earlier statement and serve the goal of getting the jury to credit the earlier statements as more accurate. Additionally, they make it difficult for opposing counsel to rehabilitate the witness's current testimony by contrasting the importance of trial testimony with the insignificance of the pre-trial statement. While certain pre-trial statements or documents will be harder to build up (e.g., a casual comment or informal notes taken at a meeting), the benefits of doing so make the effort worthwhile.

C. Expose the Inconsistency with a Narrow, Leading Question

Now that you have built up the significance of the pre-trial statement or document, the moment is at hand to lay out the discrepancy for all to see. Once again careful consideration should be given to how to make the point most effectively. At this stage, when the witness is anxious to find any way out of the dilemma caused by her inconsistency, it is critical that you frame your question as narrowly as possible. If you paraphrase or characterize what the witness said in her earlier statement, you risk failing to crystallize the issue for the jury or at least wasting time in doing so. With respect to the robbery victim, discussed above, whose description became more specific at trial, such ineffective questioning could go this way:

Q: Ms. Moore, in your statement to the police after the robbery, you gave a rather general description of your assailant, didn't you?

A: Not really. I told them about his height, weight and hair shade.

Q: But you gave only general information about each of those?

A: I don't know what you mean, but I did the best I could under the circumstances.

Contrast that with the following questions:

Q: Ms. Moore, obviously you wanted the police to arrest the man who attacked you?

A: Of course.

Q: So, is it fair to say that you told them everything you noticed about your attacker that could identify him?

A: As best I could from what I saw.

Q: You told the prosecutor on direct examination that your attacker was 5'7 to 5'9". Is that correct?

A: That is what I said and what I saw.

Q: Immediately after the incident, when the image of your attacker was fresh in your mind and you wanted to tell the police as much as you saw, you described the height of your attacker (quoting from the police report) only as "average."

A: If that is what it says.

Q: And while you described the perpetrator's weight to the police as between 150 and180 lbs., now you claim you could tell it was between 160 and 175 lbs.?

A: Okay.

Q: You described the assailant's hair only as "dark" after the robbery, but you testified on direct that it was black, and now claim to remember that it was long as well.

A: More details come to mind now.

Q: In fact, you did not say a word to the police about sideburns when you spoke with them after the attack?

A: If that's what it says on the report, I guess not.

Q: Between the time of your initial description of the assailant and the more detailed account you provided today, the police have shown you my client, Henry Hobbs, on several occasions. Is that correct?

A: I have seen him a couple of times.

The questions posed above were narrow in scope and sought largely undeniable facts from the witness. No opportunity was offered to the witness to characterize or explain the changes in her description. Furthermore, the cross-examiner resisted the temptation to get the witness to join in the conclusion that the earlier description was substantially less precise. The hope is that the jury will get the message that the witness did not get nearly as good a look at her attacker as she now claims, and that the police helped her fill in the gaps concerning what she saw. During summation, perhaps combined with other information concerning the suggestive methods of identification used by the police, the attorney, without the witness present to challenge his conclusions, will remind the jury of this testimony and suggest that the victim's identification of the defendant was not worth much. It is important when dealing with an inherently sympathetic witness, such as the victim of a crime, that the cross-examiner (except in extraordinary cases) not be seen by the jury as attacking the witness or suggesting that she is lying. Instead, as here, the attorney's questions might be designed to show that the witness's recollection changed regarding important facts due to problems with memory caused either by natural circumstances or police zeal.

D. Read the Witness's Earlier Statement Yourself

In cases involving the use of prior statements that can be read verbatim (such as the transcript of a deposition), some attorneys prefer to have the witness read the inconsistent testimony aloud to the jury. The benefit of such a technique is said to be the potent effect on the jury when the inconsistency is heard delivered from the witness's own mouth. My experience is that the potency of such testimony is more often than not diminished due to the manner in which the witness reads his or her prior testimony. It is often read too quickly or too softly, mumbled or spaced in a way that deprives the statement of its actual meaning and much of its impact. Remember, the adverse witness is not there to help the cross-examiner by emphasizing the inconsistency. At this point, the lawyer either has to try to get a better reading the second time from the witness or read it herself. At best, this is redundant and time consuming; at worst you risk the judge sustaining an objection that the question has been asked and answered. By contrast, when the cross-examiner reads the inconsistency, she can ensure it is clearly understood and can place emphasis where needed to obtain the maximum effect. The voice can be a powerful tool of persuasion, and the cross-examiner's voice, rather than that of the adverse witness, is the one that the jury should hear deliver the inconsistent statement.

E. Stop!

It is now time to practice the most difficult part of any successful impeachment. STOP! You have made your point and, now, as the devastating cross-examiner you are, you want to drive the point home. You want to finish off the witness, expose him for the fraud that he is and have him figuratively crawl off the stand in disgrace. "How can you possibly say that now when you said something else previously?"; "Do you expect the jury to believe that?"; or, my personal favorite, "Were you lying then or are you lying now?" are examples of questions designed to accomplish those ends. Resist such questions. You will give the witness a means of explaining away or minimizing his inconsistency. Asking such follow-up questions could also lead to bickering with the witness, creating sympathy for him and taking time to get to the position you were in before asking the additional questions (see discussion above in section on limiting the response).

F. Different Approach When Attempting to Show Overall Unreliability of Witness

A slightly different method of impeachment may be warranted when the purpose in impeaching is not to show the significance of any particular discrepancy but, instead, to demonstrate the overall unreliability of the witness's recollection of events through the use of different versions appearing in earlier statements. If the in-court testimony of the party to an auto accident regarding the events of that day is somewhat different from what he gave in his deposition, and both are somewhat different from what he told the police after the accident, showing the number of discrepancies can be the best means of shedding doubt on the witness's current testimony. In such a situation, the cross-examiner should establish the need for the witness to be accurate in each prior statement and then highlight for the jury the frequency of mistakes made by the witness. Such impeachment sets up a final argument which will suggest that a witness offering versions of a story different in so many ways either does not recall events accurately or has chosen to embellish the story.

G. Introducing the Prior Statement into Evidence

One issue that often confronts the cross-examiner is whether to have the inconsistent statement offered into evidence. The federal rules distinguish between prior inconsistent statements offered for the purpose of impeachment and those offered affirmatively as substantive evidence. Prior statements offered merely to impeach the current testimony are considered to be non-hearsay, as they are not offered primarily to show their truth but only to cast doubt on the testimony offered by the witness at trial. Therefore, assuming their relevance, such statements are generally admissible for impeachment purposes. When the attorney seeks to have prior inconsistent statements used as substantive evidence, he or she should consult FRE 801 (d)(1) for the types of prior statements that are admissible for such a purpose. Additionally FRE 613 should be read in order to understand the procedures required when cross-examining through the use of prior inconsistent statements.

Unless the statement is needed to affirmatively prove or rebut some element of the case, however, it is usually of little practical consequence whether it is admitted as substantive evidence or merely to impeach the witness's testimony at trial. This is because, regardless of the clarity of the judge's instruction on this point, most jurors will neither understand nor care about whether the witness's earlier statement that the light was red is offered substantively or only to impeach his trial testimony that the light was yellow. What matters to the jury is that there is a difference in the two accounts.

The primary decision, then, for the cross-examiner, is whether the strategic benefits of having the prior inconsistent statement admitted into evidence (for whatever purpose) outweigh the disadvantages of such an approach. Although the answer to that question depends upon the importance of the inconsistency and on what type of document the inconsistency is contained in, the attorney in most instances need not, nor should she, introduce the document into evidence. The attorney is permitted to elicit the inconsistent portion of the document without the requirement that the entire document be placed into evidence or even that the remainder of its contents be brought to the jury's attention. After an inconsistent statement in a document is elicited, the direct examiner can insist on having the consistent portions of the document read to the jury *only* to the extent necessary to understand the witness's statement or to put it in context. As the document that the inconsistent statement appears in is likely to be largely consistent with and supportive of the witness's current testimony, it is generally not helpful for the cross-examiner to put that document before the jury.

Illustrative of this point is a case I prosecuted in which a man was accused of raping an 8-year-old girl. After the child testified on direct examination that she had been attacked on a park bench, the defense attorney impeached her with her statement to the police that she first was attacked while still in the playground. He then made the mistake of introducing into evidence the entire statement that the child had made to the police shortly after the attack. During my closing argument, I discussed in great detail the importance of *Defendant's* exhibit #8, the child's statement to the police. If the jurors had any doubts about the child's version of the attack or her identification of the defendant, all they needed to do was read *Defendant's* exhibit #8 at their leisure during deliberations. There they could see how, immediately after the event, she described the crucial aspects of the attack in essentially the same way she did during her direct examination. Furthermore, they could read the description of her assailant that she provided to the police and consider again how strikingly the defendant matches that description. While some of this information would have been presented to the jury independent of the document, it is a clear advantage when the only written account of events the jury has with them during their deliberations is the largely supportive account of the key witness. Had the defense attorney not introduced the document into evidence, there is no way I could have gotten this valuable document into the jury's hands.

There may be specific situations, however, when it can be advantageous for the cross-examiner to introduce into evidence the document containing the impeaching statement. Where the entire document contains little in the way of material supportive of the witness's testimony or the inconsistent statement involves a core issue in the case, the strategic balance may shift toward introduction of the document. Additionally, if the cross-examiner is permitted to introduce only the impeaching portion of the document or the document is replete with statements inconsistent with the trial testimony of the witness, the cross-examiner might benefit from the jury having the document with it during deliberations.

H. Impeachment by Omission

One valuable, but often overlooked, method of impeaching a witness through use of a prior statement is impeachment through omission. For evidentiary purposes, and for strategic considerations as well, the omission should be viewed in much the same way as the inconsistency. When a written or oral statement omits a relevant fact that appropriately should be contained in the statement, the cross-examiner is permitted to use that statement to impeach the trial testimony of the witness. If the omission involves facts that would not be expected to appear in the earlier statement, the statement cannot be used to impeach. Even if the attorney were permitted to use such an omission to impeach, such impeachment makes the attorney look silly or desperate. When the party to the auto accident is asked at deposition to relate everything he saw immediately after the accident, the fact that he omitted the presence of a grocery store on the corner is meaningless. The robbery victim whose testimony at trial included the fact that her attack occurred on a sunny day neither can nor should be impeached by her statement to the police, taken shortly after the attack, that omitted this fact.

Assume, however, that the party to the accident discussed above included in his answer to the same question at trial the fact that the driver of the car that hit him emerged from his vehicle with a bottle of vodka in his hand. That such an important fact was omitted from the witness's earlier statement is significant and should lead to impeachment through use of the deposition. Similarly, if the robbery victim's testimony at trial includes the fact that her assailant had a 2-inch scar on his left cheek (as does the defendant) but her description of her attacker shortly after the crime omitted this fact, impeachment by omission is the appropriate strategy for the cross-examiner.

The method of impeachment by omission is similar to that of impeachment by prior inconsistent statement discussed above. First, build up the reliability and significance of the earlier statement. Next, elicit the difference between the statement and current testimony in the most effective way possible and, finally, move on without allowing explanation or interpretation by the witness of the earlier statement. When developing an inconsistency through omission, the additional step that the cross-examiner should take is to establish the point that the act of omitting the fact in question is significant. The simplest way of showing this is to elicit why (without actually asking "why") the omitted fact should have been in the earlier statement. For example, the robbery victim above could be questioned, in part, as follows:

Q: *Obviously, you wanted the man who robbed you to be caught as quickly as possible?*

A: Of course.

Q: *And you knew how important your description of your attacker would be in helping to catch the man?*

A: Sure.

Q: *So you told the police everything you observed about the man who robbed you?*

A: As best as I could.

Q: *Did you tell the police about the 2-inch scar you claim today to have seen?*

A: I don't think so.

The build-up questions above are safe, non-hostile questions that are virtually certain to obtain the desired answers. Their purpose is to make clear the significance of the omission and suggest the unlikelihood of the witness's having actually seen something so important and omitting it from her description. Should the witness claim she told the police about the scar or that she does not recall whether she did so, the officer and his report can be used to impeach her testimony.

CHAPTER 5

EXHIBITS

It is said that a picture is worth a thousand words. At trial a diagram, document, weapon, x-ray, video or part of an airplane engine can also be as valuable as any words the jury hears from the witness stand. Understanding the importance of exhibits, the issues surrounding their admissibility and the various purposes to which they can be put is a necessary prerequisite to planning for the effective use of exhibits at trial.

I. Purposes

The most obvious reason for the use of exhibits at trial is that they can establish or support a particular point that the attorney is attempting to make. This point may relate directly to a specific element of a crime or cause of action that the attorney has to prove or negate, or the exhibit may be used to support and confirm other testimony. A letter can show that a manufacturer was or should have been aware of a product defect; a photograph can demonstrate that an eyewitness had an unobstructed view; a hospital record proves that the patient was administered the correct medicine, and a time card suggests the defendant was at work when the crime was committed. Perhaps less obvious, but also of critical importance, is the benefit exhibits can achieve in emphasizing or dramatizing certain testimony or, at times, making the testimony less abstract to the jury.

While the victim of a serious construction accident may have testified persuasively regarding how severely his life has changed since the accident, a "day in the life" video can dramatize graphically just how difficult his life has become. The robbery victim's oral testimony about the fear she felt when the defendant pointed a gun at her can be emphasized by giving the jury the opportunity to see the gun. The x-ray of the plaintiff's knee, accompanied by a chart showing how the knee functions, serves to make the orthopedist's description of the injury less abstract to the fact finder.

A still less obvious, but equally important, benefit that comes from the use of exhibits relates to the manner in which jurors acquire and remember information. In most trials, much of the information the jury learns about the case comes through the oral testimony of witnesses. As the trial progresses, the jury is apt to tire of listening to the repetitive nature of such testimony. When a listener tires of listening, he or she is easily distracted and less likely to focus on what is being said. Providing the jurors with something they can read, look at, touch or even smell offers them a welcome change from oral testimony and makes the testimony more memorable for them. As the jury recalls only a portion of the reams of testimony produced at most trials, the lawyer's efforts to make strategically important aspects of his or her case more memorable can play a significant role in the jury's deliberations.

Another purpose for the use of exhibits relates to one of the requirements essential to any effective direct examination: enabling the witness's testimony to come across as clearly as possible. Jurors who are confused by or unable to understand aspects of the witness's testimony are unlikely to expend the intellectual energy to figure out the testimony on their own. The effective use of tangible and demonstrative evidence can clarify parts of a witness's testimony that otherwise would be difficult for the jury to understand and follow. Imagine a witness to an auto accident asked to describe what she saw testifying as follows:

> A: I was driving west on Elm St. when a truck passed me heading east. He made a left turn onto Oak St., I believe that is north. Then a pedestrian crossed Oak St. at the crosswalk heading from left to right. About two thirds of the way across the street, the truck hit the pedestrian. She was then propelled down the street some 20 to 30 feet. I was able to see the truck turn three quarters of the way around after the collision.

The use of a diagram to accompany and augment the testimony above would enable the jury to have a clear image of the details provided by the witness and a better overall sense of how the accident occurred. Given how difficult it is for many people to visualize directions and distances, it is invariably helpful to allow the witness to explain such testimony through the use of a diagram. Photographs, charts, and documents are among the other types of exhibits that can play a useful role in clarifying and explaining important aspects of testimony to the jury.

II. The Drill

Despite the considerable benefits that can be achieved from using exhibits, too many attorneys eschew the use of such evidence, in part because of their discomfort in dealing with exhibits and the insecurity that attends laying the foundation for their use. Other attorneys handle the presentation of exhibits in such a clumsy and disorganized manner that the value of the exhibit is substantially diminished or, at times, the opposing lawyer is able to prevent the use of the exhibit altogether. None of us wish to look bad, and even experienced trial lawyers, confident in their abilities as oral advocates, can feel uncomfortable at the prospect of introducing and using some exhibits. Fortunately, there is a method, easy to learn and applicable to most types of exhibits, that the attorney can employ to begin the process of getting exhibits admitted into evidence. Referred to simply as "the drill," this method allows the attorney to use basically the same approach with regard to most types of evidence and to be secure in the correctness of that approach. The drill includes the following steps:

1. Choose the correct witness or witnesses to lay the foundation.
2. Have the exhibit marked for identification.
3. Show the exhibit to opposing counsel.
4. Allow the witness to examine the exhibit.
5. Ask the witness what the exhibit is.
6. Lay the foundation necessary to get the exhibit admitted into evidence.
7. Offer the exhibit into evidence.
8. Use the exhibit to establish, demonstrate, emphasize or clarify the relevant point.

Each of these steps requires some discussion.

A. Choose the Correct Witness or Witnesses

In deciding the best manner to get an exhibit admitted and to use it productively, it is important to choose the correct witnesses to testify with respect to the exhibit. The attorney first must decide which witnesses are necessary to lay the foundation, and then those who can incorporate the exhibit most effectively into their testimony. Each exhibit requires a different foundation in order to be admitted. To have a photograph admitted into evidence, someone with knowledge of how the scene appeared on the day and time in question must testify that the exhibit is a fair and accurate representation of the scene at that time (see discussion of photographs below). Offering a letter into evidence requires, at least, a witness who can authenticate that the letter was written by the party alleged to be its author (see discussion of documents below). The introduction of a tangible item might necessitate that the proponent of the evidence establish a chain of custody and therefore may need to call each person who handled the exhibit (see discussion of tangible items below).

The testimony of most foundation witnesses, elicited only to satisfy evidentiary rules, is usually dry and of little interest to the jury. Therefore attorneys should seek to get through such testimony as quickly and efficiently as possible, generally calling only those witnesses required to lay the foundation. With this in mind, attorneys should be aware that some exhibits are self-authenticating and others admissible per se pursuant to statute. Federal Rule of Evidence 902 provides a list of self-authenticating documents and any conditions that may need to be met with respect to each type of document covered by the rule (see discussion below). No witness may be needed in order to get such exhibits entered into evidence. Additionally, admissions made by the opposing attorney in discovery may obviate the need to call one or more of the witnesses that otherwise would be needed to lay the foundation. For example, pursuant to a request for admissions, the opposing attorney may have conceded that a certain document was prepared and maintained in the regular course of business. This does not mean that the document and all information contained within it is automatically admissible, but it should permit the proponent of the record to avoid calling the records custodian. Finally, an attorney offering an exhibit should, where feasible, seek to obtain a stipulation from his or her opponent as to the admissibility of the exhibit. It can save both time and money if attorneys can avoid calling witnesses whose only purpose is to lay the foundation through testimony that is not in dispute. It is advantageous to both attorneys if they can work out before trial an arrangement to stipulate to those exhibits whose admissibility is uncontested.

Once the attorney has determined which witnesses are necessary in order to lay the foundation, he or she will next decide who should be called to put the exhibit to its best use. Recalling the variety of purposes which exhibits can achieve (discussed above), the attorney should consider who can best explain the exhibit or whose testimony can be clarified, emphasized or dramatized through its effective use.

B. Mark the Exhibit for Identification

The first step in getting an exhibit into evidence is marking it. Marking the exhibit ensures that the record takes cognizance of the exhibit. This is why when speaking of a letter that she will later offer into evidence, the attorney should refer to it not as "this letter," but as "the letter marked as Defendant's #7 for identification." The judge, the opposing attorney and the record will then be aware of the specific letter to which the attorney is referring. This avoids delay in the questioning and confusion on appeal or if the record needs to be read back later in the trial. That is also why every exhibit referred to during trial, even those that will never be offered into evidence, should be marked. Marking an exhibit is unobjectionable. Therefore, in cases involving many documents, it saves time for the attorneys to mark the exhibits prior to trial and then notify their opponent as well as the clerk regarding how the exhibits were numbered. Remember to mark the exhibit "for identification," as it has not yet been admitted into evidence.

C. Show the Exhibit to Opposing Counsel

Before the exhibit is presented to the witness, the attorney should show the exhibit to opposing counsel. Even if he or she has seen it previously, opposing counsel should examine the exhibit closely to ensure it is in the same form as when previously seen. If the proponent of the evidence neglects to show the exhibit to opposing counsel prior to presenting it to the witness, the judge, on request, will order it shown, and the examination will be interrupted needlessly.

D. Allow the Witness to Examine the Exhibit

Next, the attorney should hand the exhibit, if it is not too large or cumbersome, to the witness. Some judges require attorneys to seek their permission before approaching witnesses, while others prefer the attorney to proceed without such a request. It is wise to speak with courtroom personnel who have worked with the judge, or with the judge personally, to see which approach the judge prefers, as the attorney does not want to be admonished in front of the jury for approaching the witness and handing him a document without the judge's permission. If the attorney has neglected to find out the judge's preference in advance, he or she should ask to approach until the judge indicates such a request is unnecessary. After handing him the exhibit, make sure you afford the witness adequate time to examine the exhibit before questioning him about it. Note for the record that you are showing the witness the letter that has been marked as Defendant's exhibit #7 for identification.

E. Have the Witness Identify the Exhibit

The next step is to ask the witness to identify the exhibit. Simply note for the record that you have handed the exhibit marked Defendant's exhibit #7 for identification to the witness, and ask him what it is. After the witness identifies the exhibit, you might want to ask him how he is able to identify it.

For example:

> Q: *Officer, I show you what has been marked State's exhibit # 2 for identification.*
> *Would you tell the jury what the exhibit is?*
> A: This is the .38 caliber revolver I recovered from the defendant when I arrested him.
> Q: *How do you know this is the same gun?*
> A: I noted the serial number at the time on my report and the exhibit you handed me has the same serial number.

F. Lay the Proper Foundation

Before laying the foundation for an exhibit, the attorney needs first to consider whether the exhibit will be offered into evidence or whether it will be used merely as an illustrative tool. If the latter, the attorney may still need to lay some type of foundation in order to use the exhibit, but such questions may be different from those required for admission of the item into evidence. As noted above, each type of exhibit requires different foundational questions, but certain common principles apply to laying the foundation for most exhibits. Where permissible, attorneys are well advised to lead the witness as much as possible through foundational questions. This is one of the few times during the trial when the attorney is pitching to the judge rather than the jury.

Accordingly, the proponent of the evidence is less concerned at this point with making the testimony clear and memorable for the jury, and more interested in ensuring that the exhibit is accepted into evidence by the judge. Judges are accustomed to hearing precise foundational questions that they know satisfy the evidentiary prerequisites for the admission of an exhibit into evidence. Should the judge's mind wander a bit during the drudgery of having to listen to an attorney laying the foundation for a piece of evidence, that judge's decision whether to admit the evidence may rely upon whether he or she recalls hearing the familiar foundational questions that relate to such exhibits. Upon hearing such questions responded to affirmatively by the witness, the judge is, therefore, far less likely to question whether the foundation had been adequately laid. Only through leading questions can the attorney ensure that the elements of the foundation will be elicited efficiently and precisely. Contrast the following two attempts to lay the foundation to have a photograph admitted into evidence after the witness's familiarity with the area has been established:

Scenario 1:

> Q: *What is exhibit #4?*
> A: It looks like a picture.
> Q: *A picture of what?*
> A: The area around the school.
> Q: *Where was it taken?*
> A: It looks like from the street near where the accident happened
> Q: *What date does it seem to have been taken?*
> A: Around the time of the accident

Scenario 2:

> Q: *I show you the photograph that has been marked Defendant's exhibit #4 for identification. Do you recognize it?*
> A: Yes. It is where the accident occurred
> Q: *Is Defendant's exhibit #4 a fair and accurate representation of the way the area immediately surrounding Elm and Oak Streets looked at 3:30 p.m. on Dec.6, the date and time of the accident?*
> A: It is.
> Q: *I offer Defendant's #4 into evidence.*

Through the use of leading questions, proper because they deal with introductory matters designed to lay a foundation, the examiner in *Scenario 2* was able to successfully lay the foundation and quickly get the photograph into evidence. In *Scenario 1*, there may have been no objection or the judge could have leniently admitted the evidence over objection. It would not be surprising, however, if the judge concluded that the foundation had not been met and the proponent would be required to inquire further. This would delay the attorney's ability to use the diagram to aid the jury in understanding the witness's testimony and risk making the lawyer's presentation appear unprofessional. One caveat, however: questions that deal with key facts, even if they are part of laying the foundation for evidence, may be successfully objected to if they are leading. "Mr. Taylor, is this the letter that you wrote back to the plaintiff in which you declined his offer," would be such a question.

At times, the precise words that should be used to lay the foundation come directly from the words of the authorizing statute or rule. Once again as judges are accustomed to hearing the foundational questions from the rule, the attorney should frame his or her questions exactly as they appear in the rule. An example of this is the introduction of a document as a business record. The document is an out of court statement, and if it is being used to prove the truth of some matter asserted within the document, it constitutes hearsay. To overcome a hearsay objection, the document could be offered as the record of some regularly conducted business activity. In federal courts, such documents are covered under FRE 803 (6), and the words of that rule should be used to lay the foundation for the document. After some preliminary questions identifying the document and inquiring as to its creation and maintenance, the attorney should ask the following questions derived directly from the rule:

> Q: *Was the document made at or near the time of the event discussed within it?*
> A: Immediately after the event occurred.
> Q: *Was it made by a person with knowledge of the event described within?*
> A: Yes.
> Q: *Was the document kept in the course of a regularly conducted business activity of your firm?*
> A: Yes.
> Q: *Is it the regular practice of your firm to make such documents?*
> A: Yes.
> Q: *I offer Plaintiff's exhibit #2 into evidence.*

Each of the questions above corresponds exactly to a requirement that must be met in order to have a document recognized as a business record. The last two questions above, although they sound similar, actually call for somewhat different information. As the rule includes both requirements, both questions should be asked. Another benefit of tailoring the foundational questions to the rule is that it removes the danger that the attorney will omit an element needed to have the exhibit entered. It is not uncommon, for example, for attorneys to forget that they must show that entries in business records are made contemporaneous with the events observed.

G. Offer the Exhibit into Evidence

After the foundation is laid, the document should be offered into evidence. If it is admitted, remember to have the identification tag on the exhibit changed to reflect its admission. At times, such as when a chain of custody must be shown, more than one witness may be required in order to complete the foundation. In such a situation, the first witness identifies the exhibit, testifies as to his portion of the foundation and then concludes his direct and cross-examinations. The second and third witness then offer their relevant testimony and, when the foundation is complete, the exhibit can be offered. The attorney in such situations should keep track of what elements of the foundation were required of each witness and whether those elements were satisfied through the testimony.

As you are using exhibits during the trial, some being admitted into evidence, others not, it is essential that you keep accurate records of the status of each exhibit. One way of keeping track of the status of exhibits during the hurly-burly of a trial is to devise a chart with columns that can be checked off when the appropriate step has been taken. For example, devise a chart with the following column headings: EXHIBIT #; DESCRIPTION OR TITLE OF EXHIBIT; WITNESSES NEEDED TO LAY FOUNDATION; FOUNDATIONAL ELEMENTS; ADMITTED. Especially during lengthy trials and those with numerous exhibits, it is helpful to have at your fingertips the status of each exhibit. Additionally, by seeing what is not yet checked off, the attorney should be able to avoid the embarrassing situations of forgetting to ask a witness a required foundational question or neglecting to offer the exhibit into evidence.

III. Frequently Used Exhibits, Frequently Arising Problems

A. Tangible Items

Used effectively, tangible items can bring oral testimony to life. Rather than just hearing about what happened, jurors can see and literally feel the significance of the testimony for themselves. Listening to the police officer describe the damage to the plaintiff's car after it was hit from the rear by the defendant's truck is one thing, but viewing the twisted piece of metal that once was the trunk of the car makes the testimony less abstract and more memorable to the jury. Testimony from the assault and battery victim concerning how she was hit with a metal pipe takes on added meaning when the jury is given the pipe to examine. Feeling how hard the pipe is, the jurors can imagine the pain and injury it must have caused in a more profound manner than had they merely heard the pipe described. Before the attorney can achieve these benefits from displaying tangible exhibits to the jury, certain hurdles must be successfully negotiated.

1. Chain of Custody

Your client had just finished the canned beef he was eating for dinner when suddenly he became quite ill. The paramedic who arrived with the ambulance asked your client's wife to show him what her husband had recently eaten. She handed the paramedic the can of beef that was still on the kitchen table. After arriving at the hospital, the paramedic gave the can to a lab technician for testing. The technician tested the beef in the can and found it to contain e-coli. Two years later, your client's suit against Big Bad Canned Beef, Inc. has come to trial. You are attempting to have entered into evidence the can of beef and the laboratory report that shows the presence of e-coli in the can. First, however, you must establish a chain of custody for the can and its contents.

Chain of custody, in its broadest meaning, is a phrase used to describe each person or organization that has handled an item, from the moment that it became relevant until the item arrived in the courtroom. Before setting about to establish the chain of custody, you need first to determine what type of chain needs to be demonstrated in order to have the evidence admitted. When dealing with an object whose size, nature and chemical makeup is either irrelevant or unchangeable, a much more abbreviated chain of custody is sufficient. For example, if the police recover the robbery victim's wallet from the pocket of a suspect, an abbreviated chain of custody is permissible as the nature of the object is not in issue. The foundational questions in such a scenario could proceed as follows:

Q: *Officer, after arresting the defendant, what did you do?*
A: I searched him and found a wallet in his right rear pocket.
Q: *Please describe the wallet you found.*
A: It was a black leather wallet which contained $28 and a number of credit cards in the name of "Howard Silver."
Q: *What did you do with the wallet after you recovered it from the defendant?*

A: I placed it in an evidence bag, marked the wallet and the bag with evidence tags, and turned it in to the police evidence custodian.

Q: *I show you what has been marked State's exhibit # 2 for identification. Do you recognize it?*

A: This is the wallet I recovered from the defendant.

Q: *How do you know that?*

A: My mark still appears both on the wallet and the plastic envelope in which the wallet is contained.

Q: *Is the wallet in the same or substantially the same condition it was in when you recovered it from the defendant?*

A: Yes.

Q: *I offer State's exhibit #2 into evidence.*

Questions related to the manner in which the police evidence custodian maintains evidentiary items and whether the wallet was removed by anyone and then returned (such as if it was removed for the victim to identify) are unnecessary to establish the chain of custody for this item, the nature of which is not in issue. Demonstrating that the officer could identify the wallet, that it was the same wallet recovered from the defendant and in essentially the same condition as when seized sufficiently lays the foundation for its introduction.

Were that same wallet found on the ground near the defendant when he was arrested and the defendant could be linked to the item through a fingerprint match, the chain of custody necessarily would be more involved. In such a situation, the prosecutor would need to show that the wallet was picked up in a manner that did not affect the integrity of the later fingerprint analysis. Then she would be required to describe the manner in which each witness handled the wallet until the analysis was completed. Each person handling an exhibit on which chemical tests are performed or whose nature or quantity is changeable and at issue should be viewed as a link in the chain of custody. If any link on the chain is missing, i.e., a handler of the exhibit unaccounted for, the chain is broken and the evidence may not be admitted.

In the case described above, involving the infected can of beef whose chemical nature is a crucial issue, a complete chain of custody must be shown from the time the beef was eaten until the contents of the can were tested. The plaintiff's wife should testify to having seen her husband get sick after eating the beef and to the can's remaining on the kitchen table untouched until she subsequently handed it to the paramedic. Next the paramedic should testify to how he preserved the evidence (i.e., placed the can in a sealed plastic bag) and transported it to the hospital, where he turned it over to the laboratory technician. The technician then needs to explain how the evidence remained undisturbed until the tests were conducted and that, in performing the tests, all efforts were taken to ensure that the results were untainted by external factors. At this point, the chain of custody has been established.

Each witness in the chain of custody must be able to identify the exhibit. The attorney should be aware that the manner of this identification will vary with the witness, depending on how certain that particular witness can be that the exhibit is what it purports to be. A robbery victim who was threatened with a gun that he described only as "black" should testify when shown the gun recovered from the defendant that, "this looks like the gun the robber pointed at me." The admissibility of the gun is not dependent on the victim's being certain that the exhibit was the weapon used in the robbery, and he risks losing credibility if he positively identifies a gun that looks like thousands of others. This should be explained to the victim during the witness preparatory session. The police officer, however, can and should be positive that the gun he recovered from the defendant is the exhibit being displayed at trial because he noted the gun's serial number and labeled it with definitive evidence marking.

In the case of the tainted beef, the wife's testimony regarding the identification of the can should be elicited as follows:

> Q: *I show you what has been marked as Plaintiff's exhibit #1. Do you recognize it?*
> A: It is an eight ounce can of Big Bad Beef that looks like the one my husband ate from before he got sick.

The paramedic's identification of the item would be somewhat different:

> Q: *I show you what has been marked Plaintiff's exhibit #1. Do you recognize it?*
> A: It is the can of Big Bad Beef that I was handed by the plaintiff's wife on Dec. 17 and that I turned over to the lab technician.
> Q: *How do you know that?*
> A: I affixed my label and the date on the outside of the can before placing it in the plastic envelope. That label is still on the can today.

If the paramedic put the can in the plastic bag without affixing a personal label on the can, that should pose no problem in establishing the chain of custody. Even though he cannot be sure that the can he is shown in court is the one he received from the plaintiff's wife, he can still state with certainty that the can he was given by the plaintiff's wife was in fact the same can that was turned over to the lab technician. When the technician testifies how she isolated and labeled the exhibit and is therefore certain that the can she was handed by the paramedic is the one that was tested and the one produced in court, the chain of custody is unbroken and both the test results and the can should be admitted.

While it is preferable for the sake of clarity to call the chain of custody witnesses in the same sequence in which they handled the evidence, this is not a requirement. Therefore, in the case above, if the paramedic is leaving town before the plaintiff's wife is scheduled to testify, it is permissible to obtain his testimony first about how he received and handled the exhibit. At a later point in the trial the attorney can elicit what the wife observed before the paramedic arrived.

2. Handling the Exhibit

The first visual exposure the jury is likely to have to any tangible exhibit is when the proponent of the exhibit handles it for the first time. Bearing in mind the importance of first impressions, the attorney should handle the exhibit in a manner consistent with how she wants the jury to regard the evidence. In an assault case involving a threat with a gun, the prosecutor's handling of the gun should reinforce in the minds of the jurors the terror that the victim faced when the gun was pointed at his head. Picking up the gun in a cavalier manner, while perhaps showing the prosecutor's familiarity with weapons, works against the message she is trying to communicate to the jury about the exhibit.

When more than one item is being offered into evidence on a specific subject matter, if the attorney wishes the jury to consider each item for its individual worth to the case, she should handle the exhibit accordingly. This means the identifying witness should be handed and asked to identify each item individually and the significance of that item should be made clear before moving on to the next item. In the incident above involving the tainted beef, if, in addition to the can, traces of contaminant were found on the plaintiff's plate and fork, the attorney would be offering each of those items into evidence. As it is significant that three separate items touched by the beef had traces of contaminant, the attorney's handling of the items should emphasize the point that each of the items is independent proof of the beef's contamination. Rather than handing the plaintiff's wife all three exhibits to identify and describe together, the questioning should proceed as follows:

Q: How did your husband eat the beef from the can?
A: He put it on his plate with a fork and used that same fork to eat it.
Q: I show you Plaintiff's' #3 for identification. Do you recognize it?

A: It looks like the forks we used for dinner that night and the one my husband used to eat the beef.

Q: *What about the fork looks familiar?*

A: I recognize the pattern as being the same as our silverware.

Q: *After the ambulance arrived, what happened to the fork?*

A: The paramedic asked me for the fork my husband used. I picked it up by the handle from right next to the plate my husband ate from and handed it to the paramedic.

The plate and can of beef should be handled, identified and their significance made clear to the jury individually in the same manner. With respect to certain aspects of the chain of custody, however (i.e., those of a technical or ministerial nature about which there is no dispute), the items can be treated jointly to avoid time consuming repetition. Finally, the attorney should consider asking the court to allow the jury to examine each exhibit.

After an item is admitted into evidence, it is often wise to ask the court to allow the jury to examine the exhibit. Frequently bored with purely oral testimony, jurors look forward to receiving exhibits and personally examining them. After the significance of the exhibit has been made clear to them from witness testimony, the jury's interest in, and curiosity about, the exhibit is likely to be at its highest. In satisfying that curiosity, the attorney also makes the jurors feel more directly part of his case. Attorneys should be aware that jurors who are handling exhibits are unable to simultaneously pay full attention to the testimony from the witness stand. Therefore, when the jury is handed the exhibit, the attorney should pause in his questioning to ensure that each juror has an adequate opportunity to examine the exhibit and then re-focus on the oral testimony.

The court, in its discretion, can refuse to permit the exhibit to be examined by the jury with the witness on the stand. This is often done because the judge wishes to avoid delay. In such a case, the court may permit the jury to examine the exhibit only during its deliberations at the conclusion of the case. With respect to certain exhibits, the court may not allow direct handling by the jurors at any time even though the exhibits are accepted into evidence. Exhibits that might pose a danger to the jurors, those that are unduly cumbersome and items whose handling by the jury may result in improper prejudice fall within this exclusion. For example, such prejudice can occur when jurors conduct their own "experiments" on the exhibit during deliberations. The conditions under which jurors test the exhibit may be substantially different than those that existed when the exhibit was used during the events that led to the lawsuit. Therefore, the result of the jury's test can lead it to an inaccurate and prejudicial conclusion about an important fact in the case. Judges concerned that jurors may use exhibits in such a fashion may prefer to allow juror examination of the exhibit only during the trial.

B. Documents

The introduction of certain documents into evidence may be necessary to establish the elements of a cause of action or a specific defense. The plaintiff needs to get into evidence the written contract that is the subject of a suit alleging breach of contract. The defense must introduce the portion of the insurance policy containing the exclusionary clause to support its defense that denial of insurance coverage was proper.

Other documents may not be required to establish or answer a cause of action but may prove valuable in other ways. A notation in a business record, for example, can confirm the witness's testimony that a certain event occurred or an action was taken in precisely the same manner as the witness testified. Sometimes, just seeing something in writing gives it added credibility and significance in the eyes of the jury. In some proceedings the factual finding of a public official after conducting an investigation can be elicited through oral testimony. When the jury is shown the official document containing her report and finding, that conclusion will carry more weight. See FRE 803 (8)(c) regarding the admissibility of such public factual findings. If nothing else is achieved from placing the report into evidence, the jury will have the report available during its deliberations to serve as an instant reminder of the witness's oral testimony. As with tangible items, the attorney must take certain steps before offering documents into evidence.

1. Authentication

Before the contents of a document can be admitted into evidence or read in court, that document must be authenticated. That is, there must be a showing that the document is what it purports to be. This usually means that the proponent of the exhibit must establish who *authored* or *adopted* the document. Article IX of the Federal Rules of Evidence offers illustrations of how to authenticate exhibits. Rule 902 provides for the self-authentication of certain documents, such as newspapers, public documents and business records. Attorneys utilizing this rule should pay careful attention to the particular conditions that must be met with respect to each type of document to be self-authenticated. Certain documents covered under FRE 902 must include a particular seal or signature, others must be certified, and still others require that the proponent of the exhibit notify opposing counsel and allow inspection of the exhibit well before it is offered into evidence.

While the most obvious way to authenticate a document is to have the author identify it and testify to its production, the author may be unavailable, or difficult and expensive to call as a witness. Alternatively, the author may, due to associations with the adverse party, be a person who the attorney would prefer to keep off the witness stand for strategic reasons. Fortunately, there are several methods of authenticating documents without the need to call the author.

Among the most common methods for authenticating a document is calling a witness who is familiar with the signature on the document through having seen that signature on previous occasions. The witness would testify as to when, how often and under what circumstances he has seen the author's signature previously and that the signature on the document at issue appears to be the same. The witness need not be a handwriting expert to render such testimony. Of course, an expert can be called to testify that a comparison she has made between the handwriting on another document known to belong to the alleged author of the subject document and the handwriting on the subject document indicates that both likely belong to the same person. As such expert testimony is time consuming and expensive, it should be utilized only when no other means of authentication is available.

One simple means of authenticating a document is to produce a witness who was present when the document was prepared. That witness would attest to the identity of the author and other matters concerning the document that may be pertinent to the particular case. In lieu of such direct evidence, attorneys are permitted to authenticate documents through the use of circumstantial evidence. If the document appears that it was sent by ABC Widget Co. because it was written on the company's distinctive stationery and mailed from the company's address, that is strong circumstantial evidence that the document was, at least, authored by someone from the company. If the contents of the document are likely to be known or written about by the alleged author, that too suggests the document was in fact written by that person. Take, for example, a letter purportedly written by a foster parent to a birth parent about the child who links them together. The letter speaks of the child's recurring rash on his chest and that he forgot to bring his favorite red toothbrush to the foster parent's house. Although the birth parent cannot identify the foster parent's signature and has no direct evidence that the letter was written by the foster parent, the contents of the letter serve to establish its likely author.

Another means by which a document can be authenticated through its contents is a showing that those contents reflect the details of a conversation that the author of the document had previously. One who was present during this conversation can testify that what the alleged author of the document said at that time is later reflected in the subject document. If the witness spoke to the alleged author of the document over the telephone, the details of that telephone conversation that later show up in the document can be used to authenticate the document. In such a situation, the attorney must first have the witness authenticate the voice on the telephone. This can be accomplished by the witness's recognition of the caller's voice from previous conversations or by complying with the requirements of FRE 901 (6) (if the witness placed the call to the document author).

Assume that ABC Widget Co. wishes to introduce a letter it received from Mary Smith, a person with whom it has not corresponded previously, requesting to purchase 3 widgets. The letter could be authenticated as follows:

> Q: *I show you what has been marked as Plaintiff's #2 for identification. Do you recognize it?*
> A: This is the letter I received on May 12, 1997 from Mary Smith.
> Q: *How did you know it was from Ms. Smith?*
> A: The contents of the letter reflected the details of a telephone conversation I had with Ms. Smith on May 5.
> Q: *How did you know it was Mary Smith that you spoke with on the telephone?*
> A: I have spoken with Ms. Smith on several prior occasions and recognized her voice when she called on May 5.

When the voice sought to be authenticated is that of the person *making* the telephone call, as above, showing merely that the caller identified herself by name is insufficient. In the case above, further testimony would reveal that a person who identified herself as Mary Smith and whose voice the witness recognized telephoned to discuss the purchase of 3 widgets. Ms. Smith indicated she would send a written request for the widgets. When a letter requesting to purchase 3 widgets was received the next week signed "Mary Smith," although the signature was unfamiliar, there is enough circumstantial evidence to authenticate the document.

2. Best Evidence Doctrine

Another problem frequently encountered by attorneys when offering documents into evidence is satisfying the Best Evidence Doctrine. Stated simply, this doctrine requires attorneys to use the original or exact duplicate of a document whenever possible. If the original or an exact duplicate cannot be obtained despite the best efforts of the attorney, provisions exist for permitting the introduction of other evidence of the document's contents. Article X of the FRE is the basis for the Best Evidence Doctrine in federal courts.

Rule 1001(4) adopts the modern approach to the definition of duplicates, including not only documents made from the same matrix (i.e., carbon copies), but also those made by means of photographic or other mechanical means. Printouts of data stored in a computer are considered to be originals by Rule 1001(3). Under Rule 1003, duplicates may be offered in lieu of the original except when the authenticity of the original is genuinely in dispute or use of the duplicate in place of the original would be unfair to the other side. This means that, in most instances, a photocopy of a document satisfies the best evidence doctrine without any need to account for the location of the original.

If neither the original nor an exact duplicate of the document is available, the attorney may still have some evidence of the document's contents admitted by taking advantage of Rule 1004. That rule allows for other means of proving the contents of a document if the proponent can show the original is lost or destroyed (and not done so deliberately by the proponent), or not obtainable because it is in the hands of the opposing party or out of the reach of judicial process.

For example, if the plaintiff sent a document to the defendant that the defendant claims not to have received, the plaintiff can take advantage of Rule 1004 to introduce a memorandum that embodies the essential contents of the document. As far as the plaintiff knows, the original letter, which had been properly addressed and posted, is either lost or in the hands of the defendant. Under Rule 1004, this enables him to offer other evidence of the contents of the letter, such as the memorandum.

3. Public Records

Too few attorneys make use of the broad authority given to judges to admit into evidence reports containing the factual findings of government officials. Formerly, these findings, when based in part on information acquired from outside sources, such as eyewitnesses or statistical studies, were generally inadmissible due to hearsay objections or lack of first-hand knowledge. With the passage of FRE 803 (8)(c), such factual findings are considerably more likely to be admitted.

While the reports of public officials can normally be admitted over any hearsay objection under the business records exception (see discussion and example of offering a business record into evidence under FRE 803 (6) in above subsection, "The Drill"), there may be important benefits for the attorney in using the public records exception, FRE 803 (8)(c). This Rule permits the introduction of factual findings appearing in public reports and records when offered by the defendant in a criminal case or either party in a civil case. Should the findings at issue involve information acquired from non-public officials, such as eyewitnesses, the document would face possible objections including lack of firsthand knowledge or hearsay within hearsay if the findings were offered as part of a business record. If certain conditions are met, those same factual findings may be insulated from a successful objection if offered as part of a public record. Specifically, if the factual finding results from an investigation made pursuant to law and neither the sources of the information that led to the finding nor the method in which the report is prepared lack trustworthiness, the report and its factual finding are admissible.

C. Photographs and Diagrams

During the war in Vietnam, there were numerous reports in the American media about the brutal methods used by the South Vietnamese police. All of these reports cumulatively did not compare to the effect on the American public of the display of just one photograph. This now famous picture showed a police official firing a gun into the head of an already subdued man. Although this photo merely corroborated previous reports and reinforced the view that many already possessed, the significant role it played in influencing public opinion serves as a reminder of the power of visual images.

While most trial lawyers are unlikely to ever have a photograph as powerful as the one discussed above, the use of visual images or representations can clarify, demonstrate, emphasize and dramatize parts of a witness's testimony. Something as simple as a diagram of an intersection can help to make the witness's description of the accident understandable. This, in turn, will prevent the jury from getting confused and, thereafter, losing interest in the witness's testimony. The defense investigator's testimony about the improved physical condition of the victim of a construction accident can be effectively emphasized by a video showing the plaintiff working on his roof and riding a bicycle. Photographs of the supermarket taken at various times show how long food items were left on the floor unattended. With a drawing of the bones in the arm, the doctor can demonstrate the nature of an injury.

1. Evidentiary Requirements

In order to have a photograph or diagram admitted into evidence or merely used as an illustrative tool, a witness with knowledge must authenticate the exhibit. In all but the rarest situations, it is unnecessary to call the photographer or the preparer of the diagram as a witness. Remember, in most cases, the relevance of a photograph or diagram relates not to the tangible exhibit itself but only to what it depicts or represents. The proponent, therefore, is generally not obligated to show how the exhibit was prepared or maintained, only that it accurately represents its subject. In the rare case where the legitimacy of a photograph is at issue, the photographer may be needed to testify to its integrity. The person who prepared a chart or diagram will need to testify if the exhibit is being proffered as a scale drawing. In that case, the witness will testify to how the drawing was prepared and what scale was used.

As a matter of strategy, it is usually unwise to call the photographer. At a minimum, the attorney has probably wasted time and money in doing so. Worse still is the possibility that calling the photographer will invite cross-examination on the subjectivity involved in photography, the bias of this paid witness, the ways in which the photographs could have produced better images and other matters that will diminish or, at least, delay the productive use of the photograph. Where the photograph required some incredibly sophisticated technology (i.e., one showing a Lincoln dime on the moon), perhaps, then, the photographer is worth calling. Normally, however, a person with knowledge of the scene depicted at the relevant time is the appropriate witness to call. For example, consider the testimony below of a police officer regarding the use of a diagram of the scene of an auto accident.

> Q: *Officer, what do your duties entail?*
> A: I patrol the streets in the northwest corner of town.
> Q: *Does that area take in the intersection of Main and Oak Streets?*
> A: Yes.
> Q: *Are you familiar with that intersection?*
> A: Yes, I have driven past it hundreds of times.
> Q: *Were you present at that intersection on the night of January 2, 2007 at 9:00 p.m.?*
> A: Yes.

> Q: *I show you what has previously been marked as plaintiff's exhibit #8. Do you recognize it?*
>
> A: It looks like a diagram of that intersection and the area around it.
>
> Q: *Is plaintiff's exhibit #8 a fair and accurate representation of the intersection of Main and Oak Streets as it looked on January 2, 2007 at 9:00 p.m.?*
>
> A: It is.
>
> Q: *Would the use of this diagram be helpful to you in illustrating the location of the things you saw upon arriving at the scene?*
>
> A: It would.

The above questions and answers would allow for introduction of the exhibit and its use as an illustrative tool.

One situation the attorney needs to be aware of with respect to when to have the exhibit admitted concerns the witness's ability to mark on the exhibit. The technical approach taken by some judges is that once the exhibit has been admitted into evidence it cannot be altered, for example, by marking on it. The attorney does not want to be in the position of having her witness precluded from drawing his location at the time of the accident on the diagram because of such a ruling. With such a judge, the witness should make required markings on the exhibit after the foundation is laid but before the exhibit is admitted into evidence. On the other hand, just to make the trial lawyer's life interesting, some judges prohibit any marking of the exhibit *until* it is received into evidence. In such a situation, have the exhibit admitted and then have the witness work with it as needed. Once again, the best advice for the lawyer is to inquire of the judge, or of others who have been before the judge previously, the preferred method in that courtroom.

Once the exhibit is entered into evidence, another problem could develop if the attorney plans on having more than one witness place markings on the exhibit. Imagine one witness has already drawn on the diagram where the pedestrian was walking at the moment he was hit by defendant's car. When a subsequent witness is asked to point to or mark the pedestrian's position on the diagram, the previous marking makes the question leading (albeit visually rather than orally leading) and objectionable. Additionally, the question can be viewed as violating the rule requiring the sequestration of witnesses. To avoid this problem, the attorney can have the pedestrian represented by a cut-out figure that can be easily attached to and removed from the diagram. Other means of avoiding visually leading questions are to use an overhang of the exhibit that does not show the markings made by previous witnesses or to have a separate diagram available for the second witness. While there are more elaborate and imaginative means for dealing with this problem, the use of visually leading exhibits can be avoided simply and inexpensively.

The attorney may confront a problem dealing with changes that occurred in the scene between the time of the incident in question and when the photograph of the scene was taken. In a typical auto accident case, photographers should attempt to replicate as closely as possible the conditions that existed at the time of the accident. This means taking the photographs with traffic and lighting conditions similar to those existing at the time of the accident. The proponent of the evidence does not want to be in the position of having his photographs attacked as being unfair and inaccurate depictions of the scene. Even if the opponent is unsuccessful at keeping such photographs from being accepted into evidence, the value of the exhibit may be substantially diminished if the jury accepts the opponent's characterization of the photograph.

At times, due to changes in the subject matter occurring after the date and time at issue but prior to the taking of the photograph, the photographer will be unable to duplicate precisely the conditions that existed at the moment at issue. These changes may be due to a permanent alteration in the scene or because particular conditions that existed at the relevant moment cannot be recreated. In such situations, the attorney offering the photographs into evidence should account for the differences prior to offering the photograph into evidence. In the accident case alluded to above, those changes could be handled as follows:

> Q: *Officer, are there any differences between the photograph marked as plaintiff's exhibit #8 and the way in which the accident scene appeared on January 2 at 9:00 p.m. when you arrived?*
>
> A: Obviously, the cars in the accident are not shown in plaintiff's #8. Additionally, the photo shows a small house on Main St., somewhat south of the intersection with Oak St. On the day of the accident that house had not yet been built, and the area was a construction site.
>
> Q: *But for the differences you discussed, is plaintiff's #8 a fair and accurate representation of the area surrounding the accident scene as it appeared on January 2 at 9:00?*
>
> A: Yes.

To be admissible, a photograph does not have to be an exact representation of the scene as it appeared at the relevant moment. In order to fairly represent the scene, the photograph does have to be substantially similar to what it purports to depict. This means that the proponent of the photograph should account for any differences and minimize them. In the above situation, the court should have no difficulty admitting the photograph once it is clear that the presence of the small house does not substantially alter the scene, or the view a driver would have upon approaching the intersection. Note that the qualifying words ("but for ...") were put in the question to enable the witness to answer "yes" without qualification.

2. Using the Exhibit Effectively

Having successfully laid the foundation for the admission or use of demonstrative evidence, it is now time to put the exhibit to the best use possible. Some attorneys think carefully about how to overcome evidentiary problems involving the exhibit but pay little attention to making effective use of the exhibit and maximizing its impact. Every judge can cite numerous examples of attorneys using diagrams that were either too far away or too small for the jury to see. Witnesses are asked to mark up photographs on the witness stand that nobody but the witness can see. Charts are located in such a way that the witness illustrating on the chart blocks the view of half of the jurors. Attorneys should remember that the purpose of using the exhibit is to explain, clarify or emphasize a point by showing the *jury* something. Thus, the elementary, but crucial, first principle to keep in mind regarding the effective use of demonstrative evidence is MAKE SURE THE JURY CAN SEE THE EVIDENCE.

Upon learning in which courtroom they will be trying the case, attorneys should tour that courtroom, especially if they have never previously tried a case there. Part of the attorney's preparation for trial is choreographing his or her movements in the courtroom. For example, by getting a feel for where the counsel tables, the witness stand and the jury box are located, the attorney can make a more informed decision about whether and where to stand when conducting direct and cross-examination. Specifically with respect to the use of exhibits, attorneys can select the optimum location for placement of the exhibit to ensure that the jurors will be able to see it clearly. The attorney can determine where the witness who is illustrating on the exhibit should stand so as not to block the view of any of the jurors. Seeing the distance that the exhibit will be placed from the jury box will aid the lawyer in deciding how large the exhibit needs to be. In planning these matters, the attorney should inquire of the judge or court personnel whether the judge permits the exhibits to be displayed in the location and manner that the attorney desires. Since judges are invariably concerned with juries being able to see the evidence clearly, they are usually cooperative in responding to requests regarding locations for the exhibits.

Before calling upon a witness to show or mark something on a diagram, the attorney should have adequately prepared the witness specifically for this aspect of his or her testimony. While the markings on a diagram and the manner in which it depicts the item or area in question may be abundantly clear to the attorney who had the diagram prepared and has been working on the case for months, that same diagram may appear as a strange collection of lines and shapes to the witness seeing it for the first time. During the preparatory session, the witness should be shown the diagram that will be used at trial, have explained to her all of the items included in it and then asked the questions that will be posed to her during the trial concerning the exhibit. Have the witness point to the precise location where the pedestrian was standing immediately before the accident. Better still, have her draw that location on a diagram that is a duplicate of the one that will be utilized during trial. This simple preparatory step should avoid the witness's pointing to a line she thought depicted the crosswalk but was, in fact, a stop line, or the witness's drawing a pedestrian who is twice the size of the car shown on the diagram.

Regarding the appropriate size for an exhibit, one trial judge says attorneys should always follow the rule, the bigger the better. Blow up that photograph, use a projector to display that diagram on the wall, label that chart so jurors don't have to squint to make out which bone is the fibula. Seeing isn't enough. You want to make sure your exhibit has a profound impact on the jury, and that they will remember it during their deliberations, especially if they cannot take the exhibit back with them. Jurors are unlikely to forget the life-size photograph of a victim's battered face taken shortly after the incident.

Attorneys should be aware of how the appearance of the diagram can contribute to its strategic benefit. For example, the use of different colors to demonstrate different items on the diagram can make it easier for the jury to understand the diagram, while simultaneously emphasizing key aspects of the exhibit. Having models of items that can be affixed by the witness to the exhibit can serve to make the exhibit more real and memorable for the jury. A simple cut-out of a car and a stick figure of a woman, to be placed by the witness at the location on the diagram where he saw the accident occur, will remain as a graphic reminder to the jury that the pedestrian was walking outside the crosswalk.

Even paying attention to precisely how the witness marks the diagram can contribute to the more effective use of the exhibit. Do not put the onus of figuring out how to mark the diagram on the shoulders of your witnesses. Tell them how to do it. "With the red pen, please place the letters 'MJ' where you saw Mary Jones walking immediately before the accident. Now, with the blue pen, put 'JS' where you were standing immediately before the accident." Note that the question contains a tight time frame to avoid confusion in the witness's answer or uncertainty about an important fact when the jury looks at the diagram later. When marking diagrams, some attorneys appear unaware that the alphabet contains 26 letters. As a result, jurors looking at the diagram will see "X" marking the location of virtually everything on the exhibit. To better enable the jury to remember what has been demonstrated through the use of the diagram, have the witness use markings, such as initials, that relate to the person or item depicted. Finally, remember to reflect for the record what the witness has drawn on the diagram. Doing so preserves the record for appeal, or in the event that the jury asks later for a reading of that testimony, and allows you to tell the jury what the witness just did. "Let the record reflect that the witness just placed the letters 'MJ' on plaintiff's exhibit #3 in a location north of the crosswalk, to illustrate where Ms. Jones was walking immediately before the accident."

While some attorneys will have access to the resources necessary to produce demonstrative exhibits of which Steven Spielberg would be proud, all of the suggestions above to improve the manner in which exhibits are presented can be implemented relatively simply and inexpensively. It takes but a little planning and even less creativity.

IV. Limited Admissibility

Certain exhibits can be used by the fact finder for more than one purpose. Although one of those purposes might be improper, there may be an independent lawful purpose for which the exhibit is admissible. A photograph of the scene of an auto accident taken shortly thereafter may be admissible to depict the conditions existing at the time but may contain a graphic, even grisly, shot of the plaintiff that is overly prejudicial to the defense. A police report of the accident is generally admissible under the business record [FRE 803(6)] or public record [FRE 803(8)(c)] exception to the hearsay rule in order to show the observations and actions of the investigating officers. The statements of eyewitnesses to the accident included in the report, however, may not be admissible. Those statements are hearsay within hearsay and, unless the statements qualify themselves for hearsay exceptions, they would be inadmissible under FRE 805. An unsigned written statement by an eyewitness to the accident that contradicts her later testimony at trial may be admissible for the purpose of impeachment through prior inconsistent statement . That same statement cannot be used as substantive evidence of the matter asserted within it, as that would constitute hearsay. As the statement is unsigned, it would not meet the requirements to be treated as non-hearsay (and thus admissible without limitation) under FRE 801(d)(1).

Each of the exhibits alluded to above raises substantial questions of admissibility. The actions of the attorneys proposing and opposing the exhibits can result in the admission of the entire exhibits, the exclusion of the entire exhibits or the admissibility of portions of the exhibits. Additionally, once the exhibit is admitted, the court can permit the jury to consider the exhibit for all purposes or can instruct the jury to limit the purposes to which the exhibit can be used. It is important, therefore, for attorneys to understand the concept of limited admissibility and to be prepared to argue effectively for the most advantageous use of the exhibit.

A. Types of Relief

1. Redaction

Where an exhibit contains portions that are admissible and others that are objectionable, either attorney can request the court to redact, or delete, the objectionable parts of the exhibit.

This enables the exhibit to be admitted and, in most circumstances, to be examined by the jury with only the objectionable portions deleted. In the auto accident case alluded to above, the photograph taken of the scene after the accident would be admitted and shown to the jury after the prejudicial image of the plaintiff has been removed or covered over. The police report would be admissible once the double hearsay statements of the civilian witnesses were redacted.

The mechanics of entering a redacted copy of an exhibit should not prove difficult. The attorney proposing the redaction should have a copy of the exhibit with the objectionable parts cut, whited out or in some way made invisible. While he or she may never need to make use of the redacted version of the exhibit, having such a copy at the ready makes the attorney look professional and can influence a judge's decision regarding whether and in what form the redacted version should be admitted.

2. Limiting Instruction

Where the objection to the exhibit arises not from the fact that it contains certain improper material that can be redacted but instead because the exhibit can be used by the jury for the wrong purpose, another form of relief is needed. If the attorney opposing the exhibit is unsuccessful in keeping it from being shown to the jury, he or she should consider seeking a limiting instruction from the court. The limiting instruction directs the jury either not to use the exhibit for a specific purpose or, alternatively, to use it only for a certain purpose.

Returning again to the accident case, let us assume the attorney opposing admission of the prior inconsistent written, but unsigned, statement of the witness has been unsuccessful in keeping the statement from being admitted. Now the attorney should weigh the benefits and drawbacks of asking the court to instruct the jury that the statement can be used only as it sheds doubt on the witness's testimony during trial and not as substantive evidence of the matter asserted in the statement. While the attorney hopes the jury will follow such an instruction from the court, common sense suggests that many jurors will not understand, remember or care about such a distinction. In fact, in obtaining such a limiting instruction, the attorney risks magnifying the importance of the inconsistency in the minds of the jury. Still, there are times when a limiting instruction can cause the jury to restrict the purposes for which an exhibit is used (see discussion of curative instructions in the chapter on Objections).

B. When to Seek a Ruling of Limited Admissibility

Unless the relevance of an exhibit is explicitly limited by the court, the exhibit may be considered by the fact finder for any purpose it deems appropriate. The attorney opposing the exhibit should consider requesting that the exhibit be admitted for a limited purpose *only after* it is clear that the exhibit will in fact be admitted by the court. If an exhibit contains material that makes it inadmissible, the judge may sustain a general objection to the admissibility of the exhibit. At this point, it is incumbent upon the proponent of the evidence to save whatever portion of the exhibit is admissible. On the other hand, where the judge is inclined to admit the exhibit over an objection, the opponent of the exhibit should consider attempting to limit the purposes for which the jury can use the evidence or seek to prohibit specific portions of the exhibit from being admitted.

In deciding when to press for limited admissibility, it is important for the attorney to read the intentions of the judge correctly. If it is clear that the judge is unsympathetic to the objection, the opponent of the exhibit should speak to the issue of limited admissibility prior to the time that the court issues its ruling. Some judges do not wish to entertain any further discussion regarding the exhibit once they have ruled, and others, while willing to listen, are psychologically committed to the ruling as issued. Notwithstanding this, where the attorney is unsure of the court's view until her objection is overruled and, therefore, did not address limited admissibility prior to the ruling, she needs to raise the issue immediately thereafter. In doing so, the attorney should raise the issue of limited admissibility in a manner that makes clear to the judge that she is not challenging the ruling issued but instead seeking a second ruling.

If it is the proponent of the exhibit who is seeking limited admissibility, the process is slightly different. Again, gauging the judge's opinion early regarding admissibility of the entire exhibit can be helpful. Here, however, the attorney should normally seek admission of the exhibit in its entirety. Even if the court sustains an objection to its admissibility, the proponent can simply make a new offer of the exhibit in its revised form with the objectionable matter deleted. The making of this second offer is facilitated by the proponent of the exhibit having the redacted copy immediately available, as discussed above.

V. Opposing Exhibits

The attorney whose adversary is seeking to offer an exhibit into evidence should be aware of the two goals that can be achieved by the opponent of any evidentiary item. On one hand, if some aspect of the foundation cannot be laid or some other evidentiary principle is violated, the opponent can seek to have the proffer of the evidence rejected by the court. Failing that, there are strategies that can be employed to diminish the integrity or impact of the exhibit in the eyes of the jury.

A. Challenging Admissibility

1. Basis

The range of problems an attorney can encounter when attempting to lay the foundation for the admission of certain exhibits (i.e., the elements of "The Drill," chain of custody, authentication, best evidence and certain hearsay problems) is discussed above. The first step in attacking those exhibits lies in the opponent's determining which of the necessary foundational elements has not been satisfied. Even if the foundation is laid properly and the evidence is relevant, attorneys can still object to the admission of any exhibit whose probative value is substantially outweighed by its prejudicial impact or its likelihood of confusing or misleading the jury. Additionally, the evidence can be excluded because of the undue delay it causes in the proceeding or the fact that it is cumulative.

FRE 403 imposes on the attorney seeking to exclude relevant evidence the difficult task of demonstrating that the probative value of the evidence is *substantially* less than the prejudice it causes. This can still be accomplished with respect to those exhibits which in whole or in part unfairly prejudice the exhibit's opponent. A photograph of a party that shows the party in a highly unfavorable light for reasons entirely unrelated to the issues at trial might qualify for such an exclusion. A tangible item that is particularly grizzly, such as severed body part, is too prejudicial to bring before the jury. A document in which a party expresses ethnic or racial hatred (when that hatred is largely unconnected to the issues at trial) may be excluded even though that document may show something relevant to the case, such as the writing style of the defendant. The common thread connecting each of these items is that much of the impact of each exhibit will result in severe and unfair prejudice to the opponent. Similarly, exhibits that are misleading, such as the results of a questionably reliable test performed by an expert witness, those that may confuse, such as medical records without a doctor to explain important terms, and those that may cause undue delay also may be excluded.

2. Methods

Naturally, the simplest method of challenging the admissibility of an exhibit is to lodge an objection. Normally, this objection is timely made when the proponent of the exhibit offers the exhibit into evidence. There are situations, however, when the attorney opposing admission should consider undertaking specific procedures in support of the objection.

a. Limited Voir Dire

At the discretion of the court, the attorney opposing admission of an exhibit can ask the witness on the stand certain questions related to the admissibility of that exhibit. This is done when the exhibit is offered into evidence even though the proponent of the exhibit may not yet have finished her direct examination of the witness. The purpose of such a limited voir dire is to allow the opponent to elicit from the witness testimony that will aid him in formulating his objection to the exhibit. This is not an opportunity for a broad precross-examination of the witness. Only those questions related to the exhibit's admissibility will be permitted.

The attorney's decision whether to ask the court for permission to conduct a limited voir dire should be based upon the likelihood that questioning the witness will reveal information that would enhance an objection to the admissibility of the exhibit. Assume the last witness establishing the chain of custody has concluded that portion of her testimony related to the chain, and the proponent now offers the exhibit into evidence. If the attorney opposing admission suspects that the handling of the evidence at this final stage may have exposed it to some external taint, he should request a limited voir dire to explore that possibility. Without such questioning, the exhibit is likely to be admitted. While the opponent might uncover the chain of custody problem during cross-examination, there are consequences resulting from the evidence already having been admitted. A request at this stage to have the court change its ruling regarding the admissibility of the exhibit, even in the unlikely event such a request is successful, may not negate the damage done when the exhibit was admitted. Depending on the nature of the exhibit, the proponent may have already shown or displayed the exhibit to the jury, used it to demonstrate some point or elicited the results of a test that was performed on the exhibit. An instruction from the court to disregard these uses of the exhibit will, at most, limit somewhat the damage that has been done.

Some judges regard with disfavor requests by attorneys for a limited voir dire, considering them to cause unnecessary delays in the proceedings. If the attorney's request for a limited voir dire is denied despite his or her best effort to explain to the court the importance of the request, the attorney may wish to ask the court to reserve its ruling on admissibility until after the cross-examination. Failing that, the attorney can request that the exhibit not be handled by the jury or utilized in other ways that would prove to be prejudicial pending a cross-examination that might reveal flaws in the foundation or other evidentiary problems. When there is a risk of severe prejudice occurring before the opposing attorney is permitted to explore any evidentiary problems that might exist, the attorney should be sure to make a thorough record of the nature of the evidentiary issue and the degree of prejudice resulting from use of the exhibit. If the prejudice is severe enough, that record could serve as the basis for an appeal of any unfavorable verdict.

b. Motion in Limine

Some exhibits are so prejudicial that if the jury sees or even hears discussion of the exhibit, substantial damage may occur to the party opposing it. The defendant in a civil case wishes to introduce a large blow-up of a photograph depicting the plaintiff in a particularly unfavorable light. The plaintiff may be able to show that the prejudice of admitting such a photograph substantially outweighs whatever probative value the exhibit has. If the photograph is displayed for the witness in the presence of the jury in order to allow the foundation for its admissibility to be laid, the plaintiff's ultimate victory in having the photograph disallowed may be a pyrrhic one. The jurors have already seen the prejudicial photograph and it has left an indelible impression in their minds.

A witness in a criminal case receives a threatening letter some time prior to his testimony, and the prosecutor has some information that the letter was sent at the direction of the defendant (and, therefore, indicates consciousness of guilt). Normally, the proponent of the exhibit, in this case the prosecutor, would be permitted to lay the foundation for the exhibit and offer it into evidence before an objection is timely. In this situation, the witness, in laying the foundation, may testify to receiving the threatening letter and what evidence there is suggesting it was induced by the defendant. If the judge ultimately disallows the exhibits because there is insufficient evidence linking it to the defendant, the defendant has still suffered substantial damage. At least some jurors are likely to infer the threatening letter is connected to the defendant and hold that against him during their deliberations.

To avoid this type of prejudice, the attorney opposing the exhibit should consider moving in limine outside the presence of the jury for exclusion of the exhibit. Such a motion could be heard at the outset of the case or any time before the first witness commences testifying about the prejudicial exhibit. The important advantage of using a motion in limine is that if the attorney convinces the court that the exhibit is inadmissible, the jury has not been contaminated by any contact with the exhibit.

The court generally has discretion whether to hear the objection through a motion in limine. Some judges are more disposed to decide issues in limine, others less inclined to do so. In requesting that the judge decide on admissibility in advance, the attorney should make clear to the court the prejudice that will accrue to his or her client should the proponent be allowed to discuss or display the exhibit in front of the jury prior to a ruling on admissibility.

Where no testimony is necessary for the court to determine admissibility, the judge can rule after arguments from counsel. In the photograph of the plaintiff mentioned above, the judge would likely be able to make the necessary balance between probative value and prejudice without the need for testimony from witnesses. In the case of the threatening letter, the court would need to hear what evidence existed connecting the defendant and the letter. This could be accomplished through a proffer from the prosecutor, or the judge may require testimony from witnesses. In the latter scenario, if the court ultimately was satisfied as to the connection, the testimony could be repeated in front of the jury. If the connection was not substantial enough to establish the defendant's involvement and permit admission of the letter, contamination of the jury through exposure to prejudicial material has been avoided.

B. Diminishing or Limiting the Impact of the Exhibit

Often the attorney opposing the exhibit will be unable to keep the exhibit from the jury if the proponent knows how to lay the proper foundation. In such a situation the opponent may ignore the exhibit in an attempt to demonstrate its irrelevance or unimportance to the jury, or the opponent may take more affirmative measures to diminish or limit the impact of the exhibit once it has been admitted.

1. The Use of Objections

Merely because an exhibit has been admitted into evidence by the court does not mean the opponent is helpless to limit its strategic benefit for the proponent. During the proponent's examination, the opponent must remain vigilant to prevent the exhibit from being used improperly. Remember that questions otherwise inadmissible do not become permissible because they are asked in connection with an exhibit. Common examples of such questions are those that are visually leading and those calling for information beyond the firsthand knowledge of the witness. Assume the plaintiff has introduced into evidence a diagram illustrating the scene of an auto accident. If witness #1 drew on the diagram the location of the victim at the time of the accident, witness #2 should not be allowed to draw the victim's location on the same diagram. Because the second witness can see what the first witness drew, the question regarding the drawing is visually leading. If a police officer is asked to draw on the diagram where cars and pedestrians were located when the accident occurred and that officer was not present at the time of the accident, it is likely that her markings on the diagram will reflect what she was told by others. Unless there is some hearsay-type exception that applies to such testimony, the officer's markings lack firsthand knowledge and are objectionable.

In fact, many of the same evidentiary concerns that arise from oral examinations also occur with respect to exhibits. Even after the unfavorable photograph of the plaintiff discussed above is introduced into evidence, the opponent should prevent adverse witnesses from drawing conclusions about the way the plaintiff appears in the photograph. Witnesses testifying to the link between the threatening letter and the criminal defendant should not be allowed to buttress their testimony with hearsay statements from others.

2. The Use of Cross-Examination

During cross-examination, the opponent should frame questions that raise doubts about the legitimacy or the value of the exhibit. Perhaps the cross-examination in the accident case should elicit that taking a photograph involves subjective decisions about what to shoot, where to aim the camera and when to take the shot. In this case, the picture was taken by a photographer paid by the proponent at a particular moment that was unfairly suggestive of negative behavior. The witness may have to admit that other photographs taken at different times might reveal a different image of the plaintiff. Cross-examination of the witnesses linking the threatening letter to the criminal defendant might show the existence of other people who had cause to write such a letter. Perhaps the witness assumed without much basis that the defendant was involved with the letter and in fact no actual proof of the link exists.

3. The Use of Other Witnesses and Exhibits

At the appropriate time, the attorney opposing the original exhibit might seek to diminish its impact by calling his or her own witnesses to cast doubts on its legitimacy or value. This assumes that the exhibit is important or damaging enough to warrant such treatment. In the civil case involving the photograph, the attorney may choose to call a witness to introduce another photograph showing the plaintiff in a far more typical and favorable light. Witnesses in the criminal case might establish the likelihood that someone other than the defendant sent the threatening letter, or at least reasons why the letter was unlikely to be the product of the defendant.

CHAPTER 6

OBJECTIONS

As with their use of exhibits, the overall effectiveness of many attorneys during trial is impaired by their uncertainty regarding when and how to object to improper questions, and how to respond to the objections of opposing counsel. These attorneys may have only a superficial understanding of evidentiary principles, and applying these principles under the intense time pressure of the question and answer format can seem overwhelming. For example, upon hearing an adverse witness testify to what she was told by another person, the opposing attorney may begin to think as follows. "That sounds like an out of court statement, and it seems that it is being offered for the truth of the matter asserted, but is it being offered to show the state of mind of the declarant? If so, it could be an exception to the hearsay rule." Even if such a thought process leads to the correct application of hearsay principles to the question posed, the answer has probably been given before the attorney starts to object. Perhaps the attorney thinks that a question is improper but cannot think of the basis for the objection. Afraid he or she might be asked by the court for the basis and not wanting to look foolish, the attorney decides not to object. As a result, damaging testimony that might have been excluded or limited by the court now reaches the jury. To avoid such problems, trial lawyers must develop appropriate strategies and learn the skills necessary to handle objections adroitly.

I. Preparation

There are two attributes that good trial lawyers possess that enable them to make and respond effectively to objections. The first, *experience*, takes time to acquire. The second, *focused preparation*, requires only thoughtful planning. Experienced lawyers often report that when they hear an opponent's question that should be objected to, they feel a certain queasiness before they can think through the reason for their objection. By the time they rise to object, a plausible justification occurs to them which they are prepared to artic-ulate if asked to do so by the court. Those attorneys lacking the experience to permit them to instantly sense improper questions must prepare thoroughly to be ready to make the proper objection at the proper time, or to respond persuasively to the objections of their opponent.

After drafting those direct and cross-examination questions that best ac-complish their strategic goals, attorneys should think specifically about the ev-identiary ramifications of the questions they plan to ask. What possible objec-tions could the opposing attorney make to the substantive matters contained within the questions? Is the form of the questions objectionable? Although the question may be unobjectionable, is there something in the expected response of the witness that may lead to an objection and successful motion to strike the response? Anticipating possible objections when preparing for trial provides the attorney first with the opportunity to think about the wisdom of revising the question. Next, he or she can take the time to develop the best possible evi-dentiary response to any objection that might be forthcoming at trial. Finally, the attorney can plan for the contingency that the objection will be sustained, perhaps by envisioning an alternative method through which the desired testi-mony can be elicited. Each of these possible responses to objections is likely to be far more effective if the attorney (especially the less experienced attorney) is not considering them for the first time during the witness's examination.

Because of the strategic importance of getting certain information to the fact finder and the evidentiary issues that are likely to arise in eliciting such information, the proponent may wish to prepare a chart that lays out the re-quirements for ensuring that particularly valuable information is presented correctly. This chart's four headings might be, "MATERIAL TO BE ELICITED," "EVIDENTIARY BASIS FOR ADMISSIBILITY," "ELEMENTS THAT MUST BE ESTABLISHED TO SATISFY EVIDENTIARY BASIS" and "FACTS THAT MAKE OUT NECESSARY ELEMENTS" (see related chart in chapter on Exhibits). Assume in a trial for sale of illegal drugs that the pros-ecutor intends to ask the undercover police officer about a statement made to him by one of the participants in the deal. The obvious objection to such tes-timony is that the statement to the officer constitutes hearsay. The most likely response to such an objection is that the statement is that of a coconspirator under FRE 801 (d)(2)(E). Accepted law requires that the proponent of such a statement must establish that the statement was made during and in further-ance of the conspiracy, by one who is a coconspirator, and that there is inde-pendent proof both of the existence of the conspiracy and the defendant's par-ticipation in it. The chart alluded to above would contain the declarant's statement under "MATERIAL," reference to the coconspirator exception and the applicable statute under "EVIDENTIARY BASIS," the elements of the coconspirator exception under "ELEMENTS," and those facts that will need to be adduced showing the required elements under "FACTS." In the event an element of the coconspirator exception has not yet been met, the prosecutor can request the court to admit the statement subject to later proof of that element, as permitted by FRE 104(b). For example, if the witness who will show the defendant's involvement in the conspiracy independent of the statement at issue has not yet testified, the prosecutor can proffer the content of that testimony to satisfy that element of the rule.

With respect to preparing for possible objections to the other attorney's questions, there is an added degree of uncertainty because the opposing attorney cannot be sure exactly what questions the proponent will ask or the form that those questions will take. While the attorney cannot envision every question his or her opponent will ask, discovery permits the attorney to make an educated guess regarding many areas that are likely to be inquired about or exhibits that will be offered into evidence. The attorney should prepare a chart (similar to the one described above) of the foundation needed before a certain question can be asked or an exhibit accepted into evidence. When arguing against admissibility of the statement above, the defense attorney will then be prepared to cite specifically what element of the exception has not been sufficiently established. Additionally, the attorney should prepare for appropriate objections unrelated to the foundational elements and be ready to argue the criteria for those objections as well.

II. When to Object

Among the most difficult decisions to make at trial, especially for the less experienced attorney, is when to object. I suggest two questions that in most cases should be answered affirmatively by the attorney before he or she enters an objection. The first is, "Do I have a plausible evidentiary ground that supports the objection?"; the second, "Does the question or response contain material I wish to keep from the fact finder?" Each requires some explanation.

A. Plausible Evidentiary Basis for Objection

While there are some questions and responses that are clearly inadmissible, many more fall into a gray area of uncertain admissibility. Some questions raise evidentiary issues for which the court is called upon explicitly to use its discretion in determining admissibility. For example, FRE 403 require that the court balance the probative value of evidence against its prejudicial impact. Other questions involve evidentiary rules that do not explicitly, or always, require such discretion, but often do. Was the declarant of a hearsay statement under sufficient stress to qualify for the exited utterance exception to the hearsay doctrine under FRE 803(2)? Is a question sufficiently leading, and does it relate to a non-introductory matter so as to be improper? Are the facts relied upon by an expert witness in forming his or her conclusion typical of those used by others in the field so that the conclusion is admissible even though the underlying facts may not be (see FRE 703)? Is the question argumentative? Is the conclusion of the lay witness admissible because it is based on a perception of that witness (see FRE 701)? These and many other evidentiary issues don't readily lend themselves to immediate and certain determinations regarding admissibility. Therefore, the attorney should not refrain from objecting merely because he or she is not certain that the objection is "correct."

On the other hand, making frivolous objections can diminish the attorney in the eyes of both the judge and the jury. Objecting frequently with no support is likely to eventually bring some admonition (subtle or overt) from the judge that can harm the attorney's stature with the jury. If the attorney creates such a negative climate, the judge is more inclined to regard unfavorably even those objections that may have merit. Additionally, the attorney does not want to stand there with nothing to say should the judge ask the basis for the objection. While juries expect attorneys to object, the attorney who objects often and unsuccessfully risks being perceived by the jury as an obstructionist. Therefore, it is appropriate to object only when there is some plausible basis for the objection.

B. Determining the Question or Response Is Likely to Be Damaging

The second determination that should be made before the attorney objects is that the question or its likely response does some harm. Objectionable questions asked by one's adversary may cause no harm for several different reasons. First, the information called for is unimportant or undisputed. Second, the information will get in anyway. "You are left handed, aren't you?" is clearly leading, but a proper question that yields the same information will surely follow the sustaining of your objection. Similarly, I occasionally hear attorneys object to the witness's testifying through narration. Unless the objecting attorney believes that the narrative will result in improper damaging testimony being elicited without there being adequate opportunity to object, the objection is usually without purpose. When my witnesses had their narratives interrupted by such an objection, I followed with, "what happened next?" and the same response ensued. Third, if allowed to answer the improper question, the witness's response may actually be helpful to the attorney who withholds his or her objection. This arises most frequently during cross-examination. If your witness is deftly responding to your opponent's questions, there may be no need to object to a question that has been asked and answered. *Generally*, you should be pleased to have your witness respond on cross-examination to questions calling upon them to draw conclusions that may be improper for witnesses to draw. "You testified about the look on the driver's face, but you have no idea what he was thinking?" The attorney can object to this, but might be better served by allowing the response, "He sure seemed to be sorry for what he did." Of course, the attorney does not always know what the response will be and, therefore, may want to object if a harmful answer is likely.

C. Other Tactical Considerations

One other consideration that impacts upon the decision whether to object involves pure trial tactics. Whether the attorney should object merely to "break the flow" of his or her opponent's questions is a subject of some debate among trial lawyers. As discussed above, frivolous objections are improper and usually counterproductive as well. Where some plausible (even if not strong) basis does exist for objecting, however, attorneys should consider the possible effects on the witness and jury of interrupting their opponents questioning. On direct examination, if the witness is telling the story in a particularly compelling manner, the opposing attorney may wish to object to interrupt somewhat the unbroken flow of damaging testimony. During a rapid-fire cross-examination, the attorney may lodge an objection to give a confused witness the opportunity to collect his thoughts before facing more hostile questions. Such a tactic should be used sparingly, if at all, as repeated objections made solely to "break the flow" are transparent, and ultimately harmful to the attorney making them.

Attorneys thinking of objecting to a particular question or moving to strike a response should consider the impact of their action on the jury in other ways as well. Jurors anxious to hear the answer to a question may assume the objecting attorney has good reason to fear the answer. Thus, even if the objection is sustained, the jury may conjecture the worst possible answer. If overruled, the result of the objection can be to heighten the impact of the answer on the jury. Once the jury hears a response, a subsequent motion to strike the response or a request for the court to give a curative instruction can emphasize the effect of the harmful information on the jury.

Notwithstanding these considerations, it still may be the correct decision for the attorney to object or move to strike a response. Regardless of what the jury envisions, it is often more important to do everything possible to keep certain damaging information from the jury. A successful objection might accomplish that goal. The form of the question used by the proponent may result in improper advantage for her, such as feeding information to confused witnesses through leading questions. Objections can stop that. While curative or limiting instructions from the court may be lost on the jurors or ignored by them, when communicated effectively by a concerned judge, they can somewhat ameliorate the damage of a particular response. Many jurors are unlikely to understand or care about the difference between using a hearsay statement for the truth of the matter asserted or merely to show the state of mind of the declarant. Hearing that a criminal defendant's prior criminal background can only be considered with respect to his credibility as a witness is not likely to prevent at least some jurors from thinking, "He did it before, he's done it again." However, when a judge, often seen by the jury as the embodiment of the judicial principles of fairness and neutrality, emphasizes to the jury the importance of disregarding something that was elicited or limiting its use in their deliberations, such an instruction can be effective.

As trial lawyering is an art and not a science, no firm rule exists that tells the attorney in all situations whether or not to seek judicial intervention. Knowing the benefits and potential problems of doing so, however, allows the attorney to balance the necessary factors in making a thoughtful decision about whether to object and what relief to seek.

III. How to Object

A. General or Specific Objection

Once the decision to object is made, the attorney next has to consider the best means by which to lodge the objection. Attorneys first need to be aware of the difference between the Federal Rules of Evidence and the rules existing in some states regarding preserving the issue for appeal. In those states, unless the court requests the grounds for an objection or a specific rule requires specifying the grounds, the act of objecting alone allows appellate courts to use any basis for finding error in the trial court's ruling (see e.g. Maryland Rule of Evidence 5-103 (a)(1)). This contrasts with the federal requirement that the grounds for objections must be specified in order for the court's ruling to be found erroneous, unless the grounds are apparent or constitute "plain error"(see FRE 103 (a)(1) and (d)).

Accordingly, in these state courts, attorneys should generally object without offering a basis, unless asked to do so by the court. This enables them to argue any basis for the objection on appeal. Stating a basis is generally construed to limit the appeal on the objection to just the basis offered at trial. In federal courts, however, attorneys need to call the nature of the error to the attention of the trial judge. In choosing how to object, understanding this difference is useful, but it should be considered along with the fundamental purpose of lodging objections. Usually, we object to keep the testimony or evidence from the fact finder AT TRIAL. If the trial judge in the state courts alluded to above seems unsure of the basis for your objection or you believe further explanation of your grounds will be persuasive, you should make every effort to be heard, notwithstanding that you may be limiting the grounds you can argue on appeal. Successful appeals based on evidentiary errors are certainly the exception and, therefore, the attorney's primary goal must be to win the argument with the trial judge.

B. Standing or Seated

When I tried cases in New York, if an attorney dared to utter a word on the record without standing, the judge would immediately order the attorney to stand. In many other jurisdictions, most judges allow attorneys to question witnesses either standing or sitting (see chapter on Direct Examination for discussion of how to make the choice). In addressing the court, however, the attorney should always stand. All arguments to the court, therefore, in support of or in opposition to an objection should be conducted with the attorney on his or her feet.

In most instances, the attorney should stand as well when first saying "objection." In addition to showing the court respect, rising also ensures that the judge will notice the objection immediately. Additionally, a witness is less likely to continue with his response if the attorney is on her feet objecting. Where the attorney finds herself needing to object repeatedly to her opponent's questions, to avoid looking like a jack-in-the-box, it may be wise (assuming the judge approves) to object while still seated. Should argument be required, the attorney would then stand.

C. In or Out of the Presence of the Jury

Except for those objections made through motions in limine, the lodging of the objection will almost always take place in open court. Discussion of the objection, however, may or may not occur in the presence of the jury. FRE 103(c) provides that where there is a danger that inadmissible evidence will be presented to the jury during argument on objections, that argument or an offer of proof in connection with it should be held outside the jury's presence where "practicable." This affords the judge a great deal of discretion regarding whether to require counsel to conduct arguments at the bench or in front of the jury. Some judges (recall Judge Ito in the O.J. Simpson murder trial) require attorneys to conduct the bulk of their arguments at the bench. While this reduces the risk of jury contamination, it slows down the proceedings (recall Judge Ito in the O.J. Simpson murder trial) and could alienate jurors who wonder why they are being ignored so frequently. Other judges call counsel to the bench only when they sense concrete danger of jury contamination, or when one attorney asks to approach.

Where does this leave the attorney trying to decide whether to request the court to hear argument on objections outside the presence of the jury? Obviously, when the argument on the objections is likely to elicit information that is damaging to his or her case, the attorney should request that argument to be taken at the bench. If the judge seems reluctant to bring counsel to the bench, the attorney should make clear that real prejudice will occur if the objection is argued in open court.

At other times, the attorney may wish the jury to hear the grounds for the objection. Certainly, the attorney should not risk mistrial or incurring the wrath of the judge by arguing in open court in a manner that improperly communicates inadmissible material to the jury. Short of that, however, the objecting attorney may wish the jury to hear that the witness being cross-examined is being badgered, not allowed to complete her answers or being asked argumentative questions. If the attorney is objecting during direct examination, she may want to inform the jury through her objections that the witness is being improperly led through his testimony, being asked to testify about matters that go beyond his first-hand knowledge, or that an area of inquiry is irrelevant. In such situations, unless instructed otherwise by the court, the attorney might be well served to make her argument in front of the jury.

D. Manner of Arguing an Objection

Many attorneys are unaware that, as with examining witnesses and addressing the jury, the manner in which an attorney makes and argues the objection can play a significant role in the court's ruling. Judges are human beings, not evidence computers. Combine this with the notion discussed above that many evidentiary rulings are not clear-cut, and attorneys should realize that the manner in which they make and argue objections can play a role in persuading an undecided judge.

First, make the objection as if you believe in its validity. The way in which some attorneys object communicates uncertainty. The objection, because of the tone of voice used or the words that accompany it, sounds more like a question to the court rather than a firm statement that an improper question was asked. If the attorney seems unsure of the validity of the objection, it is considerably easier for the court to overrule it.

Second, where an argument is needed, make it politely, persuasively and professionally. The argument should always be addressed to the court and not the opposing attorney. Face the judge and direct all remarks to him or her and not opposing counsel. In all but the rarest situations (i.e., when arguing in open court that opposing counsel is about to say something that will improperly contaminate the jury), do not interrupt opposing counsel's argument. Let him or her complete the argument and then respond. When arguing, do not make speeches. Judges wish to hear, as concisely as possible, the points that support your position. Long-winded expositions are sure to make the court less favorably inclined to your position.

All attorneys, and especially newer trial lawyers, should err on the side of being overly polite to the court. Some judges view any discourtesy (even if slight and unintended) to be a challenge to their authority. Judges are less likely to decide close questions in favor of attorneys they regard as discourteous or unprofessional. Worse still the judge can make such attorneys look bad in front of the jury. Therefore, if you feel a judge has ruled prematurely in favor of your opponent, ask politely if you may be heard further on the matter. Make clear to the judge that you are not launching an attack on his or her ruling, but that there is additional important factual or legal material that needs to be brought to the court's attention. Most judges will permit you to make your argument in such a situation.

When a judge refuses to allow you to make your argument, you have a decision to make. If the matter is not particularly important, it is probably better to accept the defeat even if you regard the court's decision as incorrect.

When the ruling keeps out or lets in material that is significant and the judge has refused to let you argue the point in the manner you deem appropriate, you should request to make a record of your argument. Such a record may include a proffer of what would have been elicited and why the testimony was both admissible and important to the case. Without such a record, the issue may not be sufficiently preserved for appeal. A judge's decision refusing to permit you even to make a record of your argument for appeal creates an appealable issue itself, and, accordingly, most judges will allow you to make a record of your argument.

CHAPTER 7

Expert Witnesses

Modern litigation has been characterized by an explosion in the area of testimony by expert witnesses. This explosion has been generated in part by advances in scientific research and development and a concurrent expansion in the number of and types of lawsuits that are tried. Courts and legislatures have contributed to this trend at times by relaxing the evidentiary standards for the introduction of expert testimony, and by enacting laws that smooth the path for, or even require, the admission of certain types of such testimony.

In response to this growth in the use of expert witnesses, it has become increasingly important for trial lawyers to develop the best approach for confronting the unique opportunities and problems that accompany expert testimony. Today, issues such as choosing the best expert witness, preparing him or her for trial, meeting the relevant evidentiary requirements, organizing the direct examination and limiting the damage done by the other side's expert arise in virtually every trial. Only if the attorney can deal successfully with each of these issues will the expert testimony have the most powerful impact it can upon the fact finder. As attorneys confront the issues that arise respecting the effective use of expert testimony, they should keep three guiding principles in mind. These principles, encompassing the goals that must be achieved by expert testimony, are: *EDUCATE*, *PERSUADE* and *SIMPLIFY*.

I. Choosing the Best Witness

For the most part, attorneys have limited flexibility regarding which witnesses to call at trial. Those who observed the event in question, overheard a significant conversation, or otherwise possess relevant firsthand knowledge will likely be subpoenaed if they can offer supportive testimony. If the attorney is fortunate enough to have a number of such witnesses, he or she may exercise some discretion regarding which and how many to call. With experts, however, attorneys customarily have an array of potential witnesses from whom to select. As the presentation of the testimony is usually no better than the witness presenting it, the choice should be carefully made.

At times, the expert witness is called to testify because he or she had been the professional involved in the relevant factual scenario prior to the time that the litigation was commenced. The accountant who did the company's books needs to testify to the meaning of certain entries that she made. The coroner who responded to the scene of the shooting should testify about what he observed at the scene and then how the results of his autopsy show the cause of death. The treating physician can offer certain testimony regarding the plaintiff's condition and treatment that may not be known to the doctor who saw the patient much later or only examined the medical records. With respect to this type of expert witness, the attorney has limited choices as to which experts to call.

There are, of course, many other instances when the expert is being hired specifically to testify in the lawsuit. This is when the attorney has the ability to choose the best witness. In selecting the right witness, the attorney should remember the expert's functions are to *educate, persuade* and *simplify.*

A. One Who Can Educate

The first prerequisite for being able to educate is that one must possess a great deal of knowledge about the subject matter. Additionally, the educator must be able to explain what is often complex material in a manner that allows the "audience" to comprehend the lesson. If the educator is articulate and speaks in a language that his lay "audience" can understand, he is likely to be an effective communicator of the information.

In choosing the expert witness, attorneys should strive to find one who possesses the traits of the good teacher. Within obvious budget and availability limitations, find the professional who is the smartest and has the most experience. Speak with this person to get a sense of how he or she articulates and explains difficult material. It is often tempting to select the expert who is best known in the field, but further investigation may reveal that this is not the best person to explain to you or the jury what needs to be known about the subject, or to handle the rigors of your opponent's cross-examination.

B. One Who Can Persuade

The expert witness is usually called in to persuade the fact finder of the accuracy or the significance of an opinion she has formed regarding an important issue in the case. Aside from being knowledgeable and articulate, the degree to which one is able to persuade is often closely related to the personal credibility of the speaker. With occasional exceptions (such as when the expert is a court's witness or public official), expert witnesses will be compensated by the party on whose behalf the witness is testifying. Therefore, the witness will not be perceived by the fact finder as being entirely neutral. Within this framework, however, there are several things in the expert's background and manner that can make him appear more or less credible to the fact finder.

As the witness is being offered as an expert, the more prestigious his education and experience and the more he is regarded favorably by others in his field, the more likely it is that the fact finder will be predisposed to find him credible. Learn the witness's general background, as well as whether he belongs to selective professional societies, has additional licenses or certificates, has won awards or written and taught in his field.

Next, attorneys should learn whether their proposed expert testifies invariably for one side in certain types of cases. Does the psychiatrist almost always find the criminal defendant unable to distinguish right from wrong? Does the physician invariably diagnose soft tissue and other damage that no other doctor seems to identify? Computer data, the rules of discovery and simply asking around often allows the opposing attorney to gain access to such information. The revelation of this bias or inclination during cross-examination can damage the expert's credibility with the fact finder. Some expert witnesses, while testifying for both sides in the past, may be so wedded to one approach or so dismissive of practices commonly accepted in their field that they will be seen by the fact finder as closed-minded, inflexible and of limited value in determining the issue at hand. Additionally, although it is often difficult to avoid these days, attorneys should be wary of using experts who seem to spend more time testifying than practicing in their field of expertise. Attorneys should also carefully examine what the witness has said and written previously to see if there are any contradictions with what he intends to testify to at trial.

Finally, as with all witnesses, the manner in which the expert gives his testimony will have a substantial impact on how persuasive he or she is to the fact finder. Naturally, to be persuasive, the expert must be able to *educate* and *simplify* (as discussed above and below respectively). Hopefully, the expert expresses himself clearly and confidently, and in a way that maintains the interest of the fact finder. Beyond that, the attorney should endeavor to find an expert whose ego will not become too enmeshed with her presentation of the testimony. The expert should not be one who is perceived as being unduly combative with the other side or who cannot avoid becoming defensive when challenged on cross-examination. The best expert witnesses acknowledge reasonable points made by the other side but calmly diminish or explain them away. Attorneys should choose expert witnesses who do not come off sounding like hired guns.

C. One Who Can Simplify

Some well-known trials have highlighted the importance of making the frequently complex testimony of expert witnesses simple enough for laypersons to comprehend. No matter how scientifically convincing the evidence is, if it is not explained on a level that the jury can understand, the testimony is usually wasted. The DNA evidence offered by the prosecution in the murder trial of O.J. Simpson may have demonstrated that it was extremely unlikely that anyone else but the Defendant committed those crimes. The problem was that it took so long to complete the testimony (arguably not all of this was attributable to the prosecutors), and there was so much complicated scientific and mathematical evidence presented, that the jury was more confused than convinced.

In their effort to present expert testimony to juries in a manner that is understandable, attorneys should try to find experts who can skillfully simplify complex subjects. In speaking with potential witnesses, listen to whether they can overcome the tendency to speak in jargon. It is not easy to explain difficult material in terms that a lay audience can comprehend. Sometimes the most knowledgeable and credentialed of professionals do not possess this skill. If the potential expert witness cannot explain his testimony so that you can understand it, he is unlikely to be able to simplify it sufficiently for the jury to benefit from his testimony.

II. Preparing the Expert and the Expert's Preparing You

As with any other witness, the attorney has to put time and effort into preparing the expert witness. Many of the approaches discussed in the chapter on Direct Examination with respect to witness preparation apply to expert witnesses as well and will not be repeated here. Certain points require special emphasis however.

Some of the expert witnesses you will use have testified on many occasions. With most of these witnesses, you will not have to spend much time discussing with them the manner in which to give their testimony. Other expert witnesses may need to be reminded to avoid jargon and told that if they do lapse into such language during direct examination, you will ask them to explain their answers. Still other experts may need to be advised not to project an attitude that may impact negatively on the jury.

All expert witnesses need to be prepared in depth for the issues you anticipate will arise on cross-examination. For example, if there are inconsistencies with previous testimony or writings of the witness, different views expressed in learned treatises or problems related to bias, you will want to discuss with your expert the best way to handle these issues. Perhaps the best approach is to anticipate the cross-examination by asking the expert during direct examination about why other professionals in her area hold a different view than she about a particular test. Alternatively, to diminish the importance of the issue, you may decide the witness can easily deflect questions during cross-examination on topics such as her fee. If the issue is significant and cannot be successfully defused during cross, you can discuss with the expert how you will address the issue with her on redirect examination. In any event, it is often crucial that the lawyer and expert witness are on the same page with respect to how to handle the opponent's line of questioning.

Attorneys frequently underutilize expert witnesses in preparing themselves for trial. Experts are often the best, or at least the most accessible, source for the attorney trying to learn about the scientific or other complex aspects of the case. Additionally, your expert can help you prepare the cross-examination of your opponent's expert witness. He can help you locate weaknesses in the other expert's testimony and suggest areas of inquiry that may be fruitful. Earlier in the litigation, the expert can aid you in drafting the questions to ask the other side's expert during deposition. Your witness knows more about his or her area of expertise than you ever will. It is a lost opportunity to confine your expert's participation in the litigation to just his testimony at trial.

III. Qualifications

Before an expert witness is permitted to testify to the conclusions and opinions that will help the jury to understand evidence or determine an issue, it first must be established that the witness is qualified to render such testimony. FRE 702 enumerates the factors that govern whether the witness will be deemed qualified. In federal as well as most state courts, those factors are knowledge, skill, experience, training and education. Attorneys should bear these factors in mind when developing the qualification questions for their expert witnesses.

When qualifying any expert witness, it is particularly important for attorneys not to lose sight of who their audience is. On one hand, the attorney must satisfy the judge that the witness's credentials are sufficient and appropriate under the law to qualify as an expert. The other reason that the expert's credentials are meaningful is because they can help convince the jury of the accuracy of the witness's testimony. Especially where the case comes down to a battle among experts, attorneys should do their best to persuade the jury that their witness really is an expert in his or her field of endeavor.

Sometimes the most difficult decision to make with respect to establishing the qualifications of the expert witness is how far to go with the questioning. Clearly you want to elicit the major facts of the witness's background that will predispose the jury to accept his or her testimony, yet continuing ad nauseam with background questions is likely to bore the jurors, turn them off or even antagonize them. It is important, therefore, to prioritize among the witness's attributes, eliciting the most positive of them, those that are most relevant to his or her testimony in this case, and the credentials that make the expert stand out among others in the field. Another factor that may impact the attorney's decision as to which biographical material to highlight is the background of the opposing expert witness. If, for example, unlike your expert witness, the opposing expert does not possess a particular license or belong to a learned society in the field, you may wish to emphasize the importance of this specific credential. If you are fortunate enough to have a neutral expert, such as a government official in a civil case between two private parties, you may benefit from stressing that witness's impartiality in contrast to the other side's hired and paid witness.

With the above considerations in mind, I offer the following method for organizing the questioning of expert witnesses regarding their qualifications to testify:

1. Personal Introduction

As with any witness, give the jury the opportunity to get to know and feel more comfortable with the witness.

2. Education and Training

Highly educated professionals are desirable as expert witnesses and, therefore, attorneys will want to elicit this education. Jurors, however, most of whom perform their jobs quite well without as much education, may react negatively to experts who sound as if their education entitles them to instant, unqualified respect and admiration. Having learned how the expert communicates during preparatory sessions, the attorney may want to prepare his or her questions according to the attitude conveyed by the expert. With experts who cannot avoid appearing somewhat arrogant, the attorney may want to limit the questions in the area of education or ask narrow questions that allow the witness less room to embellish.

Don't forget to include any specialized post-graduate training the expert has received, and any professional courses that help him or her stay current in the field. Additionally, if applicable, the attorney should ask about the licenses the expert has in the field or sub-specialty.

3. Honors, Writings, Teaching Positions and Memberships in Learned Societies

With the same admonitions as above concerning the witness's attitude and not overdoing it, the attorney should elicit the special qualifications of the expert. What makes him stand out among others in his field? Has he received any honors or awards with respect to how he performs his work? Has she written articles or books on the subject matter, and was the publication of the work (such as a refereed article) indication that other experts thought it to be of value to the profession? Does the witness belong to any learned societies, especially ones in which membership is limited to those who have demonstrated substantial achievement? Does she hold a teaching position at a prestigious institution? Any of these credentials are likely to be impressive to the jury and enhance the witness's status.

4. Experience

The primary themes here are how often and how relevant. So many matters for the jury to consider and weigh in its decisions depend on subjective evaluations of disputed facts. When there is something objective and concrete that the jurors can use in reaching their determination about some issue, they are apt to latch onto that factor. Attorneys, therefore, should always elicit from experienced professional witnesses the *number* of times they have done the same or similar work (and formed the appropriate conclusion from that work) as was performed in the instant case. When the coroner testifies that she has performed 1400 autopsies, the real estate appraiser says he has valued 800 business properties or the ballistics expert speaks of testing 500 guns to determine their operability, the jury is inclined immediately to think the expert knows his or her subject matter. Some jurors whose own backgrounds and beliefs leave them unimpressed with educational credentials may give more weight to the expert's experience in the area.

Next, the attorney should make clear how the experience of the expert is directly related to the issues in the instant case. While the coroner has performed 1400 autopsies, it is directly relevant that many of those involved death by gunshot and even more specifically germane that in such cases she invariably relies upon a neutron activation test to determine whether the deceased could have fired the gun. The real estate appraiser has examined numerous commercial properties the same age as the subject property and located in similar industrial areas. He will then testify that the methods and criteria used in those cases apply to valuing the instant property as well. One means of distinguishing between competing expert witnesses is to emphasize that the experience of your expert is more directly related to the issues in the case at trial.

5. Witness Has Been Recognized Previously by Courts as an Expert in the Area

Eliciting that your witness has been recognized by courts in this and other jurisdictions as an expert in his or her field plays to both of your audiences, the judge and the jury. Judges who may harbor some lingering doubt about the qualifications of your witness are inclined to give you the benefit of that doubt upon hearing that their colleagues have already accepted the credentials of the expert. For this reason, I suggest the question regarding the witness's prior recognition by the courts be your final one before tendering the witness to the court as an expert. Jurors, too, are apt to be further impressed to learn your witness has been officially acknowledged as an expert on many previous occasions.

6. Tender the Witness

Even where it is not required that the witness be formally tendered to the court as an expert, the attorney should do so. If the other side wishes to object to the recognition of the witness as an expert or is permitted by the court to conduct a limited voir dire of the witness, it is preferable that this be done before the direct examiner begins asking substantive questions of the witness. The attorney offering the witness does not want his questions dealing with the issue at hand to be interrupted by the opponent's objection that she was never given the opportunity to challenge the witness's qualifications.

The other reason for tendering the witness is the opportunity to have the court place its imprimatur upon the witness. It can only help the attorney when the jury hears that the judge regards his witness to be an expert in her field. Be advised that some judges, wanting to avoid just such an impression, will merely tell the attorney he or she can continue rather than declaring the witness is found to be an expert. In any event, no harm is done in tendering the witness, and there is much to be gained in so doing.

7. Responding to the Premature Stipulation by Opposing Counsel

Some attorneys opposing the expert (particularly when opposing inexperienced attorneys offering the witness) attempt to avoid the jury's hearing the qualifications of the expert by stipulating to the witness's ability to testify as to certain matters. If the attorney calling the witness merely accepts the stipulation and moves on to the substantive issues, he or she loses the opportunity to predispose the jury to accept the accuracy of the witness's testimony due to her education, experience and status. This attorney has forgotten that establishing the qualifications of the witness is done for the benefit of the jury as well as the court.

When the opponent offers such a stipulation, the attorney should accept the stipulation and request that the court allow him to continue his questioning so that the jury can be fully informed of the witness's qualifications to testify to the matter at hand. Unless the questioning as to qualifications has already gone on far too long, judges will seldom prohibit the attorney from continuing to elicit the witness's full background.

IV. Direct Examination (Organization and Content)

In order to maximize the expert witness's effectiveness and ensure that the jury fully comprehends his or her testimony, the attorney must carefully organize the examination. As the testimony of the expert witness is often complex and confusing, it can be difficult for the attorney to present the testimony in a manner that is easy for the jury to understand. Particularly when the attorney's questions seem disjointed, out of sequence or repetitive, the jury can find it a frustrating task keeping track of exactly what the witness is explaining. Accordingly, after the witness's qualifications have been established, I suggest the following method for sequencing the questions posed to most expert witnesses:

A. How Did the Witness Come to Be Involved in the Case?

After the qualifications have been established, an appropriate place to begin is to elicit from the expert witness how he or she became involved in the case. The jury will undoubtedly be curious about this, and the question forms a logical bridge between the qualifications and the subsequent actions taken by the expert.

B. What Is the Typical Way the Expert Proceeds in Such Cases? Did He Proceed That Way in the Instant Case?

The initial point here is to let the jury know that the method in which the expert performed his job in the instant case is entirely characteristic of the manner in which he usually acts. If there are some differences in the expert's manner of proceeding in the instant case, it is usually wise to account for them. If, for example, the coroner failed to order a powder burns test to be conducted on the clothing of the gunshot victim, perhaps it was because the large amount of blood on the clothing would have washed it away. The economist testifying about the value of a business may have gone beyond the customary valuation criteria in arriving at her conclusion due to the unique potential of a product in the process of development.

The ultimate purpose of these questions is to inform the fact finder of the thorough and professional manner in which the expert gathered the data to arrive at her conclusion. Prior to forming a conclusion about the mental state of the criminal defendant, the psychiatrist reviewed the history of the patient's previous behavior and treatment, read the hospital records for the defendant's stay in the mental hospital after the instant crime, interviewed the defendant in depth on several occasions, spoke to witnesses who observed the defendant's behavior at the time of the crime and assessed the results of a battery of psychological and anatomical tests performed on the defendant. The jury now knows that the expert has a thorough basis upon which to form her opinion about the defendant's mental state. Prior to determining the speed at which the truck was being driven at the time of the accident, the investigator who is reconstructing the accident took measurements of the skid marks, measured other relevant distances, examined the truck and its speedometer and spoke to a number of eyewitnesses. The jury thus learns that this expert did everything possible to enable him to arrive at an accurate speed figure.

C. Did the Expert Form an Opinion to a Reasonable Degree of Certainty (or Probability) for a Professional in That Field? What Is That Opinion?

1. Elicit the Opinion before Asking the Basis for the Opinion

After establishing the procedures undertaken by the expert, many attorneys then launch into a detailed account of what the expert learned from all that he did. In other words, prior to eliciting the expert's opinion regarding the primary issue, they attempt to reveal to the fact finder the basis for that opinion. FRE 705 allows the attorney (unless the court requires otherwise) to elicit the opinion before the basis if the attorney so desires. While there is a sequential logic to eliciting what specific data led to the expert's opinion and the significance of that data before asking for the opinion itself, I suggest using the reverse order and obtaining the opinion first, as permitted by FRE 705.

The most important part of any expert witness's testimony is the opinion he or she formed on the primary issue in contention. Therefore, this opinion must be presented at a time and under circumstances that will maximize the jury's ability to absorb and remember the opinion. When expert witnesses discuss the bases for their conclusions, their testimony often is quite complex and difficult for lay jurors to follow. Even if the expert is adept at simplifying this testimony for the jury, the relationship between the information he or she acquired and the opinion this information ultimately led to can take substantial time to explain. Some jurors are unable to grasp the more technical and confusing aspects of the expert's testimony concerning the basis for her opinion while others become bored and lose concentration. If this occurs, when the attorney finally does ask the witness to state her opinion on the primary issue, the jury collectively is well past the moment when the opinion will have its maximum impact. Additionally, many attorneys become bogged down in attempting to get a clear explanation from their expert of the basis for his or her opinion, thus disrupting their planned organization of the testimony. This also can cause the opinion to have a diminished significance when it is finally elicited, because the opinion is revealed, almost in passing, as part of the expert's explanation of his basis. At times, when the attorney in such a situation does ask the fundamental questions to ascertain the expert's opinion, they may be repetitive and objectionable. Worse still, some attorneys become so involved in the process of getting their witnesses to explain their bases that they neglect to ascertain the witness's opinion at all.

The attorney opposing the expert's opinion should be aware of the qualifying language contained within FRE 705. Judges in federal and some state courts have the discretion to require the direct examiner to establish the basis for his or her opinion before rendering the opinion itself. Such discretion is likely to be exercised only when the opponent can demonstrate the existence of a substantial question as to whether the expert's opinion has an adequate basis in fact. Although such a situation will not arise frequently, when it does, the opposing attorney should ask for the court to exercise its discretion so that the jury will not be prejudiced by hearing an expert's conclusion that later may be ruled inadmissible.

2. Ask the Opinion Questions in the Correct Form and Maximize Their Impact on the Jury

While not every judge requires that the questions eliciting the expert's opinion be asked in the correct form, enough do to make it worthwhile for attorneys to regularly use the correct manner of structuring such questions for expert witnesses. The standard generally required for an expert to offer her opinion is that she do so "to a reasonable degree of certainty for one in your profession."

Remember, the opinion is the crux of the expert's testimony. You want to emphasize it in every way possible. The opinion should be elicited in two questions. The first question establishes that the witness had an opinion he or she can render to the required standard of certainty. The second question affords the witness the opportunity to state to the fact finder exactly what his or her opinion is. The questions and answers should proceed as follows:

> Q: *Do you have an opinion you can state with a reasonable degree of medical certainty regarding the condition of the plaintiff's leg after the accident?*
> A: I do.
> Q: *What is that opinion?*
> A: Mr. Evans suffered from a compound fracture of his left tibia and a severe sprain of his left ankle.

During preparation, the attorney should make clear to the expert that his first answer should be limited to the fact that he has the opinion. This prepares the jury to pay full attention to the next answer in which the witness will state his opinion.

The attorney should also be conscious of how her own style of questioning can help enhance the impact of the expert's statement of his opinion. As discussed in the section on Direct Examination, the attorney should use her voice and body language to magnify the importance of this key information in the witness's testimony. For example, the attorney can change the volume of her voice, slow down the pace of her words, alter her position in the courtroom or preface her question with a phrase likely to command the listener's attention, such as, "now could you please tell the members of the jury."

3. Meet the Required Evidentiary Standard for Scientific Testimony

a. Novel Scientific Testimony

FRE 702 permits the introduction of expert testimony when that testimony will aid the trier of fact in understanding the evidence or in arriving at a determination about a relevant issue in the case. There is a significant difference, however, between federal and some state courts regarding how this standard is applied to novel scientific testimony.

Until recently, both court systems had required that for novel scientific testimony to be admissible, the subject matter of that testimony had to be generally accepted by the relevant scientific community. Referred to as the *Frye* test (after *Frye v. U.S.*, 293 F. 1013 (D.C. Cir. 1923)), this approach made it fairly difficult to introduce scientific testimony when the subject matter of that testimony had not previously been allowed in by statute or accepted by other courts. The federal approach to novel scientific testimony changed significantly, however, with the Supreme Court's holding in *Daubert v. Merrell Dow Pharmaceuticals, Inc.*, 509 U.S. 579 (1993).

In *Daubert*, the Court held that the "general acceptance" requirement was omitted from and "incompatible" with the Federal Rules of Evidence. The Court ruled that FRE 702 requires the judge to act as a gatekeeper in determining what type of scientific and technical evidence to allow at trial. While general acceptance of the subject matter of that testimony by others in the field is relevant to the court's determination, it is but one factor that the judge should consider in assessing the overall reliability of the testimony. Other factors include whether the procedure or information has been tested to determine its accuracy, whether it has been subjected to peer review, and whether the potential for error is unacceptably high. While some federal courts have used the gatekeeper role to continue to restrict the admission of new scientific techniques, others have seized upon *Daubert* and permitted expert testimony that would not pass the *Frye* test.

Subsequently, the Court held in *Kumho Tire Co. v. Carmichael*, 526 U.S. 137 (1999), that federal courts could use the *Daubert* criteria referred to above in assessing the reliability of nonscientific expert testimony as well. FRE702 basically codifies the holding in these two cases.

When attorneys use expert testimony in state courts, they should make themselves aware of whether the jurisdiction in question uses a Frye approach, the federal approach as it appears in FRE 702 or a combination thereof.

b. Ultimate Issue Rule

With one exception, an expert is no longer prohibited from testifying to an opinion merely because it embraces the ultimate issue before the fact finder [See FRE 704 (a)]. FRE 704 (b) maintains that prohibition only with respect to testimony about the mental state or condition of the defendant in criminal.cases. The abolition of the ultimate issue rule allows the witness to aggregate his previous factual answers and testify to the opinion that flows from those facts.

Bear in mind, however, that such conclusions can still be disallowed by the court if they are not helpful to the fact finder in determining a relevant issue (see FRE 702), or their probative value is substantially outweighed by their prejudicial impact or the confusion or waste of time that would result from the testimony (see FRE 403). For example, consider the proposed testimony of a police officer responding to an auto accident who formed his opinion as to which driver was responsible largely on his assessment of the comparative credibility of the eyewitnesses. In such a case, the court should reject the opinion testimony because the jury could adequately assess the witness's credibility without benefit of the expert's opinion, and, therefore, the testimony is not helpful. Additionally, legal conclusions drawn by expert witnesses are often disallowed as being not helpful to the jury.

D. Explain the Basis for the Opinion

Allow the witness at this point to explain the way in which he arrived at his opinion. This means not only reporting the results of tests, observations, calculations and other procedures undertaken, but also clearly explaining to the fact finder the relationship between those results and his opinion. Too often, expert witnesses report the actual results of their examination of the facts and the conclusion these facts led to without describing the bridge that allowed them to connect one to the other.

The traffic investigator needs to do more than just report the length of the tire skid marks he measured and his subsequent conclusion as to the speed that vehicle was traveling at the time of the accident. Without getting too technical, he should explain how the length of the skid marks is used to gauge vehicle speed. The radiologist testifying that he diagnosed the compound fracture from looking at the x-ray will be a far more effective witness if he shows the jury what specific shapes on the x-ray depict the fracture. The real estate appraiser should not be content to testify that she arrived at fair market value from looking at comparable properties but should highlight for the jury particularly significant features of the subject house and explain how similar features affected the value of the comparable properties. In each of these situations, informing the jury of *how* the factual results led to the ultimate opinion makes the witness's testimony clearer and more persuasive, as well as increases the likelihood that the jury will remember this crucial testimony.

Generally, it is wise to ask the expert witness an open-ended question to allow the expert to explain in his own way, uninterrupted by the direct examiner, how he arrived at his opinion. Here the witness serves in his role as an educator, informing the jury of how professionals in his field use their knowledge and training to develop their opinions. Some expert witnesses are quite adept at explaining how they arrived at their conclusions in a manner that lay jurors can readily understand. Other experts lapse too often into the jargon of their profession. It is incumbent upon the direct examiner to ensure that the jury can follow the testimony of the expert as it proceeds. Jurors who feel confused or lost at stages of the testimony may turn off the witness entirely. Therefore, the attorney must be ready to follow up an unclear response from the expert with a question calling for an explanation of his or her testimony. At times, as where the expert lapses into jargon, the attorney may need to ask for an explanation of the witness's explanation. Therefore, while the general approach is not to interrupt the expert witness as he offers his explanation, where the attorney senses that the jury is losing touch with the witness, she should gently intervene with clarifying questions.

> Q: *Thank you for that explanation of the cause of the thrombosis, Doctor Balder. Did I understand you to say that this means that a large amount of blood clotted in a vessel in Ms. Ayre's left leg, causing a substantial blockage of her blood flow?*

Note that this question is not leading, because the witness has already so testified, albeit in somewhat different words. Furthermore, most judges look favorably on the efforts of attorneys attempting to clarify confusing testimony coming from expert witnesses.

E. Emphasize Important Aspects of the Expert's Testimony

As with most witnesses, there will undoubtedly be aspects of the expert's testimony that are particularly strong or significant to the outcome of the case and others that detract somewhat from the substance of the expert's opinion or the credibility of the witness herself. As discussed in the Chapter on Direct Examination, the attorney will want to consider how to emphasize the former and minimize or explain away the latter.

We emphasize portions of a witness's testimony because we want to ensure that the fact finder will particularly understand these matters and remember them during deliberations. As the jury evaluates all of the testimony it has assimilated during the trial, the jurors inevitably will prioritize among these pieces of testimony. It is that evidence which is most important in demonstrating our theme of the case that we want the jury to regard as crucial. There are several methods through which direct examiners can achieve their goal of having the key parts of the expert witness's testimony understood, remembered and relied upon by the fact finder. The following 3 methods serve as effective ways both to explain the basis of the expert's opinion and to emphasize important aspects of the testimony.

1. The Use of Charts, Diagrams and Other Demonstrative and Tangible Evidence

Allowing the jury to look at as well as hear the testimony makes it both easier to understand and to remember. Additionally, the mere fact that the expert witness has prepared an exhibit to demonstrate a particular point suggests the importance of that portion of her testimony. Consider the following examples using a chart and an item of tangible evidence:

Example 1:

Q: *Ms. Ryan, do you have anything that would help explain how you arrived at your conclusion regarding the value of the subject property?*

A: I have.

(The attorney then marks the exhibit and lays the foundation for its use, including how the expert prepared the chart.)

Q: *Would you please explain how the chart works?*

A: As you can see, I've listed the subject property and the three comparable properties across the top of the chart. In order under each property, the chart contains the number of rooms, size and other features that I have discussed in my testimony. You can see how the subject property compares favorably to the other houses in terms of …

Q: *Why did you highlight on the chart the 14 foot ceilings and the fourth bathroom?*

A: I did so because none of the comparable properties contain those features, and as I explained earlier, both significantly increase the value of the subject house.

Example 2:

Q: *Officer, I show you what has been marked as State's Exhibit #6 for identification. Do you recognize it?*

A: This is the gun I recovered from the defendant after I arrested him. (The attorney then lays the foundation and has the exhibit admitted into evidence.)

Q: *Officer, have you already checked Exhibit 6 to make sure it is unloaded?*

A: I have.

Q: *Would you do so again in front of all of us just to make sure?*

A: (Officer checks gun) I have done so.

Q: Now, would you please show us how the gun is operated

A: (Officer explains how gun is loaded, the hammer cocked, safety released and trigger pulled, using the exhibit to demonstrate each aspect of his testimony.)

Q: Could the defendant then have fired the weapon without first taking the time to cock the hammer?

A: As you can see, (officer demonstrating) the trigger cannot be pulled if the hammer is not first cocked.

In each of the above cases, the expert's use of the exhibit makes the testimony easier for the jury to understand and remember. The exhibits also serve to emphasize key strategic points in the expert's testimony.

2. Hypothetical Questions

There was a time (particularly in federal courts) when expert witnesses who lacked first hand knowledge of the facts that led to their opinions were permitted to testify to those opinions only in response to hypothetical questions. FRE 703 makes it clear that facts made known to the expert may now help form the basis for his or her opinion without the need to rely on the hypothetical question. Where those facts are the type reasonably relied upon by others in the expert's field, they do not have to be admissible in and of themselves (i.e., hearsay not covered by an exception) in order to contribute to the basis for the expert's opinion. For example, a psychiatrist may testify to her opinion about the mental status of an individual although the opinion is based in part on what others related to her about the behavior of that individual. As long as that type of information is typically and reasonably relied upon by other professionals in the field, the expert can be asked her opinion without the need to pose the question in hypothetical form (i.e., "Assuming that ..."). Accordingly, the use of hypothetical questions with expert witnesses is not as prevalent as in the past.

As hypothetical questions can help to summarize the expert's previous testimony or sharpen the connection between the facts and the expert's opinion, attorneys should still consider their use. In doing do, it is important to realize that, notwithstanding that a fact is in dispute, it can still form the basis for a hypothetical question.

Q: Officer, assuming that the car was traveling at 50 mph, would you consider that an unsafe speed given the weather and road conditions on the night of the accident?

Opposing Attorney: I object. We have put in evidence facts that dispute the car's speed as 50 mph.

Court: Objection overruled. A disputed fact may form the basis for a hypothetical question.

A: 50 mph was an exceedingly unsafe speed to be traveling on a night when the rain was falling in torrents, the wind was blowing hard, the roads were slick and visibility was greatly limited.

While the facts may be in dispute, the attorney should always prepare the hypothetical question carefully so it is not an inaccurate or unfair characterization of the facts or testimony. The expert should be fully prepared for and comfortable with all the facts contained within the hypothetical to avoid his having to give a qualified answer. Consider the following hypothetical question:

> *Q: Ms. Scientist, assume the following facts are true regarding the damage that was shown to exist to the right lung of Mr. Fale. (Attorney then lists the elements of damage to the lung to which this and other witnesses have testified.) Assume further that Mr. Fale smoked approximately 2 packs of cigarettes a day for the last 30 years of his life. Do you have an opinion you can state to a reasonable degree of scientific certainty as to the likely cause for the damage to Mr. Fale's lung?*

3. Examples and Analogies

Quite often, the best way to explain and emphasize aspects of the expert's testimony that may be complex or confusing to lay fact finders is to offer a commonly understood or experienced example or analogy that demonstrates the witness's point. Consider the following use, respectively, of an example and an analogy:

> *Q: Doctor, you said that the Plaintiff, as a result of the accident, could suffer permanent injury if he strained the muscles in his back. What type of activity could cause such a strain?*

A: The Plaintiff has a 2-year-old daughter. Just picking her up to put her in a crib could cause him permanent damage.

* * *

> *Q: Mr. Engineer, you testified to the force that impacted on the plaintiff when the scaffold fell from the building and hit him on the leg. Can you translate that degree of force to the impact caused by a car when it hits a person?*

A: The force that hit the plaintiff was about the same as the force that would be felt by a pedestrian hit by a mid-size American car traveling at 40 mph.

The first question and answer above takes medical testimony concerning an injury and puts it in terms which not only clarify the extent of the injury but also humanizes the testimony considerably. The second scenario takes an event with which no juror is likely to be familiar and compares it to the speed of a car with which all jurors are likely to be familiar. Although most of the jurors are unlikely to have experienced the impact of a car traveling at 40 mph, they will find it easier to conjure up this image due to their greater experience with cars of this size traveling at that speed.

F. Deal with Potential Problems in the Testimony

As discussed in the Chapter on Direct Examination, when faced with a weakness in the substantive testimony or credibility of her witness, the attorney must decide whether to bring up the subject herself during direct examination or let the witness deal with it on cross and perhaps redirect examination. The same decision frequently must be made regarding the testimony of expert witnesses. There may be something lacking in the expert's credentials, some procedure he could not or did not perform, facts that point to a conclusion different than the one reached by the expert or indications of possible bias present, just to name a few potential problems. As to each potential problem, the attorney, in consultation with the witness (experienced experts often can inform the decision by letting the attorney know their preference) must determine whether it is best to act preemptively. While anticipating the cross-examination may highlight the issue somewhat, it can also allow the witness to minimize any damage before the cross-examiner has an opportunity to exploit the problem. Consider the following examples of anticipating the cross-examination:

Example 1:

Q: *Dr. Allen, you stated that this is the first time you performed this surgery. What gave you confidence that you could perform it effectively?*
A: Shortly before the surgery, I attended a conference that focused exclusively on how to perform this procedure. There we were given the opportunity to perform the procedure on anatomically correct models. I read all of the literature pertaining to this type of sur-

gery. Additionally, I have performed other procedures on many occasions that are similar in nature to the one I performed here.

Q: *Is this typical of what surgeons do before they perform a procedure for the first time?*

A: Yes.

Example 2:

Q: *Ms. Ryan, are there other methods you could have used to assess the value of the Jones house?*

A: I could have used a cost evaluation method. With this approach, you estimate the value of the land and then add in the cost of all the parts of the house, factoring in depreciation

Q: *Why did you not use this method?*

A: Even factoring in the value of the land does not give the appropriate weight to the location of the house. Generally, location is the most important factor in determining the value of residential property. That is particularly true in this case, as the public school district that serves the Jones house is considered among the best in the State. Potential buyers with children (the most likely purchasers of this 5-bedroom house) are often concerned more about the quality of the school district than anything else. Charting the sale price of comparable dwellings in the area, as I did, reflects this factor far better than using the cost approach

Example 3:

Q: *Dr. Wise, you have testified to a number of acts that the defendant committed that involved senseless violence and also that you diagnosed the defendant as a paranoid schizophrenic. How did these facts impact your conclusion that the defendant was competent to stand trial?*

A: Well, of course, I took them into consideration. The acts of apparently senseless violence are more likely attributable to the defendant's anti-social behavior than anything else. While paranoid schizophrenia is a mental disease, it is apparent from studying the Defendant's background and speaking with him at length that he understands fully the charges against him and can participate in his defense (and already has).

Example 4:

> Q: *You have testified on many previous occasions to the causal connection between the death of patients from lung cancer and the fact that they were heavy cigarette smokers for long periods of time?*
>
> A: That is correct.
>
> Q: *Have those previous findings affected your ability to draw a scientifically objective conclusion in this case?*
>
> A: They have not. The changes to the lung caused by carcinogens is my area of specialization. The studies confirm that the ingredients contained within cigarettes cause these changes more than any other factor. It is not surprising that I have frequently found this connection. Besides, I have concluded in some cases that cigarettes could not be shown to be the likely cause of the malignancy.

G. Don't Treat the Jurors as Idiots

One of the benefits to writing a book such as this is that it allows the author to vent his or her pet peeves. With respect to the examination of expert witnesses, I am always troubled by attorneys whose questions separate the jurors unfavorably from all others present in the courtroom regarding their ability to understand the expert's testimony. Consider the following:

> Q: *Doctor, could you please explain to the members of the jury what you mean by a compound fracture?*

Such questioning can come across to at least some jurors as follows:

> Q: *Doctor, we lawyers and the other intelligent folks in the courtroom understand what you just said, but could you explain to the morons in the jury box what it means when you say one plus one equals two?*

The chances are that several jurors will already know what a compound fracture is. That does not mean the attorney should not ask the question, as it is important to ensure that the entire jury understands the term. Instead, the attorney should ask it in a manner that does not suggest that he or she has a negative view of the jury's intelligence. The following simple change solves this problem:

Q: *Doctor, could you explain ("to us" or "to all of us") what a compound fracture is?*

V. Cross-Examination

The goals and techniques discussed in the chapter on cross-examination are, for the most part, applicable to the cross-examination of expert witnesses as well. Due to the special nature of the testimony that experts can render (opinion testimony and responses to hypotheticals) and the level of experience as a witness that the expert often possesses, attorneys need to be aware of additional considerations and methods for approaching the cross-examination of the expert.

A. Preparation

It is important to get hold of everything possible that the expert has said or written on the subject matter of his or her testimony. Through discovery, the attorney should learn what books, articles or papers the expert has written. Computer technology has facilitated access to newspapers and other places where the expert might have written or spoken about the subject.

It can be particularly helpful to investigate the expert's testimony in other cases. This not only provides a prior statement from which the witness may be impeached, but can be illuminating with respect to what types of cross-examination questions were more or less effective. The first place to learn of this prior testimony is through discovery procedures that require some disclosure of prior testimony at previous trials and depositions. Identify the attorney who cross-examined the expert in previous cases, and attempt to ascertain his or her thoughts on the best approach to take with the expert. Prosecutors, criminal defense attorneys, plaintiff's lawyers and the civil defense bar all have national and local organizations that are good sources of information on expert witnesses. Here, in addition to the content of the witness's testimony, you can learn how often the witness has testified and, particularly, whether he or she generally testifies in support of one side or one theory. It can help establish bias at trial to show the fact finder that the expert's opinion invariably favors the other side, or that he or she is wedded to a particular approach to the exclusion of other viable approaches that could lead to different results.

The attorney should learn as much as she reasonably can about the witness's field of expertise. Some attorneys say that by the time the trial starts, they endeavor to know the field better than the expert. I think such an expectation is unrealistic, and can even have negative consequences if the attorney's questioning is an attempt to show he or she knows more than the expert. A sophisticated understanding of the field is important for the attorney in order to know where to focus the cross-examination. This does not mean, however, that the attorney needs to or can know more than the expert who has labored in the field for years. Almost never will the attorney want to turn the cross-examination into a competition regarding whether he or she knows the field better than the expert. The attorney will invariably lose that battle, and more importantly, the competition will divert the focus of the examination from where it belongs.

As discussed above, your own experts can be an excellent resource in your preparation for cross-examination of the other side's expert. Let them read the opposing expert's report and deposition, and ask them to point out weaknesses or other areas for possible inquiry.

B. Content

1. Qualifications

The first aspect of the expert witness's testimony that will require the cross-examiner to make decisions occurs when the proponent of the witness is attempting to qualify her. One option the cross-examiner has is to stipulate to the qualifications of the expert. Before stipulating, the cross-examiner should assess the benefits and drawbacks of the stipulation and if stipulating, should avoid offering the stipulation in a manner that enhances the status of the expert in the eyes of the jury.

The primary benefit to be achieved by stipulating to the competency of the expert witness is to prevent the jury from hearing the expert's impressive credentials. Obviously, the jury is more receptive to the opinions of an expert witness whose credentials are outstanding. If the direct examiner accepts an early stipulation and moves past the qualifications, or the judge then orders the examination to proceed to the substance of the testimony, the cross-examiner may have prevented his opponent from predisposing the jury favorably to the expert's testimony. Unless the stipulation is offered well into the expert's recitation of his credentials (or the direct examiner is very inexperienced), the direct examiner is likely to continue with the presentation of the qualifications even after accepting the stipulation. Similarly, unless the presentation of the witness's credentials has gone on too long, the judge is unlikely to order the direct examiner to move on to the substance of the testimony. Knowing this, some attorneys still stipulate at the outset of the qualifications to communicate to the jury that there is no dispute about the qualifications and that the focus should be on the substance of the testimony. Additionally, some hope to convey to the jurors that the direct examiner is wasting their time by continuing with the qualifications after the stipulation.

When deciding to stipulate, the attorney needs to be aware that timing and the manner in which the stipulation is offered can also have an impact on the jury. While stipulating after the witness has presented most of his credentials is more likely to end the presentation, the timing of such a stipulation can convey to the jury that the stipulating attorney is so overwhelmed by the witness's expertise that he or she surrenders on the issue. When stipulating, the attorney should stipulate that the witness "is competent in the field," not that he is an "expert." The specific words used by attorneys often have impact on the jury. Additionally, the stipulating attorney should be careful to limit the field to which he is acknowledging the witness's competence. The attorney may wish to stipulate to the doctor's competence to testify about the field of pathology. If that attorney will later be challenging the expert on her lack of experience regarding forensic medicine, he should not stipulate to the competence of the witness offered as an expert in *forensic* pathology. Finally, the cross-examiner should never stipulate if the possibility exists that he may later wish to voir dire the witness regarding her credentials.

The next decision faced by the cross-examiner is whether to conduct a voir dire of the witness regarding his or her qualifications before the direct examiner moves to the substance of the testimony. Such a voir dire is limited to issues relevant to the competence of the witness to testify as an expert, and is not intended to be a pre-cross-examination. If the cross-examiner thinks there is a realistic chance of the court's rejecting the witness's qualifications, he or she may wish to voir dire the witness in order to illuminate or magnify the expert's shortcomings. Additionally, the attorney can use the voir dire to make clear that the witness's expertise is limited in scope and that he or she should not be recognized as competent to testify to matters beyond that narrow area of expertise. If the cross-examiner does not foresee the likelihood of accomplishing either of these goals, it is generally wise to wait until cross-examination to raise questions about the expert's qualifications. Given the likelihood that the witness will be recognized as an expert by the court immediately after the voir dire, the cross-examiner risks appearing as if he or she launched and lost a significant battle by conducting the voir dire.

During cross-examination itself, the inquiry of the witness with respect to qualifications may be broader than is permitted in the voir dire. Now the cross-examiner should think of how the witness compares with his or her own expert witness as to specific aspects of their backgrounds. For example if the witness lacks a significant educational degree or training component possessed by her own expert, the attorney should highlight that void during cross-examination. Perhaps the opposing witness lacks the experience of the cross-examiner's expert, or the expertise of the former is not as specialized to the relevant issues as that of the latter. Consider the following:

Example 1:

Q: *Dr. Smith, you would agree with me that there is no substitute for experience when it comes to conducting autopsies?*

A: Experience is one important factor.

Q: *Now, is it correct that working in a small rural community, you have conducted only 4 autopsies in which a gunshot wound was found to be the cause of death?*

A: That is true.

Q: *Were you aware that the doctor we retained to evaluate your findings has conducted 50 autopsies involving gunshot deaths?*

A: I didn't know the exact number he did, but that's not crucial.

Example 2:

Q: *Doctor, you are not board certified as a forensic pathologist, are you?*

A: I am not.

Q: *To be board certified means that the doctor has reached the highest level of recognition within his or her field of specialization. Is that correct?*

A: I suppose that is one way of looking at it.

Q: *Were you aware that the doctor we retained to evaluate your findings is board certified?*

A: I had no idea.

The attorney here weakens the opposing expert while strengthening her own by drawing the contrast for the fact finder.

2. Bias

As with any witness, an expert can be impeached by showing that he has a bias toward or against a certain party or point of view. The obvious bias possessed by most expert witnesses is that they are testifying for the party that retained and paid them. The cross-examiner will want to make clear that the witness is working for the other side and may want to inquire as to the specific amount of money the expert is being paid. The argument to be made later to the jury is that the witness's conclusions are hardly surprising given who is paying him and how much he is being paid. Cross-examiners are well warned to tread carefully in this area, however. Unless the cross-examiner is fortunate enough to have an unpaid expert witness (such as a government official) as her own, or the opposing expert is receiving an exorbitant fee, she will look foolish when the same points are made about her witness. In such a situation, it is often best to elicit such information in one question and to move on.

Another area in which the expert can be biased is in his or her views concerning certain theories, tests or approaches within the field of expertise. To lay persons, it is often surprising how wedded some professionals are to certain methods and how resistant, almost hostile, they are to others. Through deposing the expert witness and through other methods of discovery, the cross-examiner should become knowledgeable about the expert's most and least preferred methods of arriving at professional opinions such as the one involved in the instant case. During cross-examination, the attorney can elicit the expert's hostility to an approach that is widely accepted by other professionals in the field. The attorney can later argue that this hostility may have led the expert to unfairly dismiss the finding arrived at by the cross-examiner's own expert witness or, at least, to have eschewed an approach that could have led to a different result. Consider the following:

> Q: *Doctor, you are aware that many others in your area of specialization use the XYZ test to formulate an opinion about the issue we've been discussing?*
> A: I don't think that test is nearly as effective as the one I used.
> Q: *I understand your opinion, Doctor. My question is whether you are aware that many other doctors use the XYZ test.*
> A: Other doctors use that test.
> Q: *But you never use that test to support your findings, do you Doctor?*
> A: I don't think the test is helpful.

> Q: *Had you used the XYZ test in this case, the results you arrived at could have been different. Isn't that true?*
>
> A: I guess anything is possible.
>
> Q: *In fact, you have been made aware that Dr. Ames did in fact arrive at a different conclusion using the XYZ test.*
>
> A: I have been told that.

Note that in the above cross-examination, the attorney neither negated the conclusion of the opposing party's expert nor got the witness to retreat significantly with respect to her conclusion. While such results are possible, they are highly unlikely. Realistically, the cross-examiner can expect the witness to argue that the approach she favors is the best one and to make concessions grudgingly about approaches she disfavors. The modest but important goal of the cross-examiner at this point is to make the fact finder aware that the bias of the expert to other accepted approaches raises a question about the determinative nature of her conclusion.

Another indication of bias can come from the fact that the witness usually testifies for one side as opposed to the other, or to one particular conclusion rather than the competing one. There is an infamous psychiatrist in Texas who demonstrates both aspects of this type of bias. In over 100 death penalty cases, the good doctor testified virtually every time for the prosecution and against the defendant. More particularly, regardless of any mitigating factors in the defendant's background, the doctor's examination always revealed that the defendant continued to pose a grave danger to society (a crucial finding for imposing capital punishment in Texas). It is hardly surprising that this psychiatrist became known as "Doctor Death." While most attorneys are unlikely to cross-examine an expert quite so linked to one side or conclusion, the examples below demonstrate how easy it is to bring out such bias.

Example 1:

> Q: *Now, Doctor, in your duty as a coroner, you testify far more for the prosecution than for the defense?*
>
> A: I testify whenever I am subpoenaed.
>
> Q: *I understand that. In your history as a coroner, though, isn't it true that you have testified far more for the prosecution than for defendants such as my client?*
>
> A: I suppose that is correct.

Example 2:

> Q: *Now, Doctor, I see you have testified in 25 cases in which you were asked to determine whether there was a causal relationship between the asbestos found in the home and the resident's contracting respiratory disease. Is that correct?*
>
> A: That sounds about right.
>
> Q: *In all but one of those cases, no matter the extent of the symptoms nor the contrary findings of other doctors, you have concluded there was no such causal relationship. Isn't that also correct?*
>
> A: Those were my findings.

3. Information Used by Expert in Forming Opinion

The opinions offered by expert witnesses are only as good as the information they used to formulate those opinions. The cross-examiner should look closely at how the expert gathered the information and whether better, more accurate or more thorough methods could have been employed. There are several ways through which the cross-examiner can raise doubts about the information used by the expert in arriving at his or her opinions.

a. How Was the Information Provided or Obtained?

Example 1:

> Q: *Doctor, your diagnosis stems in large part from the pain that the plaintiff reported to you. Is that true?*
>
> A: Severe pain is an important symptom of Mr. Boit's condition.
>
> Q: *The only way you know that Mr. Boit is suffering pain is that he told you?*
>
> A: That is the only way to know.

Example 2:

> Q: *Mr. Jones, your opinion that the defendant truck driver lost control of his vehicle due to the icy conditions was based in part on the information that the truck was swerving immediately before the accident. Is that correct?*
>
> A: Yes.
>
> Q: *The person who provided you with that information was the plaintiff's wife?*

A: She saw the swerving and later told me.

Q: *Did anyone unrelated to the plaintiff report to you that they saw the truck swerve before the accident?*

A: No.

In both of these situations, the opinion of the expert relied on a key fact provided by someone with a strong interest in the case that could not otherwise be verified. In other situations, the cross-examiner may wish to hone in on the fact that the expert is relying on information that is indirect.

Example 3:

Q: *On direct examination, you offered an opinion as to the condition from which the plaintiff suffers and her prognosis. Is that correct, Doctor.*

A: Yes.

Q: *How many times did you actually see the patient?*

A: I carefully reviewed her medical records.

Q: *Yes, Doctor, but how many times did you examine Ms. Low in person?*

A: I never examined her in person.

Example 4:

Q: *Doctor, your opinion that my client was able to distinguish right from wrong at the time of the crime is based primarily on your interviews with him beginning 2 weeks after the shooting. Is that correct?*

A: That, and observations of him by staff while he was hospitalized.

Q: *Had you ever met the defendant before the shooting?*

A: No.

Q: *Obviously, you were not present during the shooting?*

A: No.

Q: *Then, doctor, did you speak with any of the witnesses who were present when the shooting occurred?*

A: I read the police report.

Q: *But you never bothered to ask the two people who saw the shooting whether my client manifested any of the symptoms that would characterize delusional behavior. Did you?*

A: I saw no mention of such signs in the police report.

Q: Would you, as a trained psychiatrist looking specifically into the mental state of the defendant, likely ask different questions of the witnesses than those asked by the police officers investigating the crime?

A: I suppose so.

This final example highlights one of the more effective techniques to use when cross-examining expert witnesses about their opinions and the information they relied upon. Usually, the expert witness is quite adept at discussing the things he or she did, but less comfortable when being asked about tests not performed, data not acquired, or assumptions not employed.

b. What Assumptions Did the Expert Use?

Experts often assume certain facts in arriving at their conclusions. They then base their conclusions, in part, upon the validity of their assumptions. The cross-examiner can raise doubts about the validity of the expert's conclusion by raising doubts about these assumptions. Consider the following cross-examination of a forensic expert:

Q: Your estimate as to the distance the gun was held from the body of the deceased at the time of the shooting was based in large part on the absence of powder burns on either the clothing or body of the deceased. Is that correct?

A: Yes.

Q: Is it true that there was an excessive amount of blood on the body and clothing of the deceased in this case, due to the gunshot wound?

A: There was a good deal of blood.

Q: Would you agree that blood can wash away any signs of powder burns?

A: That can happen.

Q: So, there could have been powder burns on the clothing or body of the deceased in this case that you were unable to detect?

A: That is possible.

Q: And if there were powder burns, then you would have to change your opinion on the distance that the gun was from the body when it was fired?

A: I suppose that would play a role in my opinion.

When the assumption employed by the expert in arriving at his or her opinion is a number, questioning the use of that number over other possible alternatives can be particularly effective. In the cross-examination of an expert in accident reconstruction, consider the following inquiry:

Q: Is it true that the skid marks left by the defendant's truck begin 31 feet below the crosswalk?

A: Yes.

Q: Yet, you concluded that the plaintiff was hit while she was walking in the crosswalk.

A: I did and I explained why.

Q: What you said was that factoring in the average time it takes to apply one's brakes in such a situation and the speed at which the defendant was traveling, it is likely that the impact occurred within the crosswalk.

A: That is correct.

Q: Would you agree that different drivers exhibit different reaction times based on a number of factors?

A: Sure.

Q: *You estimated that the defendant probably hit his brakes 1½ to 2 seconds after seeing the pedestrian?*

A: That is right.

Q: *Yet, if your estimate was incorrect by as little as one half of a second, say it took him 1 second to apply the brakes, your opinion as to where the impact occurred would change as well. Would it not?*

A: To some extent.

Q: *Furthermore, if the defendant was traveling at only a slightly different speed than you estimated, that could also change your opinion as to the exact location of the accident?*

A: Somewhat.

Raising questions about the expert's numerical assumptions and showing the significance of using a different number can be especially helpful when the number has to be multiplied to allow the expert to arrive at his or her ultimate opinion. An economist called upon in a personal injury case to testify to lost future income often assumes the average annual income the plaintiff would earn for the remainder of his working life and then multiplies that figure by the estimated number of years of likely employment. The cross-examiner can show the fact finder that if the estimated annual income projected by the economist is changed by as little as 2%, that change can alter the ultimate damage estimate by $100,000.

4. Drawing Other Conclusions from the Same Facts?

Even accepting the facts or assumptions upon which the expert bases his or her opinion does not always lead to the same conclusion that the expert arrived at in the instant case. Different expert witnesses often arrive at different conclusions even when using the same data. Consider the following cross-examination of a defendant's expert witness in a case involving lead poisoning:

> Q: *You testified on direct that chemical tests you relied upon revealed that the plaintiff's son had blood levels of 16 micrograms of lead per deciliter of blood?*
> A: That is correct.
> Q: *You also claimed that anything below 20 micrograms is acceptable?*
> A: I did and it is.
> Q: *Are you familiar with CDC guidelines that regard anything above 10 micrograms as a serious health hazard for developing lead poisoning?*
> A: I am familiar with those guidelines, but my experience and research leads me to a different conclusion.
> Q: *But don't many experts in the field of lead poisoning rely on the research performed and the conclusions arrived at by the CDC?*
> A: I imagine many do.

One way of beginning an inquiry in this area is to ask the witness if others in his field could arrive at different conclusions using the same data. In most cases, the answer is yes and the witness will so concede. If the cross-examiner is really fortunate, the expert will deny this and damage his credibility with the fact finder.

C. Techniques for Cross-Examining the Expert Witness

Many of the tools and techniques used to cross-examine lay witnesses, discussed in the chapter on Cross-Examination, apply as well to the questioning of experts. Often, however, the principles discussed in that chapter apply with greater force when the cross-examination is of an expert witness. For example, while attorneys should use primarily leading questions during all cross-examinations, it is especially important to avoid asking open-ended questions of expert witnesses. Usually biased, often professional testifiers, expert witnesses should not be given the opportunity to explain (or to explain again what they said during direct examination) in their own terms why or how they arrived at their conclusions. If asked, experts are pleased to offer ample justification for their actions or inactions. Some explanatory testimony from the expert may be impossible to avoid, but the constant use of tightly framed questions calling for limited answers will minimize this risk. Expert witnesses who continually go beyond what is called for in the question can look bad to the jury. Even slightly open-ended questions, however, are an invitation to the expert to take another stab at persuading the jury of the correctness of his or her position.

Prior inconsistent statements can be a particularly valuable tool in cross-examining expert witnesses. Lay witnesses are understandably prone to mistakes or omissions in written or oral statements they make describing an event. Jurors tend to be less forgiving of mistakes made by experts preparing documents while acting in their professional capacity. It can be particularly effective to show that the expert's testimony on direct examination included a significant fact or conclusion that was omitted from his original report. Again, all efforts should be made to establish the inconsistency and then move on without allowing explanation or justification from the expert witness.

1. Hypothetical Questions

Just as the direct examiner can ask the expert witness hypothetical questions, the cross-examiner is permitted to do so as well. As the direct examiner did, the cross-examiner can use her version of the facts, even if disputed, to show how a different opinion could have been reached. A particularly effective means of cross-examining the expert witness is to use the same hypothetical question asked on direct, with one fact or variable changed. Consider the following:

> Q: *On direct examination you were asked to offer an opinion based on a hypothetical question that assumed a person smoked one pack of cigarettes a day for 20 years?*
> A: I recall that.
> Q: *Would your opinion change if instead of one pack, a person smoked two packs a day for that period of time?*
> A: It could.

Another related technique is to add a fact to the hypothetical asked on direct examination.

> Q: *Do you recall being asked on direct examination whether in your expert opinion it was reasonable police procedure to fire from a distance of 7 feet at a man who was bent down in the process of picking up a flashlight that he had dropped?*
> A: I recall the question, and I said it was not accepted procedure to fire in that circumstance.

Q: *If I were to add to the hypothetical that the flashlight appeared to the officer to be a gun at the time he fired his weapon, would that change your opinion as to the reasonableness of the officer's response?*

A: If the officer had good reason to believe the man was reaching for a gun, naturally that would affect my opinion.

2. Tests Not Performed, Procedures Not Done, Sources Not Used

Expert witnesses are usually quite proficient at explaining, in detail, precisely what tests they performed, what steps they took and what sources they relied upon in arriving at their conclusion. Often they are less adept at handling questions dealing with things that they did not do. Some of the cross-examination examples presented above demonstrated how this form of questioning can be used to challenge the credibility of both the expert and his findings. Consider as well the following cross-examinations:

Example 1:

Q: *You just acknowledged that any powder burns may have been absorbed by the large amount of blood surrounding the deceased's wound. Is that correct?*

A: That is possible.

Q: *Did you ever perform or have performed a microscopic analysis of the blood to see if it contained any gun powder?*

A: No.

Example 2:

Q: *Is it true that you attempted to reconstruct the accident by talking to witnesses and taking measurements of relevant matters such as skid marks?*

A: Yes.

Q: *You spoke with the defendant and his wife, who was a passenger in the car?*

A: I did.

Q: *Did you speak with the plaintiff?*

A: He has been in the hospital and difficult to reach.

Q: *Did you speak to any other persons who saw the accident?*

A: I could not find anyone else.

Q: So, the only eyewitness accounts that you relied on in forming your opinion as to how the accident occurred came from the defendant and his wife?

A: Yes.

The purpose of these questions is to permit the attorney to argue on summation that, had the expert done all that he should have, and accordingly had more data upon which to base his opinion, that opinion might be different. Cross-examiners should always attempt to learn about other tests that could have been performed or other sources of information that could have been accessed. Especially where there is little in the way of affirmative material with which to confront the expert, such information can be useful to the cross-examiner.

3. Learned Treatises

With most witnesses, impeachment through the use of prior inconsistent statements is limited to those statements made by the witness him or herself. Expert witnesses, however, can be impeached through the use of learned treatises if the treatise is acknowledged to be a reliable authority in the relevant field of inquiry. Before using the treatise, periodical or pamphlet to impeach, the cross-examiner must first establish that it is an accepted and reliable authority. FRE 803(18) permits the attorney to accomplish this in one of four ways: the expert can testify that she relied upon the source in helping to arrive at her opinion; she can admit the treatise is authoritative; the attorney can elicit from another qualified witness that the treatise is authoritative; or the court can take judicial notice of the treatise.

In an ideal world, the cross-examiner will find some nugget of impeachment within the book that the opposing expert has used to help form an opinion that is integral to his testimony.

In the absence of such direct impeachment, the cross-examiner should be prepared to impeach through the use of treatises not relied upon by the expert. In the event that the opposing expert will not concede the authoritative nature of the treatise, the cross-examiner's own experts should testify to its authoritative nature to satisfy the requirements of FRE 803(18). If the cross-examiner's own expert has not yet testified during the trial, he should proffer to the court that when the witness does testify, she will attest to the authoritative nature of the treatise. By being prepared with several authoritative treatises that in some manner impeach the testimony of the opposing expert, the cross-examiner forces the witness either to acknowledge the sources of differing opinions, or to seem stubborn in rejecting all sources with opinions different from her own.

4. When Nothing Else Is Available

The cross-examiner may unfortunately encounter situations when there is little that can be done to cross-examine the opposing expert witness in an effective manner. While this should occur only when the expert's testimony is either undisputed or not central to the outcome of the case, the attorney should still be ready for such situations.

One question that can be helpful to the cross-examiner when nothing else is available is to ask the witness if other experts in the field could arrive at different conclusions. Except for those experts testifying about conclusions arrived at with mathematical certainty, the witness should answer affirmatively to such a question. If he or she does, the point is made. If the witness refuses to acknowledge that others in a field not regarded as an exact science COULD arrive at different conclusions, he or she is likely to appear closed minded to the fact finder.

CHAPTER 8

CLOSING ARGUMENT

It is hard to envision an aspect of practicing law that is quite as exciting as the act of performing a closing argument in front of a jury. This is your opportunity to explain to the jury in your own words, through use of whatever techniques of persuasion you have acquired over the years, why the jury should find in your client's favor. No longer encumbered by the limitations of the question-answer format, the inarticulateness of your witnesses or the harmful responses of adverse witnesses, it is just you and the jury. This is as close as litigation comes to being an art form.

No better self-examination exists for determining whether you want to be a trial lawyer than assessing how you feel while giving your closing argument. If you experience no thrill, no excitement, no rush of adrenaline when selling your case to the jury, perhaps you should consider a future in areas of law other than trial practice. This is not to suggest that you can expect to be immune from that queasiness in the pit of your stomach that indicates an attack of nerves. Such nervousness is typical, and trial lawyers eventually learn how to use this emotion to key them up to deliver their closing more effectively. At the end of the day, however, if addressing the jury brings you no feeling of excitement or satisfaction, it is unlikely that you will ever find trying a case to be more than an unavoidable burden.

I. Goals

The evidentiary portion of the case has concluded, and it is time for you to make your final argument. This is the last time the jurors will hear from you and represents your chance to put the entire case together for them. Perhaps not since your opening statement has the jury been as attentive to your every word as they will be now. With so much riding on what you say and how you say it, it is crucial to understand what needs to be accomplished in closing argument and how best to accomplish these goals.

A. Completing the Process of Having the Jury Adopt Your Theme

The primary goal to be achieved in a closing argument is finishing the job begun in your opening statement and pursued diligently throughout the trial of selling your *theme* to the jury. It will be recalled from the discussion of opening statements that the theme is the one thing every attorney who goes to trial must possess. Stated succinctly, it is the central reason why the jury should find in your favor or the overall manner in which the case should be viewed. To understand why selling your theme to the jury is so crucial to the outcome of the case, we need to consider the approach that juries take to the trial as a whole.

Ensconced as attorneys are in the adversary process, we understandably tend to view a trial as the presentation of two different cases, ours and that of our opponent. Each side does its best to present its case most favorably to the fact finder and detract from the other side's presentation. We have our witnesses, our documents and they have theirs. In the minds of most attorneys, the jury decides between two competing cases and chooses the winner based on which side came off better.

Psychologists who have performed studies on the decision making process of juries offer a markedly different picture of how the jury views the trial. Rather than seeing two separate and competing cases, juries tend to view the trial as a presentation of one set of facts, albeit with different interpretations offered by each side. Obviously, the nature of the evidence presented in a given case affects the extent to which the jury regards the case as only one body of facts. If the prosecution in a murder case alleges the defendant is a paid hit man who shot the victim 8 times to prevent him from testifying and the defense case shows the accused to be a respected nurse who was home with his family 300 miles away at the time of the shooting, the likelihood that the jury will see the case as one set of facts is diminished.

Fact patterns so completely at variance with one another, however, are the exception rather than the rule for most trials. Far more frequent is the case where the factual disagreements seem less numerous and less important to the jury than those events that each side basically acknowledges occurred. Where the jury does find factual discrepancies between the two cases, it is apt to either minimize these discrepancies or search for acceptable ways to explain them away. Perhaps one of two eyewitnesses offering conflicting testimony was better positioned to see the entire event, or the witness testifying a bit too precisely is a good friend of one party and may be exaggerating somewhat. The jury wants to make a coherent whole of the testimony they have listened to and will not permit some understandable factual discrepancies to prevent them from doing so.

What is the significance of this understanding of jury decision making to the attorney who is preparing his or her closing argument? If the jury will accept and explain away certain factual discrepancies, perhaps the thrust of the closing should not be directed to arguing the factual nuances that attorneys often think verdicts turn upon. Instead, the primary goal of the closing should be to ensure that the jury views the totality of the case in those terms that are most favorable to the attorney delivering the argument. The attorney should remind the jury what the case is about in its essence. In other words, sell his or her theme. The jury will then apply this overall manner of looking at the case to the way it sees the body of testimony.

Let us return again to the two examples of case theme development discussed in the chapter on Opening Statements. In the personal injury case stemming from the automobile accident, the plaintiff's theme was that the case concerned the defendant driver being in such a hurry to arrive at her destination that she ran the red light, hitting the plaintiff and injuring him severely. If the jury focuses its deliberations on if and why the defendant was in a hurry and whether this caused her to go through the red light, the plaintiff has gone a long way toward winning the case well before the jury ever attempts to resolve any factual discrepancies that may exist. On the other hand, if, upon retiring, the jury is concerned primarily with whether the plaintiff's drinking resulted in his crossing the street without first looking for oncoming traffic (the defendant's theme), the defendant is likely to prevail at the end of the day. Undoubtedly, the jury will spend some time on both of these issues. In the end, however, the jury will come to regard one of these issues as the predominant one, and its resolution of which issue is most important will likely determine the outcome of the trial.

In the Terry Nichols case, imagine how much better the defendant would fare if, upon retiring, the jury focused its attention on the credibility of co-conspirator and drug user-turned-prosecution witness Michael Fortier. Should they determine Fortier to be largely unworthy of belief or compare his life to that of "devoted husband and father Terry Nichols," the remainder of the Government's case would not appear so overwhelming. On the other hand, if the jury examined each piece of physical evidence and oral testimony supportive of Fortier's testimony in conjunction with it, and approached its examination with the overall purpose of deciding whether all of the links between Nichols and the bombing could be purely coincidental, Nichols had best come to court toothbrush in hand.

In both of the above cases, the attorney who was successful in getting the jury to share his or her overall approach to the issues in the trial is likely to prevail. As this is so crucial a battle, attorneys need to go beyond merely stating the case theme. They need to sell it. To do this, attorneys should consider the type of factors that often influence people in making important decisions. For example, to aid in convincing the jury that the suggested overall approach to the case is the best one, attorneys can appeal to the common sense of the jurors, their life experiences or to commonly held views or values. To see how these decision making factors can contribute to persuading the jury to adopt a particular theme, consider the following hypothetical final arguments:

1. Common Sense

Members of the jury, you have listened to witnesses linking Terry Nichols, again and again, with the bomber, Timothy McVeigh. You have seen abundant physical evidence connecting Nichols with the building of the bomb; learned the motive he had for wishing to cause such mass destruction; and listened to testimony describing Nichols' precise role in this monumentally evil scheme.

You were selected as jurors in large part because of your common sense. The Government appeals to you to use that common sense in evaluating this evidence and decide whether these are the most astounding and unbelievable coincidences ever to befall an innocent man or, instead, whether the only reasonable explanation for all of this evidence is that Terry Nichols is guilty of the crimes charged.

2. Life Experiences

Most of you drive cars and have probably seen pedestrians so preoccupied with what they are doing that they fail to look before crossing the street. Without thinking of the consequences of their actions, these people dart out from anywhere on the sidewalk into the middle of the street, causing many accidents and even more near misses. Do you ever say to yourself, "I was lucky to avoid them"? Mary Smith was not so lucky.

The evidence in this case established quite clearly that the plaintiff and his friends were drinking liquor and dancing as they darted into the street in front of Mary Smith's car. As the judge has explained to you, if the plaintiff is at all responsible for the accident, he cannot win this lawsuit. Your job is to determine whether a man who runs or maybe dances into the street while drinking alcohol, insufficiently concerned to look for oncoming cars before entering the street, contributed at all to the accident that ensued. As you have seen, in this case the plaintiff's actions definitely contributed to the accident, and you must, therefore, find in favor of Mary Smith.

3. Commonly Held Views or Values

What type of a man blows up a building with innocent adults and children in it? What type of a man would lie about such a thing? As these are essential questions that you need to answer in reaching the correct verdict in this case, let us examine the 2 principal figures in this case and see if we can answer these questions.

You have heard uncontradicted testimony that Terry Nichols was a loving husband and father. He spent virtually all of his time trying to make his farm successful, so that he could provide for his family. One who cares so deeply for his own family is not the type of man who would cause such pain to other people's families.

Now let us look at Michael Fortier. He has used drugs on many occasions with his wife and others. He is a proven liar. He has been shown to have lied already about his background, his drug use, his involvement in this case and the involvement of others. We know that the prosecution offered Fortier a sweetheart deal if he would pin the blame on Terry Nichols. Is Michael Fortier the type of man who would lie again to save himself from going to jail for the time he deserves? You bet he is.

B. Dealing with Factual Discrepancies

While the attorney's primary purpose in the closing argument is to have the jury adopt his or her theme, the attorney should not ignore *important* factual discrepancies that arose during the trial. Not every factual discrepancy needs to be resolved or even addressed. Spending too much time during closing argument discussing factual differences may take the attorney's emphasis away from fully developing the case theme and showing the jury how the weight of the testimony relates to this theme. Furthermore, given the limited time during which the attorney will have the full attention of the jury and the ability of the jury to absorb only so much during closing argument, it is important for the attorney to prioritize among the testimony that was adduced at trial. While the attorney may wish to allude briefly to all of the witnesses, only those witnesses whose testimony is likely to play a significant role in the jury's deliberations should be the subject of detailed analysis. With respect to these witnesses, there are several ways in which to deal with important differences in their testimony.

1. Showing There Is No Actual Conflict among the Witnesses

The reaction of most attorneys confronted with factual discrepancies among witnesses is to consider the best way of persuading the jury that their preferred version of the fact at issue is more likely to be correct than the other side's version.

While such attempts during closing argument to win a battle over factual differences can (and sometimes must) work, it is often far more effective for the attorney to explain away or even resolve such different factual accounts. Recall that the jury tends to view the trial as essentially one body of facts rather than two entirely different and competing factual scenarios. It can be useful, therefore, for the attorney to reinforce this view by attempting during closing argument to resolve rather than "win" any factual disputes that emerged during the trial. For example, assume that in an automobile accident case, the plaintiff's witnesses saw the victim in the crosswalk while defense witnesses testified to his being outside of the crosswalk. As an alternative (or perhaps in addition) to attempting to show why her witnesses are more credible, the defense attorney may be better served by explaining how the testimony is not actually in conflict:

> Members of the jury, you will recall that several witnesses saw the plaintiff outside the crosswalk while others testified to having seen him within the crosswalk. Were some of the witnesses incorrect? No. A careful look at the evidence shows that the plaintiff's witnesses saw him when he first entered the street. You will recall that neither of these witnesses was actually watching the plaintiff when the accident occurred. Our witnesses did not see the plaintiff when he first walked into the street, so that they would not have known that he might have initially been walking near the crosswalk. These witnesses, however, got a good look at the plaintiff and where he was walking at the moment that the accident occurred. Both of these neutral eyewitnesses

to the accident itself swore to you that the plaintiff was well below the crosswalk at the moment of impact.

Such remarks during closing argument will appeal to the jury's desire to make a coherent whole of testimony that may at first appear to be contradictory.

This approach of resolving conflicting testimony can be applied to more than just eyewitness testimony. The defendant charged with arson for burning down his business to collect the proceeds of an insurance policy has put on character witnesses to testify that he is not the type of man to engage in such fraud. The prosecutor may have partially demonstrated during cross-examination of these witnesses or through his own rebuttal witnesses that the positive claims about the defendant's character are in doubt. Rather than dwelling on which character witnesses are more worthy of belief, it might be more effective for the prosecutor during closing argument to emphasize that even if the defendant possessed positive character traits, they were overcome by the desperate financial and emotional situation in which he found himself immediately before the fire.

Conflicts in the testimony of expert witnesses are also candidates for resolution rather than a focus on why one expert is correct and the other wrong. Perhaps the two experts arrived at different conclusions because they used different approaches in getting there, and the attorney can explain that her expert's approach incorporated conditions closer to the actual conditions of the incident in question. In some cases the testimony will allow the attorney to argue that her expert used a more sophisticated test that led to results that were not necessarily in conflict with the findings of the other side's expert, but to results that were more detailed and precise.

Attorneys should always consider resolving factual discrepancies in ways that help the jurors in their effort to put the whole case together in a manner that makes sense of all of the evidence presented. In addition to the substantive benefits achieved through resolving these conflicts, the lawyer avoids putting him or herself in the unfavorable position of criticizing the testimony of witnesses to whom the jury might be favorably disposed. While this is not always possible or even desirable (as where the attorney can demonstrate that his or her version of the facts is clearly the more credible), such a strategy can have a direct and favorable impact on the jury's deliberations.

2. Supporting One Witness over Another

At times, conflicts regarding important testimony cannot be resolved without showing that the testimony of your witness is superior to that of your opponent's witness. In these situations, the attorney will need to compare and contrast the competing witnesses and their testimony. Although witnesses may testify to the same event or subject matter, invariably the jury will come to regard the testimony of certain witnesses as more believable, accurate or relevant than that of other witnesses. In comparing the testimony of contrasting witnesses, the attorney should consider which of these features favors her witness and, therefore, should be emphasized.

a. Believability of the Witness

Every witness who takes the stand puts his or her credibility into issue. During the direct and cross-examination of the competing witnesses, certain facts may have been elicited that will lead the jury to regard one witness as more believable than the other. For example, one of the competing witnesses may have been shown to possess a bias regarding one side or the other. That witness may be a paid professional witness or someone who has a relationship with one of the parties, such as a friend or relative. On the other hand, the witness may possess hostile feelings toward one of the parties or to other people or issues involved in the case. If your witness exhibited a greater degree of neutrality than the competing witnesses, arguing bias can be an effective means of getting the jury to distinguish the competing testimony. Consider the following excerpts from closing arguments:

Scenario 1:

The two professionals who testified in this case offered completely different causes for the accident. In deciding whose testimony to accept, it will be helpful to use your common sense. We called John Smith, a police department accident investigator who was assigned to investigate the accident as part of his official duties. Officer Smith has no tie, financial or otherwise, to any of the parties involved in the accident.

The other side used Harry Slick and paid him $1000. Unsurprisingly, he came up with a conclusion that supported their claim as to how the accident occurred. Do you want to place your trust in the conclusion of an entirely neutral police officer performing his public duty, or in the claim of an investigator hired and paid by the persons on whose behalf he testified?

Scenario 2:

You heard from two eyewitnesses to this shooting, one claiming the Defendant acted in self defense and the other testifying that his attack was unprovoked. As you decide whose testimony to accept, consider who each of these witnesses is and how that may affect her testimony. The Defendant's witness is his wife, and while she may not be deliberately misstating what she saw and heard, it is understandable why she would view the shooting in a light favorable to her husband.

The Government called Edith Pack, who was sitting at the restaurant table right next to the Defendant and the victim. Ms. Pack, who knew no one involved in this case before the shooting, swore to you that the Defendant pulled a gun and shot the victim without any provocation. It is Ms.Pack, who has no interest in coming here other than to tell you the truth, whose testimony should be believed.

In addition to bias, the attorney may wish to argue believability by contrasting the background of his witness with that of the opposing witness. A prior criminal conviction or other testimony related to the witness's character or background can serve to make one witness less worthy of belief than another in the view of some jurors. Conversely, the fact that another witness has led an exemplary life can cause the jury to give greater weight to his or her testimony.

One caveat is in order regarding the decision to attack the believability of the witness during closing argument. As discussed in the chapter on Cross-Examination, while witnesses may be honestly mistaken for numerous and sometimes undiscernible reasons, juries rarely believe witnesses testified deliberately dishonestly without a clear reason for doing so. Therefore, before arguing that an opposing witness is unworthy of belief, the attorney should be sure that there is a specific reason he can point to that caused the witness to purposely misstate or, at least, exaggerate during her testimony.

b. Accuracy

There are an infinite number of reasons why one witness's version of an event or testimony about a subject matter may be more accurate than another witness's testimony on the same subject. Perhaps the first witness was better positioned to see what happened, was paying more attention at the key moment or has a firmer recollection of the incident. Perhaps one expert relied upon better and more complete data or used a more sophisticated test to reach her conclusion than did the opposing expert.

When arguing that the testimony of one witness is more accurate than that of the competing witness, the attorney can also point to the testimony of other witnesses or the existence or lack of physical evidence in support of that argument. It can be especially useful to link the physical evidence to the testimony of particular witnesses in order to bolster the overall accuracy and credibility of that witness. Consider the following argument in which the defense attorney cannot possibly resolve the differences in the testimony of two crucial competing witnesses:

> Violet Donnell believes that Leo Judd was the man in the mask who raped her. You will recall that she got only a brief look at her attacker and, of course, was terrified during that brief moment. It is not difficult to understand why she would make a mistake about the identity of her attacker. The likelihood of this misidentification becomes even stronger when we hear how the police showed only Mr. Judd's photograph to Ms.Donnell and put in her mind through their words and actions that the photograph was in fact that of the rapist.
>
> Leo Judd told you he was working at Acme Warehouse at the time the rape was committed. You will recall that through the testimony of Mr. Judd's foreman, we placed in evidence the time card that showed Mr. Judd began his shift before the rape and finished working after the rape. So when you consider whose testimony is accurate, remember the undisputed additional evidence that shows how and why Ms.Donnell made a mistake, and that proves Mr. Judd was nowhere near the scene of the rape.

In this case, obviously the defense attorney's intention is to attack the accuracy of the complainant's testimony and not her believability. In different situations, testimony from other witnesses or tangible evidence may be effective tools for supporting or attacking the believability of witnesses as well.

The prior inconsistent statement (either oral or written) elicited during cross-examination is an example of the type of evidence that can be used to challenge either the believability or accuracy of witness testimony. When discussing prior inconsistent statements, the attorney should avoid making mountains out of molehills. Accordingly, the lawyer's first task is to distinguish between those inconsistencies which were minor in nature and those that might influence the outcome of the case. The former probably deserve no mention in the closing argument (unless there are enough minor inconsistencies to shed doubt on the whole of the testimony), except as a means of emphasizing a more significant inconsistency or of building up the lawyer's credibility with the jury. Consider this portion of the closing argument of the criminal defense attorney in a robbery case in which identification is the key issue:

Carol Toms told you that she was robbed at 10:30 p.m. You will recall that Officer Lee testified that Ms. Toms told him shortly after the
crime that the attack occurred at 10:45 p.m. Although what she testified to is inconsistent with what she told the police, the mistake is
understandable and should not play a role in your decision in this
case. Contrast that, however, with her statement to the police, when
this incident was freshest in her mind, that she observed a scar on the
left cheek of her attacker. Her description in court yesterday of her
assailant mentioned no such scar. As you can plainly see Mr. Arthur
has no such scar, and as you heard, he never had a scar. In and of itself, this statement to the police by Ms. Toms provides you with more
than reasonable doubt regarding whether Mr. Arthur is the man who
robbed Ms. Toms.

Had the attorney above attempted to make points with the jury by at-
tributing an exaggerated significance to the inconsistent statement about the
time of the robbery, she would likely have implicitly diminished the impact
of the statement to the police about the scar. The jury might come to regard
the statement about the scar as just another error that the defense attorney
was trying to blow out of proportion. This possibility is furthered because
once the attorney loses credibility (see discussion of attorney credibility below)
with the jury by overstating the meaning of an apparently unimportant inconsistency, she will have a difficult time trying to convince them of the significance of the more important one.

c. Relevance

Another way in which an attorney can contrast the testimony of competing witnesses is to suggest that the testimony of her witness is more relevant
to or probative of the issue at hand than is the testimony of her opponent's
witness. The attorney can argue that the opinion of the doctor who examined
the plaintiff is more relevant to the treatment he should receive than is the testimony of the defense doctor whose opinion is based on the treatment generally prescribed for patients in the plaintiff's position. The criminal defense attorney can argue that testimony about the character of her client coming from
those who know him best may have more probative value than rebuttal testimony elicited from witnesses not as familiar with him. By contrast, the prosecutor could suggest the bias of the defendant's friends and relatives makes
their character testimony meaningless.

C. Connecting the Law to the Facts

The judge has instructed the jurors as to the law and explained that their function is to apply the law as given to the facts of the case. With this instruction in mind, the jury is apt to begin its deliberations by considering the legal elements of the crime or cause of action and attempting to determine if the evidence adduced at trial satisfies those elements. During their closing arguments, attorneys should always help the jury make the connection between principles of law, both general and specific, and those facts that strategically support these legal requirements.

1. General Principles of Law

Principles of law common to virtually all civil or criminal cases will be addressed by the judge in his or her instructions to the jury. The judge will also charge the jury on the specific elements of and defenses to the crimes or causes of action involved in the case as well as other applicable legal principles. Some judges allude to a specific piece of evidence when describing these principles, others do not. Regardless of the judge's practice, attorneys can enhance their arguments by showing the jury how their position is supported by such legal concepts as burden of proof, the presumption of innocence, the defense of contributory negligence and the myriad of other legal issues pertaining to the case.

The keys to using legal principles effectively in closing argument are to discuss the law briefly, make it understandable for the jury and especially to connect the principle directly with the facts of the case. Legal principles discussed in the abstract are not only uninteresting and confusing to most jurors, but are easily forgotten or minimized once deliberations begin. Linked to testimony that the jury will remember from the trial, however, these legal principles can form a strong basis for the jury's determination of a crucial issue.

Lecturing the jury on contributory negligence accomplishes little unless the attorney explains how specific actions of the plaintiff show his contributory role in causing the accident. Criminal defense attorneys always speak about the government's burden to prove guilt beyond a reasonable doubt, but often neglect to tell the jury, specifically, how flaws in the prosecution's case or testimony of witnesses for the defense form that reasonable doubt.

2. Elements of the Crime or Cause of Action

At some point in closing argument, attorneys with the burden of proof should remind the jury of the required elements of proof and explain how each element was met by the testimony and exhibits adduced at trial. Their opponents may wish to concede that certain elements have been met, in order to highlight for the jury that element about which the evidence is the weakest. Let us look at portions of closing arguments in which attorneys relate the elements of proof to the trial testimony:

Example 1: Those who bear the burden of proof

You have heard the judge describe what we needed to prove, in order for you to find that the Defendant violated the promise it made in the contract and is liable for the entire loss that AC Bolt Co. suffered as a result.

We had to show you there was a written agreement between the parties, and that, in that contract, the Defendant agreed to supply the steel AC needed to make its bolts. That contract was entered into evidence and will be available for you to examine. The judge told you that there needed to be consideration from AC in return for the promise to deliver the steel. You will see in the contract that this consideration took the form of AC's promise to pay $ 75,000 to the Defendant upon delivery of the steel.

Proof is required that the Defendant broke its promise to deliver the steel by Feb. 1 and, therefore, breached the contract. You heard uncontradicted testimony from Alan Anderson, the owner of AC, that despite his repeated requests, that essential delivery did not arrive by Feb 1 or, in fact, ever. Finally we had to demonstrate to you the loss that AC suffered as a result of the Defendant's failure to live up to its promise. I am sure you will recall hearing Mr. Anderson tell you how, without delivery of the steel, AC was unable to make the bolts for Ford Motor Co. and lost this account. Mr. Anderson explained in detail how this loss devastated the company, because of the money it lost on the Ford account and the cost to the Company's reputation for reliability that it had worked so hard to achieve. Now that we have seen how each required element of proof discussed by the judge has been met, let us examine how to put a dollar figure on that loss.

Example 2: Opponents of those who bear the burden of proof

> In order to prove the crime of Murder in the Second Degree, the Prosecution had to show that John Jones was killed by the actions of Joe Fox. As we told you at the outset of this case, there is no dispute that Mr. Jones died as a result of a shot fired by Joe Fox's rifle. So, all of the ballistic evidence from the police and the medical testimony from the coroner offered by the prosecution established only what Mr. Fox has consistently acknowledged about the shooting in his statements to the police and his testimony in this court.
>
> What is crucial to remember from the judge's instructions is that in order to convict someone of murder, the prosecution must also prove beyond a reasonable doubt that the defendant *intended* to take the life of the victim. In this case, the prosecution has failed to meet its burden of showing to you that Mr. Fox intended to kill Mr. Jones. In fact, the most persuasive evidence points clearly to the fact that this was an accidental shooting. Let us now review that evidence.

In the first scenario, the plaintiff's attorney enumerated each element of proof and immediately explained to the jury how the elements were established during the trial. In the second case, the defense attorney conceded that certain elements were proven in an attempt to get the jury to disregard large portions of the prosecution's case. Extensive consideration by the jury of the medical and police testimony might cause the jury to focus upon areas that can only be harmful to the defendant. At the least, it will distract the jury from where the attorney wishes the focus of the deliberations to be: on whether the prosecution proved specific intent beyond a reasonable doubt.

II. Organization and Content

A. Getting Out of the Gate

The concept of primacy and the experience of most lawyers tell us that the jury will be most attentive to the attorney at the moment when he or she begins speaking. It is, therefore, important to plan carefully how to begin closing argument.

Some attorneys like to begin their closing argument with a personal comment to the jury. One such comment is the attorney's expression of gratitude to the jurors for paying close attention during the trial. Often this statement is accompanied by a reference to the importance of this trial to the attorney's client and, thus, the particular significance of the juror's listening carefully to the testimony.

Personal comments such as this and others can help establish a positive rapport between the attorney and the jury that will continue throughout the closing argument. Additionally, they can give the jurors a chance to get settled before the attorney launches into the substantive portion of his or her remarks. Finally, a personal comment at the outset may facilitate the attorney's own efforts to achieve an easy and comfortable manner of addressing the jury. It should be noted that some trial lawyers view such personal remarks as transparent and unwise attempts to curry favor with the jury. They assert, for example, that the jury has a job to do and should not be thanked for doing it. As is true of many of the things that trial lawyers do, how the personal comments are communicated can determine their effectiveness. I suggest making personal comments brief and using them only if they can be conveyed sincerely and naturally.

Another means of beginning the closing is to refer back to some point or observation that the attorney made during opening statement. "You will recall that I told you at the outset of this trial that this was a case about a company that broke its promise and, because it broke its promise, Alan Anderson saw the company he built and the reputation he earned nearly destroyed. The evidence produced at the trial has shown you exactly how this happened." Such a reference to a comment made during opening statement conveys to the jury the sense of the attorney's case being a now closed and completed circle. Especially, as in this example, where the allusion is to the theme of the case, beginning the closing argument in this manner can create the impression with the jury that the attorney proved the case was about exactly what she said it was about from the beginning of the trial.

B. Organizing Discussion of the Testimony by Issues, Not Witnesses

In the chapter on Direct Examination, it was suggested that the examination could be organized either chronologically or by topic. Either method, employed effectively, permits the witness to communicate the necessary information to the fact finder in a coherent manner. The parallel decision to be made with respect to organization of the closing argument is whether to discuss the testimony of each witness or, instead, to divide the case into key issues and fit the witness's testimony in where appropriate. Here, one method is clearly preferable.

Less experienced attorneys often structure their closing arguments to cover the testimony of each witness, usually in the order in which they appeared. These attorneys generally sum up the testimony of each witness and attempt to work the key issues into their discussion of the witness's testimony or wait to discuss these issues until their recap of the testimony is concluded. Although a summation that chronologically follows the testimony of each witness is easier to prepare, it takes the focus of the jury's attention off the issues. Worse still, it can be exceedingly difficult for the jury to get a handle on each key issue when the discussion of Witness 1's testimony dealt with Issues A, B and C, Witness 2 contributed to Issues B and C, and Witness 3 testified regarding Issues A and C. The more witnesses that testified during trial, the worse this problem gets.

Remember that the primary purpose of closing argument is to have the jury adopt the attorney's theme of the case. For this to be accomplished, the jury must be persuaded that the key issues in the case are those propounded by the attorney. Therefore, the attorney needs to divide the case into those issues that best tie into and support his case theme. The attorney, after explaining why these are the issues upon which the jury should base its verdict, should demonstrate how the evidence adduced at trial supports his position on these issues. Additionally, the judge is likely to have instructed the jurors that their deliberations should focus on applying the facts as they see them to the applicable legal issues. Therefore, the jury is apt to be predisposed to considering the case by issue, not by witness.

Consider excerpts from the closing argument of the Plaintiff AC Bolt Co. in the breach of contract case using both methods of organizing the testimony.

Scenario 1 by Witness:

You heard first from Alan Anderson, who told how he negotiated a contract with the defendant for the delivery of the metal needed to make the bolts. Through Mr. Anderson, we introduced into evidence the contract entered into between the parties in which the Defendant promised to deliver the metal for the agreed to price. Next Mr. Anderson related how the metal was not delivered by the date agreed to or, in fact, ever. Mr. Anderson then told you how he built the company with Charles Clark and developed a reputation for reliability. Finally he told you how the failure of the defendant to honor its promise caused AC Bolt to lose the Ford contract, along with its reputation. He explained how this loss of reputation will translate into the loss of substantially more business.

Next, Charles Clark testified and told you how he and Mr. Anderson formed their business. He testified about how the metal that should have been delivered is used to make bolts for automobiles. You heard again how the metal never was delivered. Mr. Clark, as did Mr. Anderson, discussed the various ways in which AC Bolt Co. would lose business and money as a result of the defendant's breaching its contract.

Finally, you heard from Jane Ayre, an economist who is familiar with both the metal bolt and automobile industries. Ms. Ayre testified to the loss in dollars that was caused by the defendant's failure to abide by its promise.

Scenario 2 by Issue:

As I told you at the outset of the trial, this case is about the defendant's failure to live up to its promise and the terrible loss suffered by AC Bolt Co. as a result of that broken promise. Let us now examine how the evidence at this trial showed the existence of a promise, the defendant's failure to honor that promise, and the loss that AC Bolt Co. suffered, due to that broken promise.

You will recall both Alan Anderson and Charles Clark telling you about the negotiations that led to a contract in which the defendant promised to deliver the metal necessary to make the bolts for Ford Motor Co. You will get to take back with you that contract, and see for yourselves the clear promise the defendant made to deliver the metal by a certain date. The undisputed testimony of both men established that the defendant never delivered the metal and thereby broke its promise.

The final issue you need to think about is the value of the loss suffered by AC Bolt Co. On this issue you were presented with several important pieces of testimony. Mr. Anderson explained how much money would be lost on the Ford account. Mr. Clarke confirmed that loss and discussed what the loss of AC's reputation for reliability would mean in the future. Economist Jane Ayre, using her experience with the bolt and automobile industries, then put a dollar figure on that loss of reputation.

Organizing the argument by issues will necessitate more than one reference to the testimony of certain witnesses. As particular witnesses contributed to resolution of more than one issue, this is entirely appropriate. Such references should not be repetitive as they relate to different aspects of the witness's testimony or explain how the same testimony impacts upon several different issues. By contrast, discussing the same points when reviewing the testimony of each witness will appear needlessly repetitive to the jury, even more so in cases involving many witnesses.

C. Discussing Both Sides of the Case

In preparing closing argument, remember that the jury heard witnesses and received evidence from more than one side. No matter how effectively the attorney presented her own case, she needs to respond in some manner to the other side's case. This is not to say that equal attention needs to be paid to both cases, only that certain points made by the opponent should be acknowledged and responded to. The attorney who plays ostrich can cause a jury to accept certain adverse testimony as undisputed.

In some trials, the attorney believes he has dissembled the other side's case so completely that he neglects discussing his own witness. Clearly, minimizing one's own case sends an entirely undesirable message to the jury.

How much emphasis to place on your case and how much on your opponent's case will vary from trial to trial. While certain general criteria often cause attorneys to focus on one side of the case over the other, no hard and fast rules exist. For example, attorneys often will focus the majority of their argument on the side that bears the burden of proof. With the judge having just explained to the jury that the prosecution or plaintiff (in most instances) must prove the case to the appropriate degree, it is understandable that each side will address how that burden has been met or where the moving party failed in its obligation. Circumstances may cause this to change however.

At times, the moving party can divert the jury's attention from the weakness in his or her own case by emphasizing a significant problem that emerged during the other side's case.

Recall my armed robbery case, discussed in the chapter on Witness Preparation, where the criminal defendant was not told by his attorney of the need to respond honestly to standard impeachment questions concerning his prior criminal record. In that trial, the focus of my closing argument was on the defendant, a proven liar, who was trying to mislead the jury about his alibi as well as his criminal record. Why would he lie about where he was when the crime was committed unless he was the robber? This obviated the need for me to spend too much time bolstering the shaky identification made by the victim.

In some civil trials, the defendant may find little to dispute in the plaintiff's case and, therefore, will emphasize how his own witnesses refute the plaintiff's theory. The unsatisfying but best answer to the question of which side of the case to focus on, then, is to remain flexible and decide based on the circumstances particular to the case. However, never ignore your own case.

In certain cases, particularly criminal trials, one side may have presented all or virtually all of the witnesses and other evidence. In such instances, however, the party who offered little in the way of affirmative evidence should not lose sight of the importance of arguing effectively his or her overall theme of the case. Your theme is your case. Even if you don't put on *any* evidence (as in a criminal trial) you *do* have a case. In a criminal case where the defendant does not testify and calls no witnesses, but relies on insufficient evidence produced by the State (this is most often the case in criminal trials), the defendant still has a case. The defendant's case is developed through cross-examination of the State's witnesses. The theme is not "they didn't do a good enough job." Depending on the facts of the case, the theme may be "the existence of reasonable doubt." It is often a mistake to simply take defensive action to the other side's case.

For another example, consider an automobile accident case in which the defendant's theme is that he was driving in a prudent manner and had no opportunity to avoid the plaintiff as she crossed the street. The only witness produced by the defense on the issue of liability was the defendant himself, who testified consistently with this theme. The plaintiff called several eyewitnesses, and the police officer who responded to the scene, to support her theme that she entered the street carefully. In closing, the defense attorney may spend some time arguing that the eyewitnesses are biased or inaccurate and the police officer's testimony is largely irrelevant. Perhaps the focus of the argument, however, should be on how none of the eyewitnesses testified that the defendant was driving carelessly, and the police officer testified to the defendant's sobriety and full cooperation. Thus, even though the case depended largely on plaintiff's witnesses, the defense attorney focused his argument on the defendant's theme of the case.

D. Closing the Closing

1. Last Words

The tried and true manner of concluding closing argument is to request the specific verdict desired. This approach is often supplemented by characterizing for the jury what such a verdict means. Consider the following characterizations of favorable verdicts:

Scenario 1:

Therefore, members of the jury, do right by Carol Dean and all other victims of the horrible crime of rape who have the courage to come forward. Find the defendant guilty as charged.

Scenario 2:

Rape is cruel and unjust. It is too late to prevent the injustice that was done to Ms. Dean. What you CAN do is to prevent another terrible injustice from occurring, the conviction of an innocent man. Acquit Bill Thomas and send him home to his wife and children.

Scenario 3:

None of us have the power to make Karen Watts whole for the loss of her husband due to the carelessness of the automobile manufacturer. What you can do is to see that she is compensated in the only way our system provides compensation, making the negligent party pay for Karen's loss. Then, by awarding punitive damages as well, you can see to it that XYZ Motors will never again risk making defective automobiles that kill people. You can help Karen and society as well by finding for the plaintiff as to both compensatory and punitive damages.

Scenario 4:

The continuing success and vitality of our jury system depends upon jurors such as yourselves deciding cases impartially, based on the law and facts presented. Your verdict for XYZ Motors today upholds the promise you made at the beginning of this case to do just that.

2. Dealing with Not Being Able to Respond to Your Opponent's Response

In most civil and criminal cases, defense attorneys are confronted with the agonizing situation of being forced to listen to their opponent's rebuttal without any opportunity to respond themselves. When you are not the party with the final word, I suggest shortly before you conclude your argument saying something such as:

The rules in this court allow Ms. Oates to speak again after I finish and respond to what I've said. This is because it is she who has the burden of proof on every issue in this case. As I will not have a similar opportunity to address her final remarks, I would ask, in fairness, that you consider how I might respond to the points she is making were I given the chance.

If you are particularly fortunate, someone on the jury will come up with a thoughtful response to your opponent's point. Even if no member of the jury absolutely refutes your opponent, it is still helpful to have jurors putting themselves in your shoes and trying to think like you.

One other method for neutralizing your opponent's advantage in having the final word is to offer up a challenge by posing a question for your opponent to answer during rebuttal. Obviously, the question should be one that your opponent will have some difficulty answering in a convincing manner. Terry Nichols' lawyer might have said to the jury:

> When the prosecutor stands yet again to address you, perhaps he will deal with the issue of character. If so, perhaps he will finally answer the question of what in Michael Fortier's background and history suggests he possesses those qualities of character that can be relied upon in making the crucial decision that is before you.

The question should be phrased carefully, so the opponent will not be able to respond in the way he desires without avoiding the question. In the above example, undoubtedly the prosecutor will speak of the vast amount of evidence that corroborates Fortier's testimony. While this is a substantial argument, hopefully for the defense, some juror will realize it is not responsive to the question and, therefore, there is no good response.

E. Rebuttal

The opportunity to get the last word before the jury deliberates is too valuable for any wise attorney to pass up. The attorney should use rebuttal, both to respond to some of the arguments made by his opponent, and to make sure (hopefully, through non-repetitive means) that his overall approach to the case (the case theme) is what the jury takes into its deliberations.

Most jurors are likely to think the attorneys have already concluded their remarks before rebuttal and are anxious to begin their deliberations. It is, therefore, wise for the attorney to keep rebuttal brief. The attorney must resist the temptation to respond to every argument made by opposing counsel. Respond only to those points that you believe had significant impact upon the jury. Try to do so briefly and without repeating too closely the points that you made previously. Jurors looking to the conclusion of the case are particularly impatient with attorneys who repeat themselves.

It can also be strategically beneficial to save certain points for rebuttal, as long as you are confident these remarks will fall within the scope of your opponent's argument. For example, a point that you believe your opponent could respond to might be wise to save for your rebuttal.

III. Style and Delivery

A. Talk, Don't Read to the Jury

Closing argument is the moment when the attorney closes the deal with the jury. She must maintain the jurors' attention throughout her remarks and must deliver the argument as convincingly as possible. It is here that connecting with the jury is most essential. When the attorney reads her closing remarks, she is more apt to connect with her note cards than with the jurors. Attorneys should talk to the jurors, not read to them. The attorney who can't or won't look the jurors in the eye is going to have a difficult time persuading them of anything.

This is not to say that the attorney must never refer to notes during closing argument. As during direct examination, it is fine for the attorney occasionally to glance at her notes to see where she is or to ensure that nothing is being omitted. When speaking to the jurors, however, she must again direct her eyes toward them.

B. Establish Eye Contact with Each Juror

Throughout the trial, jurors #3 and #7 have seemed particularly receptive to you and your case. They have smiled at the right time, been appalled when appropriate and now are following your every word. The inclination is to direct all of your remarks at these two jurors.

You are better advised to make sure that some of your visual attention is given to each member of the jury, including the one who seems to be sneering at you. All of them will be deciding the case and if you cannot win over every juror during your closing, at least you want to make sure none of them enter the jury room feeling ignored and overtly hostile to you or your case. Accordingly, make sure each juror feels you are speaking directly to him or her at least some time during closing argument.

C. Not Too Fast, Not Too Slow

As attorneys address juries, a number of factors are present that are likely to cause the statement to be delivered too quickly. First, many of us naturally speak too fast. Second, the nerves and adrenaline rush likely to be present any time one speaks in public tend to hasten the pace of the speaker. Third, in the desire to incorporate as many things as possible into the statement without the remarks going too long, the attorney is likely (perhaps subconsciously) to speed up his delivery.

Having prepared their cases so thoroughly, attorneys possess intimate knowledge of the facts and the arguments they will be delivering. Juries (particularly at opening statement, but during closing argument as well) are far less familiar with the facts of the case, the relevant law and the reasoning that proceeds from the connection of the facts and the law. They need adequate time to absorb the numerous things they are being told.

When attorneys speak too quickly, it can be difficult for the jury (especially for jurors with some hearing problems) to pick up every word the attorney says. More common is the problem of the attorney whose words can be understood but who moves too quickly from thought to thought. Attorneys should pause where appropriate to allow the jury to absorb and reflect upon one point before moving on to the next. This pause need only last a few seconds, just long enough for the listener to process one thought and prepare for the next one.

Although not as common as attorneys who deliver their statements too quickly, there are some attorneys whose pace needs to be accelerated. They pause too frequently, taking too much time between thoughts. This can result in the jury's losing attention during the attorney's remarks. Jurors are unlikely to absorb the attorney's argument fully if they are continually waiting and hoping for him or her to reach the next point.

The goal, then, is to find a pace that allows the jury to understand every word and grasp fully every argument, while not causing the jurors' attention to wane.

D. Use Voice Inflection and Volume

The voice, used effectively, can be a powerful tool of persuasion. Additionally, it can help maintain the interest of the listener, even through long presentations. On the other hand, nothing can put the listener to sleep as quickly as a statement spoken in a monotone.

We have all heard powerful and persuasive speakers in various aspects of life and seen the degree to which they can move and influence their audience. We have seen lawyers (and actors who play them on television or in film) use their voices to produce sorrow, anger, indignation or a number of other emotions among jurors. Many of us would like to emulate these gifted speakers; not all of us can. What all of us can do, however, is use our voice, much the same way we do in normal conversation, to create the appropriate mood and feeling for the moment.

The voices of some attorneys tend to flatten out and lose inflection when speaking to juries, perhaps as a manifestation of nervousness. Many of these attorneys need only to employ the same voice modulation when addressing a jury that they use when telling a story to their friends. Others, whose natural tendency is to speak in a monotone, need to work harder at developing the voice as a tool for emphasis.

Attorneys can use the voice for emphasis by speaking slower at certain points, by speaking louder or even softer at others. We can learn from observing others whose styles we admire, but should not attempt to adopt the manner of one whose style and persona is markedly different from our own. Using an approach so contrary to one's normal means of communicating invariably makes the speaker appear to be phony. Within our own individual styles, however, we can work to use our voices more effectively to maintain the jury's interest and to create the feeling in the courtroom that will make our presentation more persuasive.

E. Be Aware of Movement and Position

Some trial lawyers move gracefully and effortlessly around the courtroom. Each of their movements seems designed to further some point they or their witness is making. Others appear barely able to avoid tripping over their own feet. Still others are constantly fidgeting or moving back and forth like a receiver in football trying to escape his defender. These movements are annoying and can distract the jury from the attorney's presentation. As jurors are bound to notice and be affected by the attorney's movement, the attorney must ensure that his or her physical actions in no way detract from the presentation.

As we are all different, no one style is best for every lawyer. The safest thing to do is to remain relatively stationary when addressing the jury so as to avoid distracting them. Some attorneys report that moving around when addressing juries enhances their performance because it reduces nervousness or helps them think better. As long as these movements are not herky-jerky or distracting in some other way, they seem to work well for some lawyers.

Hand and arm motion also can be distracting or can aid in the presentation, depending on how it is done. When the attorney's hands are in constant motion, that can be distracting to the listener. On the other hand, the use of a hand or arm motion to demonstrate something or to emphasize a point can be effective. Additionally, the attorney will not want to appear too stiff when addressing the jury, and the use of hand and arm movements can help in this regard.

The attorney should give some thought to the location from which the closing argument will be delivered. Standing behind a podium allows the attorney to refer to his or her notes relatively easily and to mask any nervous action of the lower portion of the body. Unfortunately, it also places something both literally and figuratively between the lawyer and the jury he or she is speaking to. Remember, the goal is to be persuasive by looking the jurors in the eye and convincing them of the merits of your case. That is more likely to be achieved by speaking with the jurors closer to a conversational distance and environment. Standing behind a podium is unlikely to further that goal. My suggestion is to use the podium if you find you need it, but work toward eventually feeling comfortable standing out in front of the jury. If you do stand in front of the jury, make sure you leave adequate room between you and the box so that the jurors do not feel you are encroaching on their space.

F. Practice

The best way to improve your style and delivery, especially for less experienced trial lawyers, is to practice your statement before you give it. Give your argument to your spouse, partner or anyone who will listen and offer constructive criticism. Deliver it to your mirror, so you can see for yourself whether your movements are annoying. If you have access to a courtroom, stand in front of the jury box and see how it feels to deliver your remarks from various positions. Through practice performances you can work on your voice inflection, pace and eye contact.

IV. Commonly Asked Questions

A. Should I Object during My Opponent's Closing Argument?

As discussed in the chapter on Opening Statements, most attorneys prefer not to object when their opponent is addressing the jury. There are times, however, when objections should be entered. Probably the most common are the following:

Each attorney characterizes the law and testimony in as favorable light as possible, but where opposing counsel misstates or mischaracterizes significant testimony or relevant principles of law, an objection is appropriate. Jury verdicts can be based upon evidence adduced at trial or that which can be reasonably inferred from that evidence. When counsel goes beyond arguing for such an inference and invites the jury to speculate or adds to the evidence adduced, consider objecting.

B. Should I Use Demonstrative and Tangible Evidence?

Absolutely. Telling the jury about how the fender was damaged is fine; showing them again the badly mangled part is better, and likely will stay with them longer. Discussing how the knee works may help the jury understand important testimony; showing them a model or diagram simultaneously will probably make it easier for the jury to follow your explanation. Alluding to the mistake the adverse witness made in his deposition is probably not as effective as picking up the deposition and reading it to the jurors.

C. Should I Prepare a Chart That Outlines Important Points to Be Placed in Front of the Jury during My Remarks?

The use of such a chart or computer program can serve as a method of reinforcing and reminding the jury of the attorney's comments during closing argument. The chart is also available as a ready reference for the attorney should he or she forget a point.

At times, the chart can play a meaningful role in supporting a specific argument. Suppose the time frame of events that was elicited at trial is particularly crucial in showing the likelihood that a certain act was committed. The use of a visual time line that includes the dates and times when things occurred leading up to the event in question can be particularly persuasive in linking the disputed event to the undisputed ones. Attorneys should realize, however, that if not used effectively or at the right time, charts can distract the jury from listening to the attorney's words.

Closing argument is your last moment in front of the jury. Make the most of it.

CHAPTER 9

Get Organized, Stay Organized

I. Preparing for Trial

On TV and in the movies, trial lawyers are rarely shown preparing for trial. They deliver smooth and passionate opening statements seemingly off the top of their head. Their witnesses say exactly what the lawyers expect. Their cross-examinations are stunning and devastating. Yet despite these fictional lawyers' polish and pizzazz, you rarely see them answering interrogatories, reviewing their client's testimony, or sweating the details of a demonstrative exhibit. Yet real trial lawyers know that preparation is the single most important factor for a successful trial. You too can be as polished as Law & Order's district attorneys, but it requires attention to the less glamorous tasks of management and organization.

Trial is approaching. What do you need to do get ready? Whether you have months to prepare or a matter of days, it is essential that you prioritize your pretrial tasks. Obviously, how you prioritize the necessary tasks will depend on your timeframe and the complexity of the case. Regardless, you should prepare a checklist to ensure that you do not miss any essential steps. You do not want to appear in court and realize you have forgotten to subpoena a key witness or to update interrogatories. Not all the steps listed below are required in every case, and some apply only to jury trials. It is a comprehensive list. However, it is a good reference point to ensure you are not missing anything as you get ready for trial.

A. While There Is Time

- Complete fact investigation. Identify and interview all potential witnesses. Identify and gather all exhibits. Create demonstrative exhibits.

- Complete discovery. All depositions, interrogatories, requests for production of documents, and requests for admission should be served and answered. Supplement your initial discovery responses to reflect any information you have gathered.
- Review discovery. Review what you have received from your opponent and consider how it fits within your theory of the case.
- Review the file. Assess your case theory and themes in light of your ongoing fact investigation and legal research.
- Create a checklist of proof. Make a chart outlining all the elements of your prima facie claims or defenses. Identify which testimony and exhibits support each element.

CLAIM/DEFENSE	SOURCE OF PROOF		
	Witness	Exhibit	Other (discovery, stipulation, etc.)
1.			
2.			
3.			

B. In the Homestretch

- Pursue settlement options. The intense pretrial preparation you have done for the case may generate new settlement options by revealing the strengths and weaknesses of each side's case. The judge will surely want to know if settlement has been explored, and whether or not the judge can be of assistance.
- Prepare for the pretrial conference and draft any pretrial filings required by the court.
- File motions in limine. If your opponent will be introducing evidence that you want excluded, file a motion in limine to have the court resolve the issue prior to trial.
- Create your trial notebook. See the discussion on *Managing the Case*.
- Draft your opening and closing statements.
- Draft your direct and cross-examinations. In addition, anticipate objections by the other side and how you will deal with them. Anticipate the other side's examinations and what objections you can and should make.

- Subpoena all witnesses and documents. Check the deadlines for serving subpoenas and required witness fees.
- Draft jury instructions.
- Draft voir dire questions.
- Prepare verdict form.
- Review depositions. Excerpt the portions you want to introduce at trial and consider how you want to present them at the trial (e.g., in writing, through narrative testimony, displayed via projector, etc.).
- Prepare your client to testify. Run through your direct examination with the client and explain what they can expect at trial. Moot the anticipated cross-examination with the client.
- Prepare your fact and expert witnesses to testify.
- Certify any business or public records. Many evidence codes allow you to certify these records with advance notice to the other side so that you can dispense with foundational elements at trial.
- Agree on any stipulations with opposing counsel.
- Learn about your judge and visit the courtroom.

C. Immediately before Trial

- Gather supplies needed for courtroom. You may need a dry erase board and markers, a laptop and projector, legal pads and pens, and the like. Do not forget copies of the rules of evidence and rules of procedure.
- Investigate courtroom technology. If you will be using courtroom technology, be sure you know how to operate the equipment and prepare a back-up plan if the equipment fails.
- Make sufficient copies of all exhibits. At a minimum, you should provide copies to the witness, the judge, the jury, and opposing counsel. Ensure that your exhibits are copied clearly and completely.
- Moot. If you are a new lawyer, or an experienced lawyer trying a novel or complex case, moot the trial with colleagues. Experiment with different themes, strategies, exhibits, and testimony.
- Continue to prepare your client to testify.
- Get a good night's sleep before trial.

II. Managing the Trial

Trying a case is hard. There is a massive amount of information, witnesses, and exhibits to manage. Not only do you have to keep track of your case, but you have to listen attentively and respond to the opposing side's case. You cannot juggle all these balls without being organized. A messy counsel table spilling over with loose papers, files, and books sends a message to the judge and jury that you are disorganized, and possibly incompetent. By contrast, with a thorough trial notebook, you will have all the information you need at your fingertips. You will appear polished and professional. As the final culmination of your case file, the trial notebook is essential to pulling your case together. Putting your trial notebook together is time-consuming, but time well spent. It will improve your efficiency at trial, the quality of your presentation, and your ability to respond to unforeseen developments. In turn, this will gain you the confidence and respect of everyone in the courtroom.

Your trial notebook might be contained in a three-ring binder with tabs, a set of expandable files, or a laptop. It might consist of a few sheets of paper or extend to a multi-volume set of large binders. You need to develop an organized, flexible system that works for you and that is appropriate for your case. Regardless of the format, there are several essential sections most trial notebooks contain.

(1) **Pleadings**. Include an index of all the pleadings in the case, along with the complaint and answer, discovery requests and responses (interrogatories, requests for production, and requests for admission), motions, and court orders.

(2) **Chronology and Checklist of Proof**. Prepare and keep a chronology of every event in the case, along with a reference to the sources of evidence for each. Include a separate chronology detailing the procedural history of the case. Create a chart that shows each element of your claims or defenses, with references to all testimony and exhibits that you will introduce for each element.

(3) **The opening statement**. New lawyers in particular benefit from including a full, written version of the opening statement in addition to an outline summary. If nerves get the better of you, you can always read from your full opening statement.

(4) **Witness examinations**. Set forth the complete direct and cross-examinations for each plaintiff/prosecution and defense witness. Include a list of exhibits that will be introduced for each witness and a summary of the facts you need to elicit from the witness. Add deposition summaries for each witness and any excerpts you plan to introduce with the witness. You may want to create a separate folder or file for each witness.

(5) **Exhibits**. Organize copies of your exhibits by witness. Prepare an exhibit log to keep track of each exhibit as it is admitted or excluded.

EXHIBIT LOG

No.	Description	Foundational Proof	Offered	Admitted
1				
2				
3				
4				

(6) **Closing argument**. The closing argument should be outlined in full before the start of the case. As the case moves forward, you can adapt and change the closing argument right in the notebook, especially if you leave plenty of white space on the page for notes. Include the jury instructions and verdict forms.

(7) **Legal Authority**. Organize the relevant statutes, regulations, and caselaw, along with sufficient copies for the court.

(8) **Jury information**. Include voir dire questions and juror profiles and questionnaires. Prepare a blank chart for keeping track of information gained through voir dire, such as juror number, basic information about the jurors, and the number and type of challenges available and used.

In sum, get organized and stay organized. By attending to details from the start, you will be able to concentrate more fully on the exciting aspects of trial work. No one becomes a litigator because they enjoy managing paper. Yet you will not persuade the judge or jury if you are fumbling for exhibits or forgetting key aspects of your direct examination. Solid managerial skills provide a foundation for the more exciting aspects of trial work.

CHAPTER 10

Technology-Enhanced Trial Practice[1]

Mollie, where are we on the Stanhope case? Are we ready for trial next week?

We're in fairly good shape, Fred. Tammi has completed the discovery database. I've finished our PowerPoint opening and have loaded all the documents and photographs we're offering into evidence into our trial presentation software. We have an appointment for tomorrow to visit the courtroom to ensure that our laptop computers are compatible with the courtroom's display technology.

Oh, that's great. Did I tell you that I've subscribed to the Courtroom Connect courtroom internet access service? We'll be able to have Dr. Archibald's help from Williamsburg when we cross their expert. She'll be in Williamsburg following the realtime court transcript, and we'll be use instant messaging so that she can give us a hand in our cross.

That's great, but what about Smith's testimony?

Well that's apt to be a problem. When he was interviewed they made a full-scale multi-media transcript. Any inconsistency, and we'll hear and see him up on the screen, life-size, spilling his guts along with the scrolling transcript. They burned it to a DVD, and it's loaded on their notebook computer, which, like ours, will be plugged into the display system at the podium.

What about that eye-witness, the one with cancer?

The current word is that she will be able to come to court so no one will be using the courtroom's remote testimony capabilities; we won't have to

---

1. This chapter is based on the experience and research of the Center for Legal and Court Technology, a joint initiative of William & Mary Law School and the National Center for State Courts. *See* www.legaltechcenter.net The authors would like to acknowledge the assistance of Heidi D. Simon, Esquire, CLCT Roger Strand Postgraduate Fellow, and Joelle Lazlo and Steven Johnston, William & Mary Class of 2009, in editing this chapter.

e-file those briefs on the legality of remote testimony. But, I just heard that we may not have a sign language interpreter available. We may have to use the courtroom's videoconferencing for that.[2]

Welcome to the world of technology enhanced trial practice!

I. Introduction — Frequently Asked Questions

1. What Is Technology-Enhanced Trial Practice?

In its most basic form, technology-enhanced (or augmented) trial practice is the use of technology to visually display images to judge and or jury. During trial on the merits counsel display on monitors or large screens images of the evidence. During opening and closing, counsel may also display text slides, portions of the exhibits chosen for emphasis, photographs, and other forms of visual material.

"Evidence presentation technology" includes other options as well, including multi-media depositions and interrogations and powerful software capable of producing time lines and other forms of persuasive explanatory images.

Technology-enhanced trial practice consists of far more than evidence presentation Forms of technology that can be of interest to a trial lawyer include pretrial technology, primarily multimedia depositions and case analysis software, and trial technology, which in addition to evidence presentation includes use of a realtime court record during trial, remote appearance of counsel, judge, or witness via video conferencing, and assistive technology.

2. Why Should I Care about This?

You do want to win, don't you? Although there are only a few controlled scientific studies, the consensus is that *when done properly*, visually displayed evidence is more easily understood and more likely to be remembered than evidence presented solely in the form of testimony. Many people are visual learners who learn better when they both see and hear. This

---

2. Fredric I. Lederer, *Courtroom Technology—Courtroom Technology: For Trial Lawyers the Future Is Now*, ABA Criminal Justice, Spring, 2004 at 14.

may be especially true of today's television and video oriented generations. Technology-enhanced evidence presentation is overwhelmingly visual. Technology is used, for example, to display exhibits while they are being described by a witness. The jury doesn't have to wait until the exhibit is finally given to it. Similarly, argument illustrated by visual material can be more comprehensible and persuasive than traditional argument. If there were two evenly matched lawyers with equal evidence, the technology-enhanced advocate would have a significant advantage.

There is world-wide consensus that technology enhanced trials are much faster than are traditional ones, saving huge amounts of trial time and thus potentially cutting attorney costs for trials (and technology-enabled alternative dispute resolution as well).

An increasing number of judges, especially federal judges, with high-tech courtrooms require counsel to use the supplied courtroom technology. Accordingly, counsel may not have a free choice when it comes to technology. Assistive technology helps those with difficulties seeing, hearing, speaking, and moving. As our population ages, assistive technology will become ever more important to provide meaningful access to justice.

3. Does This Have Anything to Do with Electronic Discovery?

Not directly. Electronic discovery (E-discovery) is the discovery of digital information—documents in their original computer form, for example. E-discovery (and data seizures in criminal cases) is changing the world of litigation as we know it, but strictly speaking e-discovery pertains to pre-trial matters. Note, however, that nearly all of today's documentary evidence originally was produced by computer. Just as counsel now seek to obtain in discovery evidence in "native format" (the computer format in which it was produced complete with the invisible "metadata" describing the date of creation, modification, etc. that customarily accompanies it), counsel ought to present the image of the "document" rather than print out a "hard copy" for physical distribution in court. We are in the midst of a "paradigm shift" that emphasizes the use and display of electronic information instead of viewing printouts of that material.

4. I Won't Be Working for a Huge Firm, How Can I Afford This?

All that counsel needs to be a high-tech trial lawyer is a laptop computer and a projector, and the consent of the judge. You can use the courtroom wall for your screen if need be. In fact, a growing number of courts now provide complete high tech courtrooms. Most lawyers use some form of word processing. Word, WordPerfect, or other programs, can be surprisingly effective at trial. Specialized software may be nice, but it's not likely to be critical.

5. I Plan to Do Poverty Law; Why Should I Care?

Aren't your clients worth the same professional representation we owe other types of clients? Imagine the persuasive impact of a displayed photo of a slumlord's unmaintained and crumbling apartment house in a rent suit.

6. I Don't Plan to Try Jury Trials, So How Does This Affect Me?

Although technology enhanced trial practice is especially effective and efficient in jury cases, it works well in bench trials as well. Many trial judges who serve as fact finders appreciate the clarity that visually presented evidence and argument can provide.

7. How Widespread Is This?

2003 data accumulated by the Federal Judicial Center with the assistance of the Courtroom 21 Project (now the Center for Legal and Court Technology) indicated that about 25% of the nation's federal courtrooms were high tech.[3] We now estimate that the number is close to 33% and growing. Although there are no accurate data for state courts, there are a large number of high-tech state courtrooms, and they include many different types of courts. The nation's highest tech family courtroom, for example, is in Bexar County, Texas.

Although Hollywood seems to be making a major effort to portray courtrooms and hearings in traditional form with little or no technology, the local news increasingly shows high-tech trial practice. From what we can tell, jurors not only accept lawyers using computers, but rather expect

---

3. In 2003, 363 of 1,366 United States district court courtrooms had permanently installed laptop computer wiring and 370 had monitor-type jury displays. ELIZABETH C. WIGGINS, MEGHAN A. DUNN, AND GEORGE CORT, FEDERAL JUDICIAL CENTER SURVEY ON COURTROOM TECHNOLOGY 8 (Federal Judicial Center, Draft edition August, 2003). Today, there are many more high-tech courtrooms as well as many others with cart-based equipment that is brought into the courtroom when necessary.

them to do so. In one sense, this likely is also an offshoot of the "CSI effect," in which people believe (albeit erroneously) that every case has or should have technology-based evidence such as DNA analysis.

8. But I'm Not a Computer Expert!!!!!!

You don't have to be an expert. Basic evidence presentation is *much* easier than programming a VCR. Sophisticated evidence software *does* take expertise. Happily, if you are using high end software likely you *are* an expert or have expert assistance.

9. Are there Any Problems with This?

Of course. Remember the caveat carefully inserted into the answer to FAQ 2 above, "when done properly"? Badly implemented technology-enhanced trial practice is at best confusing and distracting. At worse, you could lose your case. A trial lawyer's incompetence can be made more blatantly obvious when illustrated by technology. In addition, although often overstated, there is an ever-present risk of computer or other technology failures

10. Does This Mean I May Have to Use a Computer at Trial?

Yes!

United States District Court Williamsport, Pennsylvania

In a world in which "FAQ's" are understood and expected by millions, should trial practice remain unchanged from the days of Patrick Henry, Thomas Jefferson, and George Wythe?[4]

The world of trial practice is rapidly evolving into one in which good trial lawyers use technology to help them make their case. Our goal in this chapter is to introduce you to the basics of technology-enhanced trial practice. We have included enough detail and illustrations so that with some practice you should be able to do a creditable job in court if you choose to use technology, or are instructed to do so by the court. Please keep in mind that reading a book is not the same as acquiring skills. Just as reading the chapters on direct and cross alone won't make you a skilled examiner of witnesses, this material won't turn you instantly into a highly competent high-tech trial lawyer.[5] But, it can be a start. Even the simplest eviction case can potentially benefit from technology.

Fairfax, Virginia's Courtroom 5E

---

4. George Wythe, the nation's first law professor, a signer of the declaration of independence, and one of the era's best known lawyers and legal statesmen was a giant of his age. Unfortunately, history has not been kind to him and he is relatively unknown outside of William & Mary Law School, which he effectively began as a result of Jefferson's actions to create university based legal instruction.

5. You may wish to seek out specialized training such as the certification courses offered by the Center for Legal and Court Technology. *See* www.legaltechcenter.net.

One of the reasons why judges like high-tech trials is that they are *fast*. Counsel no longer walk around the courtroom to show exhibits to the participants, and judges increasingly prevent lawyers from reading or having witnesses read key parts of evidentiary exhibits. Technology-enhanced trial practice uses the same rules as traditional practice, but is different in important ways that are hard to describe. Try to watch a high-tech trial before appearing in one of your own. Always keep in mind that technology changes the nature of the modern trial. It is faster (affecting lawyer stress), far more visual, and emphasizes direct fact-finder involvement with the evidence.

II. Pretrial Technologies

Perhaps the most important thing to consider when thinking about pretrial technologies is the frightening reality that the case might actually go to trial. Because most cases settle before trial, some litigators assume that their case will settle rather than go to trial. As a result, in the days before legal software became multi-faceted, some lawyers invested large amounts of time and money in pretrial discovery and case analysis using specialized software that did not lend itself to trial use. Faced with trial, they needed very expensive data conversion services to prepare their evidence for use and presentation at trial. Always assume that every case may actually go to court and plan accordingly.

Pretrial technologies can be classified substantially as fitting into three primary (and sometimes overlapping) categories:

Information collection
Information analysis and organization
Case preparation for trial

It is not enough just to collect the facts and documents of a case. The raw information must be analyzed to understand how it all fits together and how it can best be presented at trial in accord with the rules of evidence.

By "case preparation," I mean preparing your information for actual use at trial. Major programs such as Concordance and Summation can be especially important for information analysis although they lend themselves to case preparation as well. Let me suggest two other possibilities as being particularly useful: electronic deposition (or interrogation) transcripts and the seemingly ever more powerful CaseMap program suite.

A. Multi-Media Depositions

Depositions are the lifeblood of civil practice. Not only are they crucial for discovery, they can be very important when used on the merits in lieu of a live witness or for impeachment. Although depositions are improbable in most criminal cases except to preserve testimony of witnesses who are not expected to be able to attend trial, they do exist, and some states such as Florida use criminal case depositions extensively.

Effective trial use requires that you can find what you need from a deposition when you need it. When a deposition is taken by a court reporter, that reporter should supply you with an electronic copy of the transcript, one which can be electronically searched like any word processing document. At trial, if all else fails, you have a good chance of finding what you need quickly if you can search the transcript—even if you failed to anticipate in advance what you might need or how best to subdivide the transcript.

At the same time, use of that deposition at trial can be much more persuasive if the judge or jury can actually see or hear the witness in open court. Making a video recording of the deposition will permit you to actually show the testimony, complete with any evasive voice tones and the like. In addition, a court reporting firm or a specialty vendor can synchronize the video to the text transcript and produce what we call a multi-media deposition. Usually played from a CD/ DVD or your computer's hard disk, this permits you to play the audio and video of the witness as well as to scroll the text transcript below or to the side. Please note that while many lawyers consider this to be incredibly powerful, others find it distracting. On balance, we'll opt for especially persuasive.

Note that police interrogations can be presented in court in the same way as depositions. Of course, unless you're a prosecutor you likely will have no input into how the police choose to record a statement given by your client or by another witness.

Although multi-media depositions and statements with synchronized audio/video and text can be created by lawyers using programs such as Trial Director, this is a specialized area best done by an expert. Many court reporting firms can do this for you.

B. Analysis Software

It has only been relatively recently that powerful case analysis software has become simple enough for the average lawyer to use. Although there are many possible software packages available, Lexis/Nexis CaseMap is especially easy to use, and it now has trial presentation possibilities. CaseMap permits you to divide your case data into a database structured by legal issues, facts, witnesses, documentary and other evidence, and other categories counsel may wish and then link all of that information.

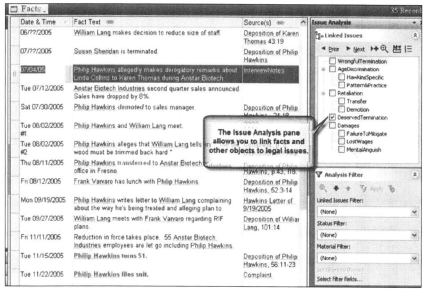

Sample Lexis/Nexis CaseMap screenshot using its sample case

Basically CaseMap is a case database which allows you to see how information is related to critical events and legal issues. The CaseMap suite includes TimeMap, a powerful program that allows you to easily create time lines showing facts, witnesses and evidence that can be displayed during trial.

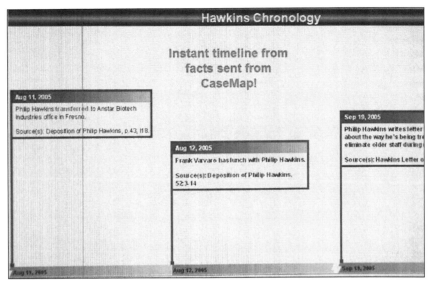

CaseMap chronology

III. Trial Technologies

There are many potentially useful trial technologies. We will concentrate on technology-enhanced evidence presentation, ordinarily the most important, but also briefly deal with trial use of the court record, remote appearances, and assistive technology. In all cases, before trial counsel should carefully plan for the use of technology. Ask yourself:

- What are your goals, objectives, and needs?
- Given what you have or what you can afford to rent, what technological options are available?
- To what extent are you competent and comfortable with your realistic technological options?

Then decide what trial technologies you will use.

A. Evidence Presentation

In technology-enhanced evidence presentation, counsel displays images to judge and jury. As a result, the fact finder is able to see the exhibit immediately after it is received in evidence rather than having to wait while a witness describes the exhibit with counsel later handing it up to judge or jury.[6] Customarily, the witness, judge and counsel will see the exhibit on 15 inch or larger monitors at their positions. Jurors are likely to see them either in similar monitors, usually with one monitor allocated to every two jurors, or on a large screen, or both.

The primary way of showing images at trial is via a document camera, a white board, VCR/CD/DVD player, or by computer.

1. Document Cameras

A document camera is a vertically mounted video camera that when connected to a monitor or projector shows images of anything placed under the camera, customarily documents, photographs, and physical objects. Often known as "Elmos," these cameras are marketed by a wide variety of companies including WolfVision, Samsung, Sony, and ELMO. All such cameras have a zoom feature that allows counsel to zoom in and emphasize key portions of the material being shown. Document cameras are the most basic form of technology-enabled evidence presentation. They are used primarily by lawyers who wish to try a traditional case using paper evidence but who wish to display images of the paper during direct and cross (as well as opening and closing) and highlight key portions.

Counsel can annotate the physical documents with markers and the like. When document cameras are used in a high-tech courtroom, counsel often can annotate the image, rather than the paper, by using a touchscreen monitor with an annotation feature. In high-tech courtrooms, counsel normally use computers, reserving document cameras for last minute evidence not yet in digital form or for back-up in case there's a problem with the computer.

---

6. The necessary procedure for laying a foundation using evidence presentation technology is set forth at [page 13], *infra*.

CLCT's Chris Taranto demonstrates a WolfVision Visualizer.

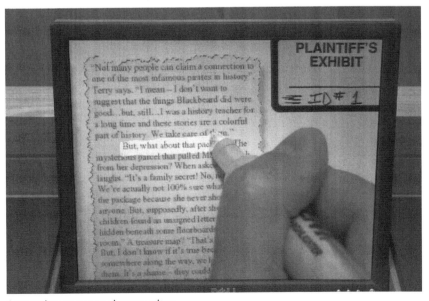

Annotation as seen on jury monitor.

2. White Boards

White boards are portable or permanently mounted boards on which counsel or witnesses can write. Traditional whiteboards are useful for quick pieces of text (often used during closing) and for drawing diagrams such as street intersections and having witnesses mark the location of events such as where defendant's automobile entered the intersection. Modern whiteboards, however, can work in accord with computers so that a computer image can be displayed on the board and then annotated by the witness (or counsel). The white board image is displayed to the fact finder. "Whiteboards" can be actual white boards, rear projection monitors, or flat screen displays.

Witness annotates an exhibit on a portable 3M Wall Display

3. Audio/Video Playback

Given how easy and inexpensive it is to use a camcorder, counsel increasingly seem to be playing recorded audio/video back in court. Many courtrooms have equipment able to play video tape, CDs, DVDs, and sometimes forms of flash memory in the courtroom. Never assume that the equipment is there. If you think you may need it, check with the court's courtroom technologist.

4. Notebook Computers

Notebook computers are the most frequent way for counsel to present images at trial. Potential images consist of case documents obtained in their original electronic form or from scanning paper documents, photographs (increasingly from digital cameras), or images created by computer such as PowerPoint slides, Excel spreadsheets, or images with annotations.

When counsel need to show images in a traditional courtroom, the easiest way is to get the judge's permission and then use a small but bright projector. Using a portable screen or even a wall, counsel can then connect the computer to the projector and show large images. Remember to get audio speakers if you need sound as well. Previously prepared multi-media depositions will need audio and video.

In a high-tech courtroom, counsel will connect the computer to the courtroom video distribution system. Notebook computers are designed so that they can be used with an external display; the user connects the computer to the display with a cable. In a high-tech courtroom the lawyer does the same thing except that instead of a single display, the cable goes from the computer to the courtroom display system. Counsel MUST know how to set the computer to display its content through the courtroom display system. The appendix at the end of this chapter includes detailed instructions on how to do this as well as how to avoid unpleasant surprises such as having your computer go sleep in the middle of your direct examination because it is trying to save power.

Depending upon the courtroom and the judge, counsel may need to use the computer at a centralized podium or lectern or may present from counsel table, either personally or with another person running the computer. Litigation support vendors can be hired for this purpose; sometimes they may be permitted to install a control station elsewhere in the courtroom.

Computer-based evidence display is the "killer application" of courtroom technology. Use of a high-end software package such as Sanction or TrialDirector will allow counsel incredible flexibility to present evidence in whatever sequence may be desired with the ability to provide instant annotation, markup, or "call-out," an enlargement of key text that is created in front of the fact finder.

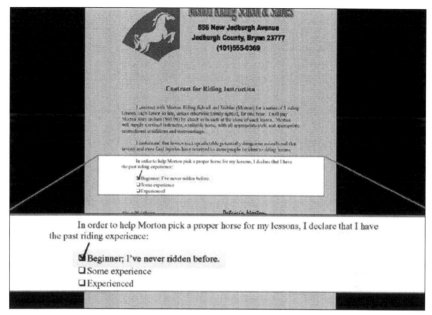

An annotated call-out of a contract provision using Trial Director (Courtesy InData Inc. and CLCT).

A word of caution is appropriate. There are two problems with call-outs. If nothing else, too many or unnecessary call-outs can prove distracting to jurors. In addition, experimental work conducted by the Center for Legal and Court Technology has shown that many jurors become distrustful of counsel who too rapidly create call-outs and in the process obscure the underlying document. Jurors think that counsel are purposely hiding adverse evidence. Either be sure that the jurors can read the underlying document in full before doing a call-out or ask the judge to advise the jurors that counsel will use call-outs to emphasize key points but that the jurors will be able to read the exhibits in full during deliberations (if that is court practice).

Evidence that is annotated during trial can be preserved for the appellate record either by printing out the annotated evidence or, provided that the court or counsel has the capability, capturing it electronically for later printing.

5. The Court Record at Trial

Trial lawyers who try cases in courtrooms with court reporters have invaluable options unavailable with different approaches to making the court record. In a traditional trial, counsel may be able to get expedited (usually "daily") copy of the transcript to assist in preparation for later direct and cross, closing argument, and in jury cases, preparation of jury instructions. Today, many court reporters can provide "realtime" transcription, an electronic feed of the draft transcript supplied directly to counsel's computer. With appropriate software, counsel can code the transcript so that key testimony can be recalled instantly. With an internet connection in the courtroom, the transcript, sometimes with streaming audio and video, can be sent back to counsel's office or even to a remote expert. Remote staff or experts can communicate with counsel by instant messaging.

Courts that use electronic recording for the court record may be able to provide counsel with the day's proceedings in audio or audio/video format. Although the court may have text annotations to assist the court in finding material, these may not be available to counsel. Searching the disk to find key terms uttered by a witness, for example, is possible but likely to require specialized and expensive software.

6. Remote Appearances

Faced with a witness who is too ill to come to court or whose travel is too expensive to support, you may be able to use two-way videoconferencing. An ever-increasing number of courtrooms now have commercial standard video-conferencing, often with the remote witness appearing in a large flat-screen display immediately behind the witness stand. Ideally, the witness would originate from another courtroom. However, companies such as Kinkos and Courtroom Connect supply video conferencing on a per session commercial basis. Ordinarily video conferencing for remote testimony works very well. Just remember that as there is a small transmission lag, and you cannot easily interrupt a witness.

It is quite possible that your court may soon permit remote motion practice. Already possible by telephone, soon inexpensive webcams attached to office computers ought to permit remote motion practice with each participant able to see and hear all the others, with a master version displayed in the courtroom.

7. Assistive Technology

A significant number of Americans have or will have difficulties seeing, hearing, speaking, or moving. Technology permits us to assist members of the community with special needs. Deaf or hard-of-hearing witnesses who use American sign language, for example, may be able to use a remote interpreter should a local expert be unavailable. Blind participants can use special scanners and computers to read documents to them. The topic is too large for this brief chapter, but please keep in mind that if you, a client, a witness, juror or judge has special needs technology may be able to assist. Check with the Center for Legal and Court Technology, www.legaltechcenter.net, for specifics.

IV. A Note on Jury Voir Dire

When selecting jurors, counsel often have to advise potential panel members of the parties and witnesses. Consider showing potential jurors pictures rather than just mentioning names. Occasionally jurors do know witnesses and parties but simply do not remember their names. If nothing else, using a document camera or computer to display their pictures is a good way of introducing future witnesses to the jury.

V. Presenting Evidence—Law and Practice

Let us assume that you have decided to use electronic evidence presentation. You have loaded your evidence into your computer in the form of electronic images,[7] and you know how to display them. They key question now is how to show them while complying with the rules of evidence and courtroom practice. Happily, this is not difficult. Let's deal with the mechanics first, assuming that your case has not been pretried with all evidentiary matters having been resolved.

A. How to Properly Present Electronic Evidence

The key to the electronic presentation of evidence is to remember that evidence normally will not be made available to the jury ("published") until admitted. Assuming that an exhibit has been marked previously, this creates three steps in the ordinary process:

---

7. Remember, however, that a juror viewing an electronic picture of a gun has a very different experience from one holding the gun in the hand, complete with its solid feel, weight, and danger. Sometimes traditional practice can be more powerful than just using a displayed image.

1. Show the exhibit to opposing counsel (and judge)
2. Lay an appropriate evidentiary foundation and then offer the exhibit into evidence
3. In a jury trial, ask the judge's permission to give it to the jury ("publish" the exhibit)

Technology-enhanced trial practice substitutes displaying the exhibit for physically handing it to others. Electronic display requires first that counsel ask the judge's permission to display the exhibit to the appropriate person or people and that the display then be implemented. Depending upon the courtroom and judge, the actual display of the exhibit may be implemented by counsel pushing the proper spot on a touch screen control panel or by the courtroom technologist (deputy clerk) or other person handling the switching.

The following is a representative procedure for authenticating, offering, and publishing electronic images:[8]

> Q: *You have referred to a {contract, letter, diary entry.... } Would you be able to identify it again if you were to see it again?*
>
> A: Yes
>
> Q: *How?*
>
> A: I would recognize {my handwriting, the handwriting, the paper because of the ink stain and tear on the paper}.
>
> Counsel: 1) Counsel asks the judge to have the clerk display Exhibit *** for Identification to the court and opposing counsel;
>
> 2) Counsel asks the judge to have the clerk display Exhibit *** for Identification to the witness;
>
> Q: *Let the record reflect that I am showing Exhibit *** for Identification to the witness. [Name of witness] what is Exhibit *** for Identification?*
>
> A: It's the {contract, letter, etc.}
>
> Q: *How do you know?*
>
> A: [I recognize the handwriting, the paper because of the ink stain, the marks on the paper, etc.}
>
> Counsel: Your Honor, I offer {Plaintiff, Prosecution, Defense} Exhibit *** for Identification in evidence as {Plaintiff, Prosecution, Defense} Exhibit *** .

---

8. FREDRIC I. LEDERER, TRIAL PRACTICE IN A TECHNOLOGICAL World § 11-32.10 (William & Mary law School 2007).

Judge: [To opposing counsel] Any objection?

Opposing counsel: Either, "no," or statement of objection. If opposing counsel objects, the judge will hear argument on the admissibility from both parties. Assuming that the judge rules that the exhibit is admissible:

Judge: {Plaintiff, Prosecution, Defense} Exhibit *** for Identification is received in evidence as {Plaintiff, Prosecution, Defense} Exhibit ***.

Counsel: Your honor, would you please have the clerk display the exhibit to the jury.

Counsel should then proceed with questions about the document.

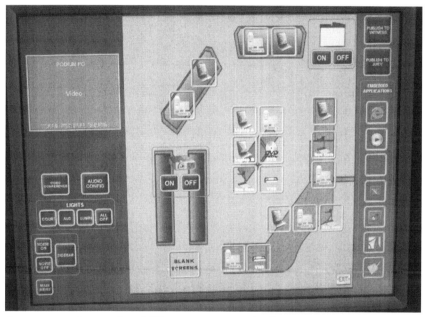

Crestron control screen from William & Mary Law School's McGlothlin Courtroom. Note "Publish to Witness" and "Publish to Jury": buttons in the upper right.

Many courtrooms are designed so that any image on counsel's computer is automatically displayed to the opposing counsel and the judge, unless counsel has prohibited the computer from sending the image to an external display. The courtroom switching system, usually controlled by a touchscreen control panel, must be used to display the image to the witness and when appropriate to the jury. Critically, if the switching system isn't used to "publish" the exhibit to the jurors they won't see it in front of them. Experience suggests that a surprisingly large number of lawyers forget that special action is necessary to publish the exhibit to the jury.

Evolving court practice has every major annotation of an electronic document treated as a separate exhibit. If a contract is plaintiff's exhibit one, the image of the contract with the defendant's name circled in red electronically may be 1A and the image with the key provision called out and enlarged in a box may be 1B.

B. The Impact of the Rules of Evidence[9]

Initially, it is useful to distinguish between evidence that is only presented or shown electronically and evidence which is itself electronic in nature or which has been converted into electronic format. Likely the simplest example of electronically presented evidence is a photograph which is displayed at trial via a document camera.... .

Having laid whatever foundation may be necessary to establish logical relevance, counsel would place the photograph on the horizontal stand of the document camera. The image would then be available to judge, witness, and opposing counsel. Counsel would then ask the witness to identify the photograph. Authentication would proceed and, assuming compliance with other applicable rules, the photograph would be offered and admitted. In this example the underlying evidence is non-electronic in nature. If the actual photograph is tendered to the fact-finder, the electronic image can be treated as the equivalent of a photocopy, used solely for convenience. This presents no evidentiary issues if the underlying admissibility of the photograph has already been established. But, if the image is what is used to establish admissibility, what is actually being offered is not the original photograph but the electronic duplicate image, in which case the witness, counsel, judge, and in a jury trial, the jury, may never see the original photograph. Instead all will view and act upon an electronic image. Is a best evidence challenge avail-

---

9. This material is taken from FREDRIC I. LEDERER, TRIAL PRACTICE IN A TECHNOLOGICAL World § 11-40.00 et seq (William & Mary law School 2007) with minor editing; most footnotes have been omitted.

able? In these circumstances, the image functions as electronically produced evidence.

Electronically produced evidence can be defined as that evidence which originates as digital material or which is, regardless of origin, produced in court solely as digital material. Perhaps the best examples are digital photographs and digital audio and video recordings.

The Best Evidence Rule, Federal Rule of Evidence 1002, ordinarily requires that, "To prove the content of a writing, recording, or photograph, the original ... is required...." Under Federal Rule of Evidence 1001(4), an electronic image of our photograph, for example, would seem to be a duplicate and under Federal Rule of Evidence 1003 ordinarily admissible to the same extent as the original; in some cases the image may even be defined by Rule 1001 as an "original."[10]

The definition of "duplicate" must be reconsidered, however, before accepting the admissibility of the image in lieu of the original physical image. Electronic visual images of original non-digital evidence nearly always differ in some particulars from the "hard-copy" originals. Current technology is such that even if a totally accurate image of the original is made or captured, the displayed image will differ in color and resolution. Except in the most extraordinary installation, it is almost certain that the same photograph, for example, displayed on two or more TV's or monitors, will have at least subtle color balance, shading, and/or brightness differences as each TV or monitor reproduces the image differently. Small markings on the original, including physical creasing and the like, may be difficult or impossible to detect in an electronic image. Can the resulting multiple differing reproductions be termed "duplicates?" This was the attack mounted by the defense in the Unabomber case when the defense moved to prohibit the prosecution from displaying the defendant's numerous writings electronically.[11]

10. If the image is produced from "data stored in a computer or similar device, any printout or other output readable by sight, shown to reflect the data accurately, is an original." FED. R. EVID. 1001(3). In the computer scenario, all data printouts are identical. In the case of the document camera, the process is closer to a photographic enlargement or reproduction and thus more likely a "duplicate."

11. United States v. Kaczynski, 1997 WL 567038 (E.D. Cal.) (CR-5-96-259GEB). The defense challenge was unsuccessful.

Federal Rule of Rule 1001(c)&(d) requires "accurate" reproduction. Federal Rule of Evidence 1003(2) permits admission of "duplicates" unless "it would be unfair to admit the duplicate in lieu of the original." A black letter rule analysis unavoidably yields the conclusion that in one sense the image and the original are not identical. Yet, even the quickest examination of the intent of the Rules yields a ruling in support of the images. In the Unabomber prosecution, had the case not been resolved by plea the government would have offered the images solely for the textual content of Defendant's writings. The color and condition of the originals would have been irrelevant. Under these circumstances the electronic image would be a true duplicate, just as a black and white photocopy would be, which is already usually considered a duplicate under Rule 1001(4). Insofar as the reason for which the evidence is offered, the image is an accurate copy of the original. Accordingly, unless the differences in electronic display and reproduction are logically relevant, any differences from the original are of no evidentiary consequence.

Document camera presented evidence is customary in at least hundreds of American courtrooms. What is less frequent but of increasing importance, especially in major cases, is scanned or imaged documentary evidence. To scan a document, photograph, or the like, one places the original on or in a scanner. The scanner in effect takes an electronic picture of the original using a process similar to that used for photocopying. The resolution and color validity of the electronic image primarily depend upon the quality of the scanner and the way in which the electronic image is recorded. Scans can be imperfect, primarily for physical reasons such as improper feeding of the original into the scanner.

Computer scanning should be distinguished from optical character recognition (OCR). When one "OCR's" a document, one instructs a computer to use special software to review a scanned document and convert the image of the document into computer recognizable text for purposes such as lawyer searching of the document. Optical character recognition is almost never perfect, and inaccurate word conversions are customary, requiring human proofing if perfect accuracy is required. In courtroom evidentiary presentation, however, it is only the electronic images that are presented in evidence. OCR versions of the documents may be used by counsel to help determine which images to offer, but it is only the images that are offered. Accordingly, offering of scanned images preserved on, for example, a CD-ROM disk, is functionally identical with use of the document camera—unless there is reason to suspect an inaccurate copying of the original. The proponent must authenticate the image and qualify it as a duplicate. Whether authentication should mean something more than our traditional methods is another matter.

There are often questions concerning the courtroom validity of digital information, given the ease with which such information can be seamlessly altered. There are methods which can at least diminish the chances of such alteration, but that is to fail to address the central issue. Suppose a witness is shown a photograph. Traditional authentication requirements will be served when under Federal Rule of Evidence 901(b)(2) the witness identifies the image as accurate—testimony of a witness with knowledge will suffice. Suppose, however, that the image is a digital one, displayed perhaps by computer; should the same result apply? To the degree that we consult Federal Rule of Evidence 901, or its common law equivalent, the answer is clearly yes. But, it has been suggested that the combination of technology and human perceptual limits could dictate a different result.

The argument goes thusly: when a person looks at an image, the person does not and perhaps cannot verify all components of the image. Instead, the person confirms some of the components. That serves to authenticate the entire image, as it is unlikely that part of a photograph could be accurate and part inaccurate, and photographic tampering could be detected. The digital critic then points out that any aspect of the digital image can be altered electronically, potentially without telltale signs of alteration. This perspective questions witness authentication of many digital images; although the witness has identified one part of the image as accurate, that tells us nothing about the remainder.

Yet, what of a traditional photograph—are the two image technologies really so very different? Photographs can be altered. Concededly, such alterations may be easier to detect. If the digital critic's assertion that the witness only verifies part of an image is correct, that is a distinction without a meaningful difference as the witness could be fooled by either technology. The critical distinction comes into play only if there is a reason to question the image and refer it for expert analysis and the expert can detect photographic alterations but not digital ones.

Given the nature of the adversary system, our evidentiary rules actually are rather undemanding. Admissibility rules such as authentication are easily satisfied, leaving it to the parties to deal with evidentiary sufficiency. American courts have dealt with real and alleged forged evidence since the beginning of the nation. In the absence of modern scientific techniques, parchment documents skillfully forged with quill pens presented formidable questions of detection and proof. Isn't the current ability to digitally alter or fabricate evidence the same problem—or is it?

Both common law and Federal Rule of Evidence 403 permit otherwise admissible evidence to be excluded when the evidence gives rise to an unreasonable risk of unfair prejudice. Electronically presented and produced evidence may present such a risk. High production quality animations in particular may convey to some jurors greater probative value than may be justified by the actual content. At the same time, the closer an animation may be to reality (i.e. a videotaped reenactment), the higher the risk that the fact-finder might subliminally interpret the animation as objective fact. Certainly a judicial instruction might cure any risk in all but the most realistic animations, and likely this risk would be less if a fact-finder were faced at trial with conflicting or dueling animations. Ironically, if production quality raises an unfair prejudice risk, in some cases proponents might be better served by foregoing any efforts at Hollywood glitz.

Note that the above discussion deals with the average case. It does not apply, for example, to an attempt to offer into evidence an electronic document complete with its "metadata." Metadata can be defined as data about data. It includes all the information that is recorded by a computer about a document including its size, when it was made and altered, and much more. Because a normal witness cannot authenticate the metadata of an exhibit just by looking at it, expert testimony likely will be necessary to authenticate an electronic document that is offered with its metadata. At the same time, the jurisdiction may have special rules for computer produced evidence. Maryland, for example, led the United States in its adoption of a special rule for such evidence,[12] which largely requires early notice to the court and opposing counsel of the intent to use such evidence as well as supplying opposing counsel with a copy of the evidence.

---

12. MD. R. CIV. P. 2-504.3, Computer Generated Evidence and Material.

VI. Openings and Closings

Openings and closings are clearly different in function; the opening introduces the case while the closing summarizes the evidence in argumentative fashion. Both, however, lead themselves to the potential use of technology.

Lawyers have used demonstrative exhibits in openings and closings for generations.[13] "Boards" containing diagrams, charts, photographs, and text are a trial lawyer's standard. Technology permits the use of inexpensive computerized graphics, including PowerPoint slide shows. The critical question is whether computer-based images will be helpful to your case. The cliche that "Pictures are worth a thousand words" is often but not always true. Use graphics sparingly—enough to make your point and to keep your fact finder interested. Ordinarily avoid sound effects and be very careful in your use of pictures and slide transitions. A trial is not and should not be a PowerPoint presentation!!!!!! PowerPoint is, however, a useful tool to make key points.

For openings, graphics can assist in communicating your case theory as well as to introduce key people, documents, and concepts. Remember, however, that openings may not be argumentative. Further, openings cannot use facts that will not be introduced into evidence or reasonably inferred from the evidence. Be cautious! In a personal injury case, however, if permissible, a photograph of the severely damaged automobile may be a useful part of the opening. Keep in mind, however, that some courts require that all images to be used at opening must be served on both opposing counsel and the judge in advance—in order to avoid unnecessary mistrial motions. Even if this rule seems to have applied only to traditional trials, assume it applies to high tech evidence images as well.

PowerPoint: The case of the negligent waiter

---

13. Courts often are concerned about the use of visual graphics during opening statement for fear that a mistrial may be necessary if the evidence referred to in openings is not successfully introduced at trial on the merits.

Closing arguments are by definition argumentative. You are both summing up and trying to persuade. Graphics can be very useful at this point, especially inasmuch as you are allowed to draw reasonable inferences from the evidence introduced. You can review the evidence complete with your annotations circling key text in documents, show time lines, argue logical causation via diagrams, and use both simple and sophisticated graphics to argue your theory of the case.

If you use text slides via PowerPoint or other programs, ordinarily keep them simple! A few words on a slide are far better than a text-filled slide that jurors must try to read while you argue. During trial, the evidence is key. During closing, your argument is key—the graphics complement it but ordinarily don't substitute for it. Then again, sometimes a picture, even a complicated one, *is* worth a thousand words.

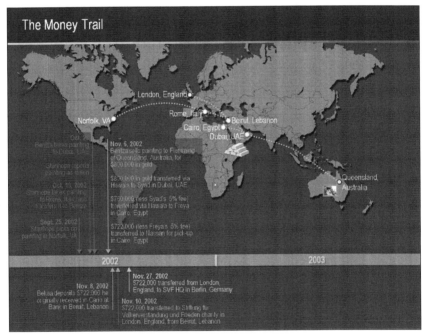

Sophisticated PowerPoint slide created by FTI Consulting for United States v. Stanhope, a courtroom 21 (CLCT) Laboratory Trial to illustrate a forensic expert's testimony and for closing argument.

VII. Jury Implications

Anecdotal evidence and the experimental experience of the Center for Legal and Court Technology support the proposition that today's jurors find nothing unusual about technology-enhanced trial practice. Indeed some jurors have expressed surprise that not all cases are high-tech. We seem to have come a great distance from the days in which lawyers worried that showing up in a rural jurisdiction with a computer and projector would make counsel look like distrusted alien "city slickers."

You should keep in mind, however, that jurors are complicated people. Many lawyers have had occasion to talk with jurors informally post trial, and it is always interesting to learn how they reacted to various exhibits or to counsel's efforts. Unfortunately, psychologists learned long ago that what jurors tell you is not necessarily how they actually reacted at trial. Worse, jurors can communicate honestly how they thought they were affected by some form of trial practice only to be wrong. This is counterintuitive, of course. Surely a juror can tell you what worked. In fact, data sometimes support the proposition that jurors reacted to various forms of evidence in ways totally at variance to what they believe. In short, be careful of accepting at face value what jurors tell you they liked or found successful in your first high-tech trials.

Many high tech courtrooms have jury display monitors installed at or below the rail of the jury box. That can present counsel with a strange feeling. You're making a brilliant argument complete with great graphics but the jurors aren't looking at you. Instead, they're looking at your graphics and all that you see are their foreheads. Relax; that's how it's going to be. You must be doing a good job or they wouldn't be concentrating on your material.

One of the real problems with technology-enhanced trials is how the jurors will review the evidence during deliberations. At present, most jurors will review evidence in the jury room with paper copies of what they were shown electronically in the courtroom. Sometimes, as when video material was displayed, they may ask for a replay and be brought back to the courtroom for it. Some years ago, the Center for Legal and Court Technology conducted a year's worth of empirical research to determine how to use technology in jury deliberations. It is not especially difficult to do so, and you should expect that to become more customary as the years go by. Until your jury can electronically review admitted evidence, keep in mind that what you show in the courtroom may not be fully reviewable during deliberations.

Appendix

How to Avoid Apparent Disaster When Using a
Notebook Computer at Trial
or
What You Need to Know To Connect and Use Your Computer Without
Needless Stress and Panic
FREDRIC I. LEDERER, TRIAL PRACTICE IN A TECHNOLOGICAL WORLD
Appendix B (William & Mary Law School 2007)

I. Introduction

Unlike some software, notebook computers themselves are fairly simple to operate. Notwithstanding this fact, they have a number of features and characteristics that can lead an otherwise highly competent and prepared trial lawyer to believe that he or she is in the midst of catastrophic computer failure during trial. The material that follows is designed to assist you in avoiding this unenviable fate.

A. Pretrial Preparation

Before trial, do the following:

1) Turn off all screen savers (your computer doesn't really need them and if it does this isn't the time for one anyway);
2) Make sure that any wallpaper you have on your desktop can be seen by judge and jury. If you would be embarrassed to have your mother see it, change it! Remember that what you think is cute may carry a different meaning to others. And, there is NO way you can be certain no one else will see your desktop, even if you're not presenting evidence from it.
3) Remove all icons that hurt your image. This is not the time for the judge and jury to learn that you, or your children, play *Grand Theft Auto*.
4) Ensure that your computer operations will not be interrupted by operating system upgrades, anti-virus checks, spyware audits, software registration reminders and the like. Pragmatically, this probably means making sure that your computer is not connected to the Internet during trial, unless you'll need it for communications to outside the courtroom. If you have built-in wireless, that can be temporarily turned off.

5) *TURN OFF ALL power management*. This is critical. Computers are designed to save power, especially laptop/notebook computers that often run on battery power. If you do not alter your power management settings to turn the feature off, your computer likely will go into hibernation and suspension during trial as the system is often set to turn of after anywhere from

Turning off Power Management—Settings

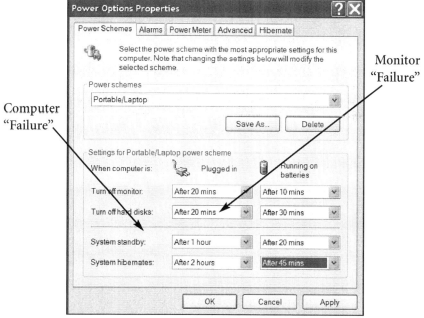

Critical Settings to prevent technical problems that appear to be "failures"

a few minutes to a half hour without being touched. Although it is not difficult to revive the system, it can take a while and throw off your entire timing. You can also wind up feeling embarrassed in front of judge and jury as well as stressed. In Windows XP or Vista, go to the Control Panel, click on Power Options, and then set your components to never turn off (to save power), as shown in the following XP screen shots (in Vista, select Presentation and ensure that the settings for turning off the display and for the computer "to go to sleep" are "Never").

B. Preferred Settings (Hard Disk Setting Is Optional)

C. Connecting the Computer for Trial

You will either be connecting to a court supplied display or display system or bringing your own and connecting to it. In either case you need to know in advance whether your computer will work with (be compatible with) the display mechanism. No matter how assured the court or firm technical experts are, there is no substitute for trying your computer out with the actual display hardware before you need to use it and when you have enough time to take corrective action.

Plug the computer into a local power outlet. Then, ordinarily you will connect a male-to-male monitor cable from the display mechanism to the computer. If you are bringing your own portable equipment, make sure you have brought monitor extension cables, power strips, and extension cords.

Notebook computers must be instructed to send a video signal out of the computer. On many, but not all, this means pressing the function (fn) key at the same time as another, often the F8 key as illustrated below. Most computers cycle among: notebook display only, external display only, both displays. We usually describe selecting the video mode as "toggling" the computer.

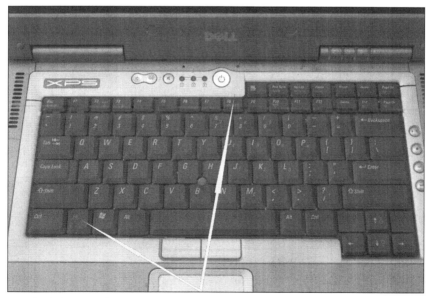

Press both the Fn and F8 keys on this Dell laptop to "toggle" the video modes.

D. Critical Note—Playing Video

Absent adjusting video card acceleration settings, some notebook computers, especially older models, may not be able to putput moving video to an external display when using windows media player, see http://www.microsoft.com/windows/windowsmedia/knowledgecenter/mediaadvice/0063.mspx, unless the computer is set only to external display. In other words, If you don't do this, your computer screen may show the video, but the judge and jury will see nothing. But, if you do toggle the system to display only on the external display system, you will have to use that system to control your own computer. Also note that if you have embedded video in PowerPoint and plan to display it by clicking on the image in PowerPoint, the computer may shift resolution on the fly. This shift may result in the external system either being unable to handle the video output or in taking an appreciable time in order to adjust to the new resolution settings. This may manifest after you play the video, making it hard for you to return immediately to PowerPoint.

E. Troubleshooting Image Display

If after connecting the computer and verifying that it is on and displaying on its own monitor it does not appear to be displaying on the external projector or courtroom system, proceed with the following checklist:

1. Verify that it is actually connected with a monitor cable to the display mechanism! Even experienced high-tech lawyers in the stress of trial have done all the hard stuff and forgotten to connect the computer. Is the cable connected at the other *end*? Is the display turned on, switched to your input and not "muted"?
2. Verify that you have toggled the computer!!!!
3. If you are connecting directly to a projector, especially one you have rented, consider whether there is a given startup sequence necessary. Some projectors require that the projector be started before (or after) the computer is connected.
4. Check to see if you have a resolution mis-match. "Resolution" usually defines the degree of detail displayed by the computer. Higher resolution gives a cleaner and more detailed image as well as potentially more information on the screen. Computer video is usually described as super vga (800x600 pixels); xga (1024x768), and then varying terms like ultra for higher resolution. Modern displays should be able to handle at least xga (1024x768) but

some projectors cannot handle that resolution. More importantly, many new notebooks have substantially higher resolutions than xga, and the display system may not be able to handle that. The usual tip off to this is a message on the display to the effect that the "signal is out of range." You could also check the instruction manual for the display system. If you think you have a resolution problem, lower your resolution through the control panel's display settings as shown below (In Vista, go to "Personalize—showing a monitor display—and then select "Display settings." Then proceed as follows.).

Display Icon

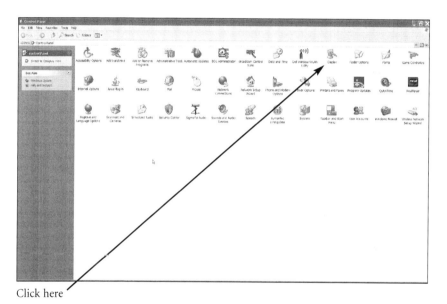

Click here

Click on Settings...

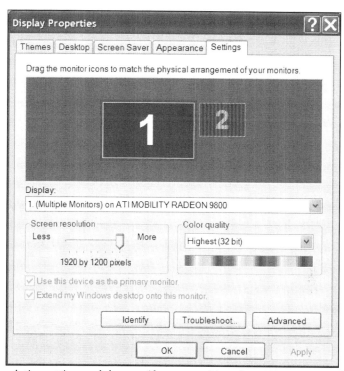

Check resolution settings and decrease if necessary. More than 1024 × 768 may be problematic.

5. If everything else checks out, and you have lowered your resolution to the lowest available in your computer (sometimes lower than 800x600), there is a small possibility that you have a frequency mis-match. That would mean that the display device cannot handle the electronic signal that your computer is sending. If that is the case, you ought not to try to adjust the frequency yourself unless you are a highly experienced computer user.

There are of course other possibilities. These include:

1. The cable isn't attached to or is loose at the display device, or the display device is video muted or, more likely, is switched to a different video input;
2. The display has a hardware problem;
3. *The monitor cable is bad.* This is a real possibility, especially if you have never used the cable before, or it has been hurt in shipping or travel.
4. If it is a high-tech courtroom, the system may have a more sophisticated problem, such as a switching difficulty, which can only be resolved by the court staff.

Note that these instructions are almost entirely oriented towards the computer user and not the court. The court system is rarely at fault. There is a realistic possibility that it is, but it's improbable. Of course, if connected to a court system, you won't be able to see anything if your computer hasn't been selected by the court control system as the display source, but we have assumed that you verified that early on.

If you are in a high-tech courtroom, the court technologist may be available to assist, but that is not the court's responsibility.

When having a problem, counsel are frequently stressed and desperate. Often someone will volunteer help. Remember that the volunteer may be helpful but may also complicate the problem. Sometimes both can be true. Watch what your technical volunteer (even the court technologist) does and take notes if possible. You may find that the immediate problem has been fixed only at the cost of a later, unexpected new problem. If you have kept notes, a real expert may be able to fix things faster than in their absence.

CHAPTER 11

Bench Trials

Despite the central place juries hold in the American imagination of the judicial system (and trial advocacy classes), most adjudications in the United States are bench trials, where judges decide both the questions of law and the issues of fact. In sheer numbers, more dispute resolution is akin to Judge Judy than to Twelve Angry Men. In recent years, several prominent cases were tried before the bench, including the Microsoft antitrust trial; the University of Michigan affirmative action case eventually decided by the Supreme Court; and the criminal trial of Kenneth Lay, the CEO of energy giant Enron who was accused of fraud. One-third of federal trials are non-jury trials. Most federal and state criminal trials are also heard solely before the bench. One out of three felony trials are bench trials, as are the vast majority of misdemeanor trials. The subject matter of mandatory bench trials runs the gamut, from small claims actions to criminal misdemeanors to patent claims for equitable relief to civil rights lawsuits to enforce the Voting Rights Act.

Moreover, even where there is a right to a jury trial, criminal defendants can waive that right, as can both parties in a civil matter. For instance, civil litigants may opt for a bench trial where they determine that the issues are too technical for a jury to understand. Likewise, criminal defendants may opt for a bench trial where they fear that jurors will not be able to separate their emotions about the crime charged from viable defenses. Deciding whether to forgo a jury involves consideration of a wide variety of factors, such as the characteristics of the jury pool, the judge assigned to the case, the strength and weaknesses of the legal claims and defenses, the anticipated testimony, and the like.

In many cases, however, juries are not an option. Juries have nothing to do with the resolution of millions of federal and state administrative cases or claims before alternative dispute resolution bodies, such as mediation and arbitration. In other words, more trial lawyers find themselves trying to convince a single legal expert than a group of laymen drawn from the community. Thus, it is imperative for both civil and criminal trial lawyers to understand the similarities and differences between bench trials and jury trials and to shape their trial skills accordingly.

I. Bench Trials Are Different

There are several differences between bench and jury trials—all driven by the contrasting role of the judge. In a jury trial, the judge serves as an umpire, controlling the courtroom, ruling on evidentiary issues, and instructing the jury about the law. The judge does not decide the case; rather, she ensures that the jurors can undertake the decision-making process free of obstacles, such as confusion, prejudicial appeals to emotion, or inadmissible evidence. By contrast, in a bench trial, the judge is the ultimate fact-finder, and thus a much more active participant in the trial who may interrogate witnesses and question the attorneys directly. This means that the lawyers cannot exert the same level of control over a bench trial as they can in a jury trial. The potential loss of control is the most challenging aspect of representing clients in bench trials.

A. Timing and Pace Are Faster

Bench trials usually move faster than jury trials. A bench trial does not require voir dire, the lengthy process of questioning a pool of potential jurors about their backgrounds in order to yield seated jurors who can decide the case without bias or emotion. Moreover, without a jury, there is no need to halt the trial to hold evidentiary hearings outside the presence of the jury or to summon the attorneys to the bench for judge-counsel conferences. Further, in a bench trial there is no need to haggle over the wording of jury instructions.

Not surprisingly, bench trials are less costly and more efficient than jury trials. Studies have shown that bench trials take half to one-third as long as comparative jury trials. At the same time, because there is no concern about inconveniencing a jury, some judges will interrupt, postpone, and continue bench trials to accommodate other court matters. Thus, a lawyer may be whipping through a bench trial or, alternatively, trying a case in disjointed fits and starts. Under either circumstance, it is essential for the trial lawyer to be prepared to accommodate the rhythm and reality of bench trial scheduling.

Understand that the judge wants to move the case quickly. It is important to be attuned to the judge's viewpoint, but not to undercut your case on the mistaken belief that bench trials require less vigorous advocacy. This is a delicate balance. You should definitely take steps to streamline your case. Keep your opening statement brief and vivid. Focus your witness examinations on the core facts. Avoid duplicative testimony and exhibits. Stipulate to as many facts and exhibits as possible with opposing counsel.

At the same time, do not sell your case short by racing through it. The judge knows nothing about the case other than what the parties present at trial. She will not fill in blanks, or assume that other evidence exists somewhere in the world to support your case. If you rush through important testimony, the judge may miss it or fail to understand its significance. By contrast, if you present a convincing and dynamic case—and tell it like you mean it—the judge will not rush you and will give your case the careful consideration it deserves.

B. Tone of Argument Is Less Dramatic

Persuading a single individual with legal training and experience is different than persuading a group of laypersons. Thus, a trial lawyer needs to alter the tone of argument when appearing before a judge. A judge is less likely to be persuaded by blatant appeals to sympathy and emotion, and may be turned off by such an approach. The judge is unlikely to fall for a David v. Goliath characterization of a case. Folksy stories, homespun analogies, and rhetorical questions have little place in presenting a case to a legal professional whose paramount interests are discerning the truth about a past event and avoiding appellate reversal. At the same time, it is important to remember that a judge is a person, and not a legal automaton. Most judges appreciate a lawyer who presents an interesting case and tells a coherent story with energy and enthusiasm.

Studies show that most people retain information from visual exhibits better than aural information, and this is no less true for judges. Accordingly, you should use exhibits to the same degree before a judge as you would before a jury. Always provide a courtesy copy of each exhibit to the judge so that he can follow along with your witness' testimony. Better yet, save everyone time and present the judge and opposing counsel with a tabbed binder of all the exhibits you plan to introduce at trial.

Vivid storytelling is particularly important when you consider that judges, unlike jurors, hear many cases, day in and day out. This makes it even harder to grab and hold a judge's attention. Accordingly, a bench trial requires vigorous advocacy shaped for an audience of one.

Moreover, judges appreciate candor over spin and reasonableness over a winner-takes-all attitude. Acknowledge weak points in your case and explain why you still should prevail. Do not make unfounded objections simply to throw off the other side. Withdraw objections that lack merit. Concede valid objections by the other side. Work with opposing counsel on stipulations. Judges look favorably on lawyers who assist in the pursuit for truth instead of throwing up roadblocks.

In any type of trial, it is a good idea to learn which judge has been assigned to handle the trial and to observe the judge handling other matters. Yet this is particularly important in a bench trial, where a single person holds all the cards. Just as you conduct fact investigation of your case, you should conduct fact investigation of your judge. This is one area in which a bench trial can be an advantage—you can research the predispositions of a judge, whereas you cannot research jurors.

If direct observation is impossible, you can still research the judge's courtroom style by speaking with experienced lawyers in the jurisdiction. You can read published opinions by the judge. Some jurisdictions even have directories that provide background information on judges, including their courtroom reputation. Moreover, if you have a pre-trial conference, you can seize the opportunity to ask the judge about her plans for conducting the trial, any courtroom specific policies, and scheduling issues that may arise. In short, know and understand your audience and prepare your case accordingly.

C. The Judge May Question Witnesses

A judge in a bench trial is likely to take a much more active role in questioning witnesses on both direct and cross. Whereas a jury must resolve competing stories shaped by a clash of opposites, judges are interested in finding the "truth." The judge wants to get to the heart of the matter, and is usually less interested in dazzling displays of oratorical skills or a winning personality. Thus, in a bench trial, a judge may take over questioning of a witness altogether, or take the witness down an entirely different road than that mapped out by trial counsel.

A carefully scripted direct examination may go off course in a bench trial when a judge jumps in to ask the witness questions focused on a specific time, person, or event. A calculated cross-examination designed for yes and no answers may unwittingly turn into an opportunity for the hostile witness to address the judge directly and, worse, at length. In a bench trial, strategies designed to hide or skip over unfavorable evidence usually fizzle before a good judge. Moreover, while skilled trial counsel can often take advantage of an unprepared or untalented opposing counsel in a jury trial, this tactical advantage diminishes in a bench trial. Where opposing counsel fails, the trial judge will often pick up the slack.

Not surprisingly, judges presiding over a bench trial do not want to hear deposition testimony read into the record. Instead, they usually prefer summaries or highlighted portions of deposition transcripts or excerpts of videotaped depositions. Be thoughtful and thorough in your selections.

Judges may be particularly active in questioning experts on direct and cross. Know the judge's policy on handling expert testimony. Most judges do not want to take time for you to establish your expert's credentials. A detailed curriculum vitae, admitted as a business record, usually suffices to qualify the expert. Some judges prefer that the expert report be submitted in writing and then allow only cross-examination and re-direct in the courtroom. On direct or cross, many judges will have targeted questions for the expert. Judges are generalists, and will take advantage of having experts available to explain complex, scientific, and technical matters.

You need to ensure that even if the judge derails your planned questioning, you still get evidence admitted to establish each and every one of your claims or defenses. Many lawyers find it helpful for their trial notebook to contain a summary checklist of important topics that need to be covered in witness examinations. Such a checklist serves as a quick reference to ensure that you lay a complete record when things do not go in the planned order. In the end, it is the trial lawyer who must create a record for appellate review. It is no excuse that the trial judge took things in an unexpected direction or emphasized seemingly unimportant facts.

Just as the trial lawyer needs to be prepared for the unexpected, so do the witnesses. No witness in a bench trial should be surprised when a judge seizes control over direct or cross. It is thus essential that your fact and expert witnesses be prepared not only to testify in response to questions by counsel, but also to respond fully, clearly, and politely to judicial questioning. Due to popular culture conceptions of trials, many witnesses do not expect to address the judge directly, and this can be unsettling without advance warning.

D. Rules of Evidence Are Applied Loosely

The rules of evidence are designed largely to ensure that jurors hear only relevant, accurate, and reliable evidence. Evidentiary rules limit trial counsel's ability to distract jurors with evidence that might mislead them or inflame their emotions. In a jury trial, the judge decides whether evidence is admissible, and the jury decides how much weight to give the evidence. Yet the screening purpose embedded within our evidentiary rules is not needed when a case is tried before a judge.

Accordingly, appellate courts hold that a bench trial judge is presumed to have considered only relevant and admissible evidence in reaching her findings. Thus, inadmissible evidence that gets into the record is more likely to be harmless in a bench trial. In short, trial judges are more likely to get into trouble on appeal from excluding evidence than from admitting it. As a result, evidentiary rules are not applied firmly in bench trials. After an objection, you are likely to hear the judge respond, "I will take the evidence for what it's worth."

This does not mean, however, that trial counsel should roll over and play dead. It is still important to lay a record for appeal by objecting to inadmissible evidence and making offers of proof when the judge excludes an important piece of evidence. You may even have to object to the judge—politely, of course!—if he questions witnesses on objectionable matters. Do not get sloppy in laying evidentiary foundations. Be alert and actively listen to the opposing side's case so that you can make proper objections. The judge is entitled to rely on any evidence that gets admitted into the record.

Evidentiary errors can affect a substantial right of a party and raise grounds for reversal. Moreover, well-founded objections can focus the judge's attention on important evidence and diminish the impact of evidence presented by the other side. Jurors can be extremely annoyed by objections or think you are hiding important evidence from them. Yet a judge is less likely to hold a valid objection against you. So, if you argue your objections forcefully and briefly, you may impress the judge and rattle your opponent.

Be aware also that you will have to deal with evidentiary issues as they arise. In modern litigation, particularly in civil cases, many evidentiary issues are resolved prior to trial in lengthy pre-trial conferences. This helps trials move more smoothly without subjecting the jury to fits and starts. Obviously, this concern does not arise with bench trials, and thus, far fewer evidentiary issues are worked out in advance. Instead, the judge will entertain objections in the context of the trial. Remember, the judge wants to save time. Anything you can do to keep things moving will dispose the judge in your favor.

E. Openings and Closings Look Like Appellate Arguments

Wander into a bench trial during openings and closings, and you might think you have stumbled into an argument before a one-person court of appeals. During both openings and closings, judges will often question counsel vigorously about the legal standards and precedent that govern the case, factual inconsistencies in the evidence presented, and the implications of the case for larger legal and policy issues.

In a jury trial, openings and closings serve distinct purposes. Openings serve as overviews of the evidence that will be presented at trial, while closings are an opportunity to argue how the facts fit within the governing legal standards. This distinction often blurs in bench trials, in which both openings and closings can become interactive dialogues between counsel and the judge. The judge may swing back and forth between the opposing lawyers in pursuing a line of inquiry. It is important for the lawyers to respond to the judge's questions and not stubbornly stick to a planned script. It is also important to remain unfailingly polite to the judge, even if you feel your case is swerving off course.

Moreover, in bench trials, the law plays a much more prominent part of the opening and closing arguments. Judges are more willing to consider factual *and* legal argument in bench trial openings. Likewise, whereas jurors must accept closing arguments as they are and cannot question the lawyers, judges in bench trials can use closing arguments to probe any and all aspects of the case. Not all judges seize this opportunity. However, for those that do, trial counsel need to be prepared for an appellate-style argument, and not simply controlled statements. Further, you can ask the judge if he or she has any questions, thereby ensuring that you tie up loose ends from an advocate's perspective. If you do not know the answer to the judge's question, offer to conduct research and quickly provide the judge with a memorandum.

Bench trial judges often want to jettison opening statements altogether, reasoning that they do not need the benefit of an overview and can easily assimilate the evidence presented into the applicable legal framework. You should disabuse the judge of that notion. Explain to the judge in one or two sentences why a brief opening statement would be helpful in your case. In other words, tell the court why your case is unique and why your opening statement will sharpen the issues in the case.

Remember, a bench trial judge is interested in saving time. Frame your request for an opening in light of the judge's perspective. You can say, "Your Honor, I realize you have reviewed the pleadings in this case. However, I believe a short opening statement of two to three minutes can assist the court in narrowing the issues in the case." You can even provide the judge with a chronology of key events in your case, a short outline of the relevant law and facts in the case, and/or a chart showing the relationships among the parties. Make the judge's job easy and you will gain credibility and respect. If, despite your best efforts, the court denies you an opening statement, you should carefully consider the order in which you call your witnesses. You should call as your first witness someone whose testimony can serve the same overview purpose as an opening statement.

F. Briefs Are Extremely Important

In many bench trials, pre-trial or post-trial briefs are required, and in many others they are accepted. Take advantage of these opportunities. Many federal and state procedural rules require trial counsel to submit findings of fact and conclusions of law at the end of a case. In pretrial briefs, you get to present the written equivalent of an opening statement. That is, you can set forth a roadmap that describes your proof at trial, describes the governing law and relevant authorities, and argues how the evidence leads to a particular legal result. Similarly, a post-trial brief can review the evidence that was presented, tie it directly to the law, and refute the evidence and arguments presented by the opposing side. Such briefs are obviously inappropriate in jury trials because jurors may only consider the evidence presented and the jury instructions from the judge. They do not get to read and reflect upon a written summary of the case.

By contrast, for a judge presiding over a bench trial, the briefs can serve as templates for a decision, and the briefs are thus vital advocacy tools that should not be overlooked. If the court does not require a brief, trial counsel should offer to submit one. Regardless of the stage of the case when you submit a written brief, do not assume that the judge is familiar with the law governing the case. Set forth the legal standards thoroughly and succinctly. Explain to the judge why the evidence presented at trial satisfies the legal standards. Attach statutory excerpts if the governing law is from another jurisdiction. In short, make it easy for the judge to rule in your favor.

II. Bench Trials Are the Same

Although the look and feel of bench trials can be very different from jury trials, the similarities vastly outweigh the differences. Regardless of the decision-maker, most trials focus on the presentation of testimony and exhibits designed to tell a consistent and believable story about a past event. Thus, all trials require thorough and creative fact investigation and legal research. All trials require mastery of the procedural and evidentiary rules that govern the forum. All trials require preparation, organization, and persuasion. In any trial, judges appreciate lawyers who speak clearly, with brevity, and with passion. In short, good advocacy skills apply to any legal forum.

III. Administrative Hearings

Much of what we discussed about bench trial advocacy applies equally to administrative hearings. These hearings are bench trials outside the judicial system. However, a trial lawyer needs to be aware of the many possible differences between administrative and judicial hearings and to prepare accordingly. Moreover, there is incredible variation in how different agencies hear cases. Thus, it is essential to know your forum.

A. What Agencies Do

Most adjudication in America happens before administrative agencies. Agency hearings far outnumber the federal and state court caseloads combined. Indeed, the Social Security system alone is the largest adjudicatory body in the Western world. It distributes retirement and disability benefits to tens of millions of Americans. While the Social Security Administration annually hears millions of claims involving relatively small amounts of money (albeit of great importance to claimants), other agencies, such as the Federal Communications Commission or the Securities and Exchange Commission, hear far fewer cases that often have millions of dollars or national policies at stake.

Administrative agencies exist at both the federal and state levels, and still other agencies are found at county and city levels. Administrative agencies touch every individual and business in this country. More people interact with agencies than they do with courts. Agencies regulate economic behavior, keep workers safe, distribute public benefits, protect the environment and public health, license professionals, prosecute discrimination, and the list goes on.

Legislators create agencies to carry out governmental programs, and agencies are located within the executive branch. Nevertheless, agencies perform both legislative and adjudicatory functions in addition to executive functions. Legislators lack the time or expertise to pass laws with the specificity needed to achieve governmental objectives. Accordingly, agencies issue detailed rules to carry out statutory objectives. These rules have the force of law. For instance, the Environmental Protection Agency issues rules that limit pollution and the Federal Trade Commission issues rules to protect consumers from fraudulent business practices. When an agency applies its governing statutes and rules to specific parties, the agency is conducting an adjudication.

B. The Rules of the Game

Be aware that agency practices differ widely, even within a single state. Thus, it is imperative to learn about the forum before appearing at an agency hearing with a client. The lawyer, client, and witnesses should know what to expect when they walk through the hearing doors.

In most agency hearings, a single decision-maker is charged with issuing a decision on behalf of the agency. Depending on the agency, this person is usually called an administrative law judge, administrative judge, a hearing officer, or similar term. These decision-makers do not have constitutional protections of lifetime tenure, but they are still expected to be unbiased, impartial, and fair. Moreover, they have many of the same powers of trial judges. Typically, they may issue subpoenas, administer oaths, rule on evidentiary matters, regulate the course and conduct of the hearing, and make or recommend decisions to the agency.

Yet administrative agencies do not use the judicial system's rules of civil procedure. Rather, to find the procedures that govern agency hearings, you need to look at the governing federal or state administrative procedure act (APA). APAs are statutes enacted by legislators to govern administrative agencies. Most APAs contain a section that explains the procedures for contested hearings. In addition, many agencies issue their own procedural rules that may supplant or supplement the APA. And, to complicate things further, some agency hearings are governed instead by the organic statute that created the agency or the statute setting forth the substantive law at issue. At the local level, you need to check municipal codes and charters for hearing procedures.

C. Informal Does Not Mean Casual

Most contested hearings before agencies are called "informal adjudications." Do not be fooled into thinking the hearing will be casual or laidback. The word "informal" is a term of art within administrative law. It means that the hearing will have fewer procedural requirements than a "formal hearing," which is nearly identical to a court trial. Still, informal hearings are not free-for-alls. Instead, they operate under procedural rules, which are often required by constitutional due process. In short, informal hearings can be quite formal indeed.

For instance, in most informal hearings, there are opening and closing statements, direct and cross-examinations, objections, and evidentiary rulings from the judge. Pretrial and post-trial briefs are sometimes required, and often recommended. Administrative judges typically must prepare written findings of fact and conclusions of law at the end of the case. While the courtroom rules of evidence do not apply to administrative hearings, most judges nevertheless use them as guidelines and give less weight to evidence that violates evidentiary rules. So, while hearsay is usually admissible, do not expect it to win the case. At the same time, you may have greater leeway to submit documentary evidence without laying an elaborate foundation.

You should be just as prepared for an informal hearing as you would for a court trial. In preparation, anticipate objections to your evidence and consider how you would respond. Review your testimony with your witnesses. Tell a compelling and vivid story about your case. Use exhibits. Treat the hearing official with all the respect you would accord a judge in court. Look the judge in the eye, express conviction in your position, and be enthusiastic.

D. Similarities and Differences

While most hearings are held before a single judge, some are held before panels of hearing officers. Woe to the lawyer who expects to argue before a single judge and is instead confronted by a raised dais with eleven panelists, all of whom ask questions! Similarly, while some hearings are held in spaces with the wood-paneled formality of a courtroom, others may be held at conference tables in cramped agency offices. Some administrative judges have law clerks and a staff, others work alone. Some wear judicial robes; some wear business suits. You might be expected to call the judge, "Your Honor," or simply by name.

Some agency judges are specialists who hear only one type of case repeatedly. Others are generalists who hear claims from multiple agencies, and are thus akin to judges in the judicial system. You can safely assume that a specialist knows the governing law, and you should focus on demonstrating how the facts satisfy the legal standards. By contrast, with a generalist, you should be prepared to educate the judge about the governing law. You can earn a lot of goodwill by giving the judge a bound and indexed set of all relevant statutes, regulations, and cases.

Many administrative hearings are adversarial, like trials. The hearing may involve two private parties in a dispute before an agency decision making body, such as a claim for workers compensation. Or, the hearing may be an enforcement action brought by a government agency against a private party charged with violating the law, such as a labor department's claim against an employer for violating fair wage and hour laws.

Yet not all administrative proceedings are adversarial. Many cases involve a single claimant who is seeking benefits from the government, such as claims for social security. In these latter sorts of hearings, there is no adversary. Rather, the judge acts as an inquisitor, developing the record, questioning witnesses, and reaching the decision. Moreover, in an inquisitorial system, the judge may call neutral experts to provide opinions about technical aspects of the claimants' case.

The appellate processes for agency hearings also vary widely. Learn them before your initial hearing. Generally, courts are very deferential to agency decisions. This means that you usually win or lose your case before the administrative law judge. Nevertheless, find out what body will hear the case on appeal, and whether that hearing will be *de novo* or on the record. The immediate appeal might be within the agency, or it may be directly to state court or to a separate administrative court. There may be multiple levels of appeal. Moreover, the standards for review of your agency decision may differ from appellate review standards for trial court decisions. Further, there are a variety of doctrines that govern the timing of agency appeals. Understanding your opportunities on appeal may impact your negotiation strategy, your client counseling sessions, and your hearing tactics.

E. Know Your Forum

In sum, most administrative hearings are like bench trials. Yet because of the diversity in hearing procedures, it is essential to learn about your forum before you appear there for the first time. Otherwise, you risk looking bumbling and incompetent. Read the governing procedural rules. Arrange to observe a similar hearing, if possible (not all administrative hearings are open to the public). Speak with experienced lawyers in the field. Contact the administrative law section of your local or state bar organization. Once you have your bearings, strong advocacy skills will carry you the rest of the way.

CHAPTER 12

Poverty Lawyering in Court

Like popular culture depictions of trials, most trial advocacy simulations focus on jury trials litigated against the background of extensive discovery. In the simulated world, no one worries about the cost, and the lawyers pour their energy into a single case at a time. However, lawyers who represent low-income clients often juggle enormous caseloads while worrying about litigation costs. Low-income clients usually cannot afford expensive experts or lengthy computer research sessions. As a result, legal services or public defender offices must make difficult fiscal choices. By contrast, in cases involving wealthy litigants, there are teams of high-paid lawyers and extensive legal support services, including paralegals, administrative assistants, jury consultants, litigation support services, document management systems, and expert consultants and witnesses.

Due to a lack of resources and overwhelming caseloads, poverty litigators face unique challenges as trial attorneys. Moreover, pro bono attorneys may be surprised at how different their pro bono cases proceed through court as compared to their "regular" cases. Despite obstacles, poverty and pro bono lawyers make dramatic differences in the lives of their clients through hardwork, preparation, and persuasive trial skills.

This chapter discusses some of the challenges a poverty lawyer or pro bono attorney can expect in cases involving low-income litigants, as well as suggestions for meeting these challenges head-on. This chapter narrowly focuses on representing low-income clients in court—it does not address the profound issues surrounding attorney-client relationships, the goals and strategies of poverty lawyering, or the lack of attorneys available to represent low-income clients. Nor does it address substantive legal issues that arise in representing poor individuals. Rather, this chapter aims to give you a realistic sense of what you can expect in a poverty law practice when you enter the courthouse doors.

I. Prepare for Anything

Many poverty lawyers regularly handle civil matters in small claims courts and other courts of limited jurisdiction. In these courts, there are often limited, if any, discovery tools. Without interrogatories, depositions, and document requests, the lawyer often walks into the courtroom with only scant knowledge of the opposing side's case. While a subpoena can ensure that necessary third parties or documents appear at trial, obtaining information on the courthouse steps certainly does not allow for advance preparation. Thus, a $2,000 small claim action can be more challenging to handle than a $20,000 contract action, in which both sides carry out planned examinations with limited surprises.

This means that the poverty lawyer has to be prepared for almost any scenario—unexpected claims and defenses, surprise witnesses and exhibits, a judge who knows nothing about the case, unforeseen procedural tactics for delay, and the like. Talk about thinking on your feet!

Fact investigation and informal discovery can sometimes alleviate these surprises, as well as lead to new claims or defenses, encourage settlement negotiations, and move the case forward. Informal discovery includes shared communication between the parties, witness interviews, observation and surveillance, and internet and public records searches. For instance, a simple phone call between attorneys can often yield valuable information and open the lines of communication.

Yet if a case does not settle, the only way to prepare for the unexpected is to know the case backwards and forwards. If the opposing side drops any huge surprises at trial, it is appropriate to request a postponement from the judge to conduct factual and legal investigation. However, a judge is only likely to grant such an extension if she is convinced that the case warrants extra time, which in turn, would make a difference to the outcome. It is impossible to make such an argument if you do not know the case thoroughly. And, if the request to postpone is denied, you need to be ready and able to go forward without a hitch.

As part of your preparation, try to visit the courthouse before your case to watch a mass justice system in action. You should know the procedural rules that govern your case thoroughly. In addition, many courts abide by quirky, unpublished rules that have developed over time. Some judges and clerk's offices even have their own rules that apply in their courtrooms; they may or may not give these in writing to lawyers who appear before them. Ask lawyers familiar with the jurisdiction whether there are any rules or practices you need to know about that cannot be found in books.

II. Respond to Rushed Dockets

The court dockets in many areas of law that impact low-income litigants are huge. It is not uncommon to walk into an inner-city courthouse and see hundreds of cases listed for a single morning in a single courtroom. In many of these cases, one of the parties will not show up, leading to a default judgment or dismissal. Other cases will result in settlements, often negotiated on the spot. Only a minority of cases will likely go to a full trial. Nevertheless, sorting through such a lengthy docket puts tremendous pressure on the judge and the courthouse staff.

This has several repercussions for the trial lawyer. First, as the trial lawyer, it is important to understand the docket pressures facing a particular courthouse and to shape your trial plans accordingly. An identical case may be allotted a two hour trial in a suburban county courthouse, but twenty minutes in a busy inner-city courthouse. Clearly, your trial preparation needs to accommodate these differences.

Second, there may be tremendous pressure from the court to settle the case. Of course, the attorney and client should consider and weigh all settlement options, the alternatives to settlement, and the implications of each. Sometimes one implication of not settling a case is incurring the wrath of the trial judge who will hear the case. However, it is ultimately the client's decision, and if the client opts for a trial, it is important not to allow the court to bully the client into an unsatisfactory resolution.

Third, the court will want to move the case quickly. This means that the judge may not permit opening statements, or will only allow a very short opening. A good trial lawyer can encapsulate his case theory into one or two compelling sentences and will seize the opportunity to make even a brief overview of the case. The court may also push counsel to focus direct and cross-examinations on certain issues or limit the amount of time permitted for each witness. Some judges will begin the case by asking trial counsel what evidence they plan to present. At that point, the court may give counsel the court's impression of the strengths and weaknesses of each side's case and then either encourage further settlement discussions or take other steps to shorten the trial.

Regardless of the time pressures you face, it is still your job to present evidence to support each prima facie element of your claims or defenses. It is no argument on appeal or excuse to clients that the judge was in a rush. It can be a delicate balance between respecting the time pressures facing the judge and presenting all the evidence necessary to make the case. If the judge is excluding evidence or preventing you from pursuing a line of questioning, make a proffer in order to preserve the issue for appeal. Being polite and respectful to the court is essential to navigating these competing pressures.

Consider time restrictions as an advantage—they force you to focus your case on its strengths, to eliminate redundant and needless testimony and exhibits, and to reinforce your theory and themes in a concise way. You may also find it useful to show the judge how you are prepared to assist him in adjudicating the case by having multiple copies of evidence and authority, as well as litigation documents at your fingertips.

You may have a type of practice in which you appear before the same judge regularly, such as a public defender who handles misdemeanors or traffic matters. If you are consistently on time, prepared, and organized in routine matters, you will get more freedom, patience, and attention from the court when you really need it. Moreover, by stepping up your style of representation on certain matters, you can set those cases apart and signal to the judge the importance of the case. At other times, you may need to signal to the judge that you are trying a marginal case at the client's insistence and implicitly ask the judge not to punish your client for exercising his right to a trial. One benefit of being a repeat player is the opportunity to work with the judge to reach sensible results. However, you need to earn the judge's trust. Preparation is the key.

While the courts struggle with large dockets, so do many poverty lawyers. You may handle hundreds of cases alone. Organization is the key to managing a large docket. Every deadline must go in your calendar, with a tickler system to remind you of upcoming deadlines. It is impossible to remember the details of hundreds of cases simultaneously, so it is essential to keep your files up-to-date and thorough. Time put in on case management at the front end will pay off later. Of course, huge caseloads can compromise effective representation. These issues are larger than a single attorney and demand the attention of the judicial system at large. Nevertheless, strong organizational skills are the foundation for persuasive advocacy under difficult circumstances.

III. Work Collaboratively with Clients

Low-income litigants often face numerous, overlapping difficulties. Take the case of Sheila R. She missed work for two days when her child had the flu. She could not find a babysitter who could provide the necessary care or take her son to the doctor. She lost her job, and could not pay the next month's rent. As a result, she was sued for eviction. At the same time, her apartment was in such disrepair that it threatened the health and safety of Sheila and her family. This provided her with a defense to the eviction action, and the possibility of having her rent abated until repairs were made. Potentially homeless and already unemployed, her life threatened to spiral out-of-control. For such a litigant, the court case is one complication in a bevy of problems.

As the lawyer, you need to be realistic about the time your client can commit to the trial. Client meetings may have to occur at odd hours to accommodate work schedules. Witness preparation sessions may have to yield to preparation over the phone or immediately before trial. The client may need your assistance gathering relevant documents or files from government agencies. Your client is your partner in the representation, but the client's time and energies may be compromised by the struggles of daily living.

Moreover, your client may not be able to read. Therefore, you should be sensitive about how literacy impacts the case substantively and as part of the attorney-client relationship. Further, your clients may not keep calendars, address books, or blackberries. To help them remember important facts and names, you will need to be patient and detailed in your client interviews.

The foregoing suggestions assume that you can easily reach your client. However, your client's phone may have been cut off for failure to pay the bill. Your client may be shuttling between homeless shelters and relatives' homes. It can be challenging to communicate with some clients. Work with your client to set up a system for regular contact, such as setting up a weekly time for the client to check in with the office or using a family member to relay messages.

You also need to be sensitive to the fact that your client may initially see you as just another cog in the wheel of bureaucracy. Many low-income clients are forced to spend inordinate amounts of time navigating social service agencies, gathering documentation, and making regular recertification meetings to obtain government assistance. These clients spend a lot of time being judged by others. Thus, you cannot assume that the client understands that your role as an attorney makes you different. In your role as a counselor, you can build rapport that breaks down the client's preconceived notions. In your role as an advocate, you can demonstrate your commitment to the client's case.

IV. Catch the Judge's Attention

There is a misconception surrounding many poverty law cases that they are factually run-of-the-mill and legally simple. Most poverty law cases do not involve large dollar amounts, and in our society, complexity is presumed to correlate with the amount of money in dispute. Yet these so-called routine cases can impact profound matters of life, health, and safety. Low-income litigants can face homelessness in housing court, loss of their children in family court, physical and mental injury in domestic violence cases, and bankruptcy in small claims court. They may be fighting for public benefits that mean the difference between eating and going hungry or between getting medical care and dying from routine illnesses. In short, the stakes for these litigants can be extremely high.

At the same time, the facts and law surrounding these cases can be complex. The governing law often involves a complex combination of constitutional law, statutes, regulations, and administrative guidance materials at the federal, state, and local levels. Increasingly, poverty law advocates are also looking to bring international legal norms into local courtrooms.

Take for instance Sheila R.'s eviction case, described above. One of the problems in her apartment was that it had peeling and chipping paint. Since it was built before 1950, the paint contained lead. Lead paint can cause mental disabilities or kill young children. The meant that inspectors from the health department would need to get involved to test the lead levels. Sheila's children would need to be tested for lead poisoning. They may need follow-up treatment. Federal and state laws and regulations governing lead paint liability and clean-up are complicated and run hundreds of pages. Sheila would need to move out of the apartment during clean-up or perhaps permanently. She would incur costs for moving, a security deposit, and the first months rent. Unable to pay these costs, she might be eligible for certain public benefits programs. However, it is not easy to determine eligibility among the possible federal and state programs, each of which has its own standards. Before you know it, a "simple" eviction case involves multiple city agencies, the health care system, and the social services department.

Yet a judge hearing a poverty law docket may come to the bench with the myths and misperceptions that the cases are cookie cutter. Depending on the position and claims of the parties, having a "run-of-the-mill" case can be a tactical advantage or a disadvantage and will influence how you paint the case to the judge. For low-income litigants it is more often a disadvantage. For instance, a tenant living in a home with no working heat in the middle of a Northeastern winter needs to catch the judge's attention with the severity of the situation. The judge may spend long days hearing about alleged defects in the warranty of habitability to the point where the tenants' lists of complaints becomes a blur. You do not want to be one of many.

So, you need to educate the judge about the stakes of the case and the applicable law. Are there children or elderly or disabled people living in the house? What was the temperature yesterday? What extreme measures are the tenants keeping to stay warm? Use storytelling and vivid detail to set your case apart from the pack. Moreover, do not assume that the judge knows the law or has read it accurately. Because so few low-income litigants have lawyers, the judge may have a one-sided view of the law. The judge may be unaware that complex federal regulatory standards overlay and perhaps supersede state law. The judge may not have considered alternative interpretations of the law or relevant legislative history.

Moreover, never assume that the governing law or the other side's interpretation of the law is valid. The statute may violate the Constitution, regulations may violate statutes, and state laws may violate federal law. If the law is unfavorable to you, consider legal strategies for challenging it. You need to be creative, thorough, and exhaustive in your legal research. Poverty law advocates have convinced courts across the country to overturn numerous statutes and regulations that harmed their clients. Being a good advocate means being proactive, and not simply dealing with the hand that you are dealt.

V. Cut Costs

Litigation is expensive. Even putting aside attorney fees, depositions alone involve the costs of the court reporter, transcripts, copies, and witness fees. It also costs money to obtain records from third-parties, such as medical records or school files. Drafting or responding to interrogatories and document requests take attorney and client time, as well as money. As the case moves to trial, you may need to pay a process server to serve subpoenas. Your case may require an expert to consult with you about scientific, medical or technical matters, and you may need an expert to testify in court. At almost every phase of litigation, there are bills to pay. But, in a poverty law practice, it is a foregone conclusion that the client cannot pay those bills.

In criminal cases, *Gideon v. Wainwright* provides that indigent defendants must be provided with a lawyer. Despite *Gideon's* promise, many defendants are still convicted and imprisoned each year without any legal representation. Other defendants obtain poorly paid lawyers burdened by hundreds of other cases, who may have little substantive expertise or lack the funds to investigate facts or obtain DNA testing. As for experts, the *Ake* case held that criminal defendants raising an insanity defense are entitled to a psychiatric expert paid for by the state. Other experts, and other defenses, do not have this guarantee.

Many people are surprised that there is no right to a lawyer in civil cases. Instead, it is estimated that only twenty percent of low-income litigants receive legal assistance. Even the Supreme Court has recognized that we live "in a time when the need for legal services among the poor is growing and public funding for such services has not kept pace."[3] Yet as a matter of constitutional principles, the Court does not treat wealth classifications as a suspect class subject to heightened scrutiny under the Equal Protection Clause, nor does it treat economic and social legislation as implicating fundamental rights. As a result, the Court has upheld filing fees for bankruptcy petitions and welfare appeals against challenges by indigent litigants because these types of cases do not implicate "fundamental rights."

Nevertheless, as a matter of state law, many jurisdictions waive filing fees for indigent civil litigants, and sometimes waive fees for transcripts on appeal. These fee waivers open the doors to the courthouse for the poor, but they do not provide assistance once the litigant is inside. The poverty lawyer must be creative, diligent, and prepared to surmount these financial barriers.

Most legal services and public defender offices have a dedicated litigation budget to cover some of these costs. Still, the pot is finite, and the need far outstrips supply. Hard decisions have to be made about where to concentrate resources. While large law firms can often spend generously on pro bono cases, the legions of pro bono lawyers in small firms or sole practitioner offices can find these costs onerous. In short, representing poor clients requires creativity to deliver superb advocacy on a budget. Here are some suggestions.

A. Put the Client to Work

Recognize your client as a partner in the representation. For instance, your client can help with fact investigation. Clients can often obtain medical records, social service files, school files, and the like faster than you can. They have personal relationships with the people who keep the files and can get their calls returned more quickly. Clients can also speak with potential third party witnesses about testifying in the case for free. Further, clients can create time-

---

3. Mallard v. United States, 490 U.S. 296, 310 (1989) (holding that a federal court cannot require an unwilling attorney to represent an indigent litigant in a civil case under 1915(d)).

lines of events, draft initial responses to interrogatories, search for documents, and list estimated damages and expenses.

B. Save Money on Copies

You may be able to convince third parties to waive or reduce costs for copies. Explain that you are doing work pro bono, your client is indigent, and the court has waived its filing fees. Many third parties will waive their fees as well under these circumstances. In some cases, clients have a legal right to free copies of their file, particularly from social service agencies. Also, be aware that many states have statutes that regulate what medical providers can charge for copies; many medical providers are unaware of or ignore these limitations.

C. Pursue Alternative Dispute Resolution

Consider alternative dispute resolution. Many courts sponsor mediation programs, in which parties can agree to submit their dispute to a mediator. Mediation can reduce litigation costs by removing the case from the adversarial process. Counseling a client about the option of mediation requires consideration of a variety of factors, including whether the parties will have an ongoing relationship, the client's values, how quickly the client wants the case resolved, the complexity of the legal issues, the balance of power between the parties, the desired remedies, the parties' need for privacy, and the desire to set legal precedent. Cost is just one factor among many to consider in weighing the mediation option, but it can be a significant benefit of mediation.

D. Create Inexpensive and Persuasive Exhibits

Exhibits are a vital part of trial advocacy. Most people retain visual information better than aural information, and in today's technological age, people increasingly expect to learn information visually. Visual aids also break up the monotony of testimony and can help clarify complex issues. Be creative in thinking about how exhibits can enhance your case. Put yourself in the fact-finder's position. What would help judge and jury envision the facts in your client's favor and better understand your witnesses' testimony?

Once you decide how exhibits can be helpful, you need to be equally creative in crafting exhibits with impact. You probably cannot afford to hire graphic designers or illustrators to design your demonstrative exhibits. Yet there is much you can do on your own with a computer, an internet connection, and a copier to give your case visual impact. Even basic word processing programs allow you to insert pictures and clips, emphasize certain text, create charts and tables, use bullet points, and customize font style and size. You can download calendars to create timelines and use spreadsheets to summarize financial information and other data.

Many publicly-available documents can be blown up and displayed on poster board, such as maps and land records. Anyone with an internet connection can now download aerial photographs taken from satellites of any location in the world. The public library, particularly the children's section, has encyclopedias and non-fiction books full of pictures and diagrams that could be useful to your case. Hobby shops and craft stores are full of miniaturized models that might be relevant, such as cars, people, buildings, and trees. Do not forget the power of witness demonstrations. They cost nothing and have lots of visual impact.

If you are working with an expert (see below), that person probably has many helpful exhibits right in her office. For instance, doctors often have anatomical models, diagrams, as well as videotapes and patient brochures describing various conditions and treatment options.

Alternatively, you may choose to make your lack of fancy exhibits work in your favor. A public defender may tell the jury, "I do not have slick maps and computerized models because I don't have an entire police department and a huge budget at my disposal." As you present your exhibits, tell the jurors to raise their hands if they cannot see them or if they need them passed around. Heighten the inequality and make it work for you. Uneven resources can backfire for the resource-rich side.

E. Network for Experts

Experts serve many roles in trial practice, but they are expensive. Experts help trial attorneys evaluate cases, assist in case development, educate counsel about specialized aspects of the case, and testify in depositions and in court. Cases involving low-income litigants often involve scientific, medical, and technical matters. Child custody cases need psychological evaluations of the parties and the children. Social security disability claims involve assessment of medical records and vocational evidence to determine whether a claimant can no longer work. Consumer cases can involve complex financial accounting; sometimes a handwriting expert is needed to authenticate a contract. Criminal cases may require expert testimony on issues ranging from eyewitness identification to DNA evidence to syndromes, such as battered woman syndrome.

One way to find an expert is to look for fact witnesses who already have helpful knowledge about the case. Treating physicians in particular can serve dual roles. The same is true for other professionals who regularly interact with low-income populations, such as social workers, teachers, and psychologists. Unfortunately, other professions do not have the same norms and expectations of pro bono service as lawyers. Yet because these professionals have a relationship with your client, they may be willing to testify for free or at a reduced fee. This is the time to break out your negotiation skills.

When there is no appropriate fact witness who is willing to serve as a low-cost expert, you need to get creative. Develop collaborative relationships with other professionals who serve similar populations. Attend trainings and join advocacy groups that are interdisciplinary. Keep track of professionals who refer cases to you. Volunteer to do community education programs for needy populations, such as teaching nursing home residents about advanced medical directives, in exchange for assistance from the staff on cases. Graduate students and recent graduates are often willing to provide services at a low-cost or no-cost in order to gain experience and bolster their resumes. Also, many experts are willing to consult on the case for free, even if they do not want to testify in court. Their insights can be invaluable to preparing for cross-examinations and in recommending background readings to you. Neighbors, relatives, and friends may be willing to provide pro bono expert services. Ask around!

Criminal defense attorneys should always file *Ake* motions, ex parte if possible (research the law in your state), asking the court for a court-appointed expert. If a wealthy litigant such as O.J. Simpson would have an expert on an issue, you should have the same expert. While you may not get the expert you seek, you are laying a record for a possible appeal.

VI. Working with and without Technology

Courtrooms that hear concentrated numbers of cases involving low-income litigants tend not to have advanced technology. You might walk into such a courtroom and find nothing more than a chalkboard — bring your own chalk and eraser. Federal courts are more likely to have courtroom technology than state courts, such as document cameras that display exhibits onto a screen, projection systems that project digital data, electronic whiteboards, and videoconferencing. New technologies provide exciting opportunities for trial lawyers.

If these resources are available, use them as long as they enhance your case. Review the chapter on courtroom technology in this book as you assess various possibilities. It does not cost you anything to use hardware the court already provides, and you do not need to buy expensive software to store exhibits on a computer or to display paper exhibits electronically. With basic powerpoint software, you can create textual and demonstrative slides, which are particularly helpful on openings and closings.

The rise of courtroom technology provides several benefits for poverty lawyers. For instance, some courtroom technology is designed specifically to assist disabled litigants, who are disproportionately low-income. Examples include real-time court reporter transcription for hearing impaired witnesses and scanning and conversion of documents into Braille for visually-impaired witnesses. These technologies can also assist disabled attorneys. In addition, videoconferencing can save on the costs of bringing remote witnesses into the courtroom.

Yet sometimes technology can be a disadvantage for poor litigants. For instance, when hearings are conducted via videoconferencing, rather than in person, the due process rights of claimants can be adversely impacted. Likewise, criminal defendants lose the right to confront their accusers. You should be current on this area of caselaw if your client will not be face-to-face with the judge. Technology can also be problematic if the opposing side brings in its own hardware, thus potentially creating a disparity between the parties. In short, technology can be a double-edged sword, and you should carefully think about whether technology can benefit or harm your case.

VII. Overcoming Language Barriers

Eighteen percent of people in the United States speak a language other than English at home. Poverty rates are higher among the foreign-born, and especially among non-citizens. The foreign born population continues to grow; it increased by 57% between 1990 and 2000. As a result of these demographic trends, poverty lawyers frequently represent clients who are not fluent in English. This affects all aspects of the attorney-client relationship, including trials. In court, you need to understand how to work with interpreters to deliver the best possible representation for your clients.

First and foremost, you need to ensure that the courtroom interpreter speaks the same language and dialect as your client and can translate legal terminology. Although Spanish is the most spoken language in this country after English, it is spoken by people from twenty-one countries, with countless dialects and regional variations.

Being bilingual does not qualify someone to serve as an interpreter. Courts should not be permitted to use clients' children, relatives, and friends as interpreters, or have such interpreters working on behalf of your adversary. If you have concerns about an interpreter's qualifications, you can conduct a voir dire and ask the interpreter about their training and credentials, native language, education in foreign language skills, courtroom experience, and familiarity with legal terminology.

As an advocacy matter, be sure that the interpreter does not block the view of the judge, jury, or counsel and that the interpreter can hear everyone in the courtroom. You can provide the interpreter with case information, a summary of anticipated testimony, and written documents in advance, to help prepare the interpreter for the case and speed up the trial. In addition, ensure that the interpreter does not improperly influence the client's answers with nodding or facial expressions. The interpreter should not answer questions from the client or give the client advice. Nor should the interpreter engage in colloquies with the client or other witnesses. Lawyers and judges should address the parties, and not the interpreter. Be sure to explain the neutral role of the interpreter to your client.

Not all courts provide non- and limited-English speaking litigants with an interpreter. As a constitutional matter, there is ample caselaw holding that criminal defendants who do not speak English should be provided with an interpreter. In federal courts, any party sued by the United States has a statutory right to an interpreter under the Federal Court Interpreters Act, 28 U.S.C. 1827, with the costs borne by the government. Some states have similar statutes for criminal defendants, and a few also extend the right to civil cases. In the absence of such a statute, the party requiring the interpreter usually has to bear the costs, which are typically allowable to the prevailing party under fee shifting statutes. Jurisdictions also vary as to whether or not they certify interpreters. Federal certification is available in Spanish, Haitian Creole, and Navajo.

If your jurisdiction provides interpreters for court proceedings, confirm with the court that the interpreter will be there at the right date and time and that the interpreter speaks the proper dialect. The court also needs to schedule additional time if an interpreter is needed and to provide breaks for the interpreter. Be prepared — cases requiring interpreters take a lot longer. Ask the court to make an audio recording of the hearing, as opposed to only a written transcript, in the event of appeal.

Finally, if you are involved in a cross-cultural representation, be sure to advise your client about how our judicial system works. In other countries, the judicial system can be far different — ranging from kangaroo courts to courts where bribes are an essential part of practice. Clients may have inaccurate expectations about our judicial system. Accordingly, they need to be prepared not simply to testify, but also about how the system as a whole operates. Finally, be alert to issues surrounding whether your client's immigration status is relevant in the proceeding, whether the court or opposing counsel are entitled to ask about your client's status, and how your client's immigration status can substantively impact the case.

Introduction to the Casefile CD

The CD included at the back of this book contains five full casefiles and three mini-cases designed to let you practice the skills and strategies discussed in the preceding chapters. The trials include both civil and criminal cases and will get you on your feet as a trial lawyer. The mini-trials allow your teacher to focus on specific trial skills. In addition to trial mechanics, these realistic simulations will give you opportunities to grow as an effective storyteller and to develop persuasive case theories. Each casefile includes a summary of the case, the relevant law, witness and expert depositions and statements, and a wide array of exhibits. A brief summary of each case is below.

I. Full Casefiles

State v. Perry: Ripped from the headlines, this case is about an arson fire that kills a woman who has been trying to help her community rid itself of drug dealers. The defendant is believed to have started the fire to intimidate the homeowner and others who might be similarly inclined. It involves the testimony of the woman's husband, who was in the house when the fire started; an eyewitness who dragged the husband out of the burning house; arson experts for each side; and an alibi witness.

Fox v. Wolfe: A woman falls on the outside steps leading to her garden apartment complex. She sues the landlord for negligently maintaining the property. Among the witnesses are an eyewitness who claims to have previously fallen at the same spot and notified the landlord of his fall, an eyewitness for the defense, and engineers for both sides who will testify about the danger of the steps and railing. There are photographs of the scene that the lawyers can use to illustrate their theories of the case.

State v. Gooner: The defendant is charged with robbing and assaulting the clerk of a pawn shop. The case rests in part on eyewitness identifications and includes a perceptual psychologist who will testify about the effects of unconscious transference in skewing eyewitness identifications. Additionally, the State will call the getaway driver who is agreeing to testify against the defendant in exchange for a favorable plea agreement.

Landmark Property Management v. Hodges: The landlord is suing to evict a tenant for breach of lease based on claims of noise, trash, and loitering. The tenant is a single, working mother of two, including a teenage son accused of playing his music too loudly. She not only claims that she is in compliance with the lease, but also that the lawsuit is in retaliation for her previously filing a successful rent escrow action. In addition to the parties, witnesses include a police officer called to the scene of a disturbance in front of the tenant's home and the tenant's son. The case is designed to be a realistic simulation for training poverty lawyers and clinic students. It includes a wide array of exhibits typically found in landlord-tenant litigation, such as the lease, warning letters, business records, and photographs.

Grant v. Ellis: A father and a child's maternal grandparents are fighting over custody of a ten-year boy after the violent death of the child's mother. The grandparents claim that the father, an ex-felon with a history of drug abuse, cannot provide a safe, stable home for the child. The father claims that he is fully rehabilitated and that the grandparents' health problems limit their caretaking abilities and that their smoking is dangerous for the child, who has asthma. Witnesses include a court-appointed expert social worker who recommends placement with the grandparents and a reverend who runs a church-based transitional housing project where the father lives and works. There is a wide array of exhibits available for litigating the case, including the expert report, medical records, school records, and photographs. The case is designed to be a realistic simulation for training poverty lawyers, family lawyers, and clinic students.

II. Mini-Cases

Interglobal Hotels Inc. v. The Band Known as Straightshooters: The members of the Straightshooters rock band trashed a number of the Plaintiff's hotel rooms that they stayed in while on their concert tour. The purpose of this action is to recover the damage done to the rooms and the cost of the room service bill that the band refuses to pay on the grounds that they did not authorize the food and beverage order. The case raises a series of evidentiary issues related to documents and photographs.

Rose v. Davy: Ms. Rose and Mr. Davy were involved in an automobile collision at an intersection in which Ms. Rose suffered significant damage to her leg. Eyewitnesses will offer varying accounts of how the accident occurred. The file includes photographs and diagrams that the lawyer can use to visually bring the case to life. The case also involves the testimony of an orthopedic surgeon who examined the hospital records and x rays and will offer opinions about how the plaintiff sustained her injuries and whether they were pre-existing.

State v. Hurley: The only witness here is a character and reputation witness in an embezzlement case. This witness offers the direct examiner the opportunity to think about how best to elicit favorable character testimony and allows the prosecutor to practice cross-examining an impressive witness.